★ ★ ★ ★ ★ ★ ★ ★ ★ ★ ★ ★ ★ ★ ★ ★ ★ ★ ★ ★

FALL FROM GRACE

★ ★ ★ ★ ★ ★ ★ ★ ★ ★ ★ ★ ★ ★ ★ ★ ★ ★ ★ ★

★ ★

FALL FROM

SEX, SCANDAL, AND CORRUPTION IN AMERICAN

BALLANTINE BOOKS

NEW YORK

★ ★

GRACE:
POLITICS FROM 1702 TO THE PRESENT

SHELLEY ROSS

All rights reserved under International and Pan-American Copyright Conventions. Published in the United States by Ballantine Books, a division of Random House, Inc., New York, and simultaneously in Canada by Random House of Canada Limited, Toronto.

Grateful acknowledgment is made to *Playboy* Magazine for permission to reprint an excerpt from "*Playboy* Interview: Jimmy Carter," *Playboy* Magazine (November 1976); copyright © 1976 by *Playboy*. Used by permission.

Illustration credits can be found at the back of this book.

Library of Congress Catalog Card Number: 87-91422

ISBN: 0-345-35381-1

Cover design by Sheryl Kagen
Illustration: Collections of the Library of Congress
Book design by Alex Jay/Studio J

Manufactured in the United of America

First Edition: July 1988

10 9 8

For David S.

ACKNOWLEDGMENTS

I would like to thank the people whose efforts greatly contributed to the publication of *Fall from Grace*. First and foremost, Joëlle Delbourgo, editor-in-chief of Ballantine Trade Books, whose belief in the project and commitment to excellence were unwavering from beginning to end; and her assistants, Jane Bess and Elizabeth Zack for their editorial support.

I would also like to express sincere appreciation to Jeanne Edmunds Apostol, former producer of CBS's "Face the Nation," who tirelessly tracked down the illustrations and contributed her inside knowledge of Capitol Hill; to Myles Berkowitz, whose exhaustive library research helped make "impossible" deadlines seem all the more manageable; and to Helen Weller who generously served as a sounding board.

In addition, I would like to mention the unsung hero at Columbia University whose scholarly fact-checking proved invaluable. I am also grateful not only to the librarians at the Library of Congress, New York Public Library, and the University Research Library at the University of California Los Angeles, but to the fellow researchers who enthusiastically contributed to my pursuit of historical scandals.

CONTENTS

A TIMELINE OF AMERICAN SCANDALS

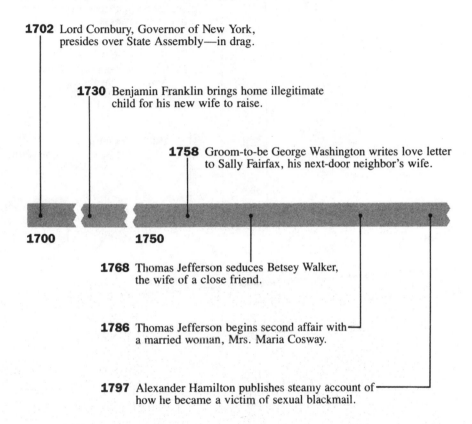

1702 Lord Cornbury, Governor of New York, presides over State Assembly—in drag.

1730 Benjamin Franklin brings home illegitimate child for his new wife to raise.

1758 Groom-to-be George Washington writes love letter to Sally Fairfax, his next-door neighbor's wife.

1700   **1750**

1768 Thomas Jefferson seduces Betsey Walker, the wife of a close friend.

1786 Thomas Jefferson begins second affair with a married woman, Mrs. Maria Cosway.

1797 Alexander Hamilton publishes steamy account of how he became a victim of sexual blackmail.

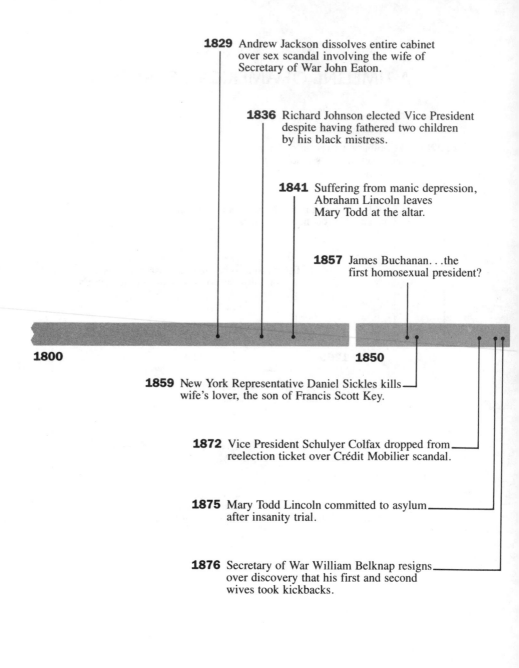

1829 Andrew Jackson dissolves entire cabinet over sex scandal involving the wife of Secretary of War John Eaton.

1836 Richard Johnson elected Vice President despite having fathered two children by his black mistress.

1841 Suffering from manic depression, Abraham Lincoln leaves Mary Todd at the altar.

1857 James Buchanan...the first homosexual president?

1800

1850

1859 New York Representative Daniel Sickles kills wife's lover, the son of Francis Scott Key.

1872 Vice President Schulyer Colfax dropped from reelection ticket over Crédit Mobilier scandal.

1875 Mary Todd Lincoln committed to asylum after insanity trial.

1876 Secretary of War William Belknap resigns over discovery that his first and second wives took kickbacks.

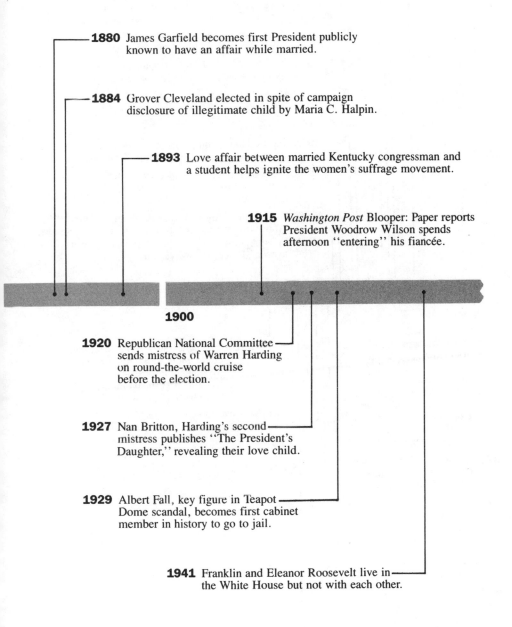

1880 James Garfield becomes first President publicly known to have an affair while married.

1884 Grover Cleveland elected in spite of campaign disclosure of illegitimate child by Maria C. Halpin.

1893 Love affair between married Kentucky congressman and a student helps ignite the women's suffrage movement.

1915 *Washington Post* Blooper: Paper reports President Woodrow Wilson spends afternoon "entering" his fiancée.

1900

1920 Republican National Committee sends mistress of Warren Harding on round-the-world cruise before the election.

1927 Nan Britton, Harding's second mistress publishes "The President's Daughter," revealing their love child.

1929 Albert Fall, key figure in Teapot Dome scandal, becomes first cabinet member in history to go to jail.

1941 Franklin and Eleanor Roosevelt live in the White House but not with each other.

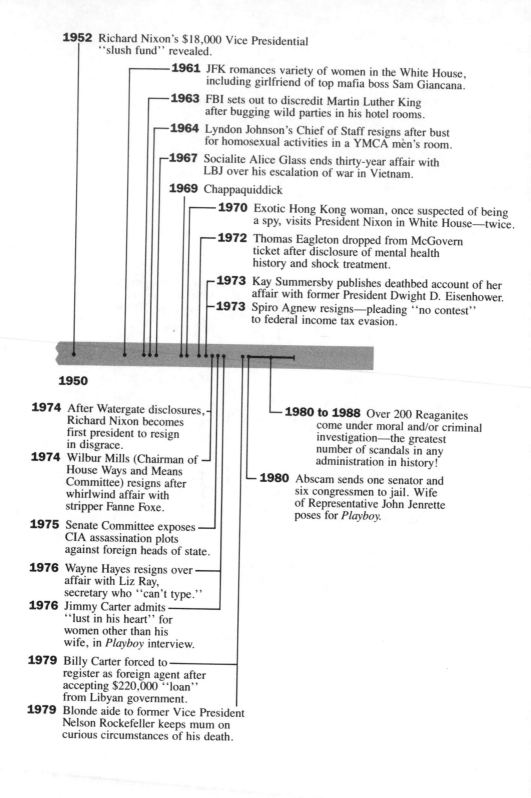

1952 Richard Nixon's $18,000 Vice Presidential "slush fund" revealed.

1961 JFK romances variety of women in the White House, including girlfriend of top mafia boss Sam Giancana.

1963 FBI sets out to discredit Martin Luther King after bugging wild parties in his hotel rooms.

1964 Lyndon Johnson's Chief of Staff resigns after bust for homosexual activities in a YMCA mèn's room.

1967 Socialite Alice Glass ends thirty-year affair with LBJ over his escalation of war in Vietnam.

1969 Chappaquiddick

1970 Exotic Hong Kong woman, once suspected of being a spy, visits President Nixon in White House—twice.

1972 Thomas Eagleton dropped from McGovern ticket after disclosure of mental health history and shock treatment.

1973 Kay Summersby publishes deathbed account of her affair with former President Dwight D. Eisenhower.

1973 Spiro Agnew resigns—pleading "no contest" to federal income tax evasion.

1950

1974 After Watergate disclosures, Richard Nixon becomes first president to resign in disgrace.

1974 Wilbur Mills (Chairman of House Ways and Means Committee) resigns after whirlwind affair with stripper Fanne Foxe.

1975 Senate Committee exposes CIA assassination plots against foreign heads of state.

1976 Wayne Hayes resigns over affair with Liz Ray, secretary who "can't type."

1976 Jimmy Carter admits "lust in his heart" for women other than his wife, in *Playboy* interview.

1979 Billy Carter forced to register as foreign agent after accepting $220,000 "loan" from Libyan government.

1979 Blonde aide to former Vice President Nelson Rockefeller keeps mum on curious circumstances of his death.

1980 to 1988 Over 200 Reaganites come under moral and/or criminal investigation—the greatest number of scandals in any administration in history!

1980 Abscam sends one senator and six congressmen to jail. Wife of Representative John Jenrette poses for *Playboy*.

Introduction

POLITICAL ETHICS. IN AMERica they seem to change as often as hemlines. What is scandalous in one decade is business as usual in another. In 1832, Representative William Stanbery (D-Ohio) was censured merely for suggesting that the House Speaker's eyes might be "too frequently turned from the chair you occupy toward the White House." But forty years later, when Representative James A. Garfield (R-Ohio) admitted accepting stock from Crédit Mobilier of America at a time when the company needed legislative favors, he not only escaped censure, he was elected president.

Varying standards have also been applied to politicians' private lives and personal morality. As far back as 1797, the political career of Alexander Hamilton survived in spite of his published confession that he was a victim of sexual blackmail. In 1836, we elected a vice president who had fathered two children by his black live-in girlfriend. Throughout the twentieth century, we winked and snickered at a variety of stories of presidential philandering, but in the 1988 campaign, we watched the demise of Gary Hart after front-page headlines about his tryst with a Miami party girl.

Throughout the rest of the 1988 campaign, voters learned of mistresses and shot gun weddings, résumé enhancement and plagiarism, pot-smoking and amphetamine addiction, cronyism and even a little-known gay sex scandal. In addition, the ghosts of Iran-Contra and Ed Meese entered the race. Beyond that, voters were asked to choose between wimps and bullies, womanizers and corn-balls, and even a John F. Kennedy impersonator or two. The media attention to the new "character issue" provided a showcase for some great political theater, although none ever matched the level of titillation inspired by Gary Hart's melodramatic resignation and controversial return. For the first time in the history of network television, a presidential candidate was asked, point-blank, if he had had an extramarital affair. Even the usually staid *New York Times* sent out an "adultery questionnaire." Needless to say, in 1988 everyone was off and running—from the *National Enquirer* to C-SPAN.

But is the media today really more probing, or do political candidates have more scandals to hide? That's what *Fall from Grace* sets out to answer.

In the context of this book, "scandal" is defined as a moral stumbling, or any action or incident which, if exposed to the public, will discredit the politician involved. The scandals reviewed include not only sex, corruption, and conflict of interest, but mental health, marriage and family problems, alcoholism, and anything else that *might* affect leadership or our pursuit of a more perfect nation. I stress might because, as history will reflect, some of our most moral leaders have been our weakest, while some with the most scandalous behavior have served the country the best. With this comprehensive look at scandals through the ages, however, those judgments will, hopefully, be left to the reader.

Today, in fact, those judgments are more important than ever. As Gary Hart put it so succinctly, "If someone's out doing dangerous things, you don't want their finger on the button." But even on a less dramatic level, political scandals can and have influenced the course of history. A colonial governor who was a transvestite served as an inspiration for the articles of impeachment to the drafters of the constitution who wanted to be sure they had a way to get rid of such characters in the future. An 1829 scandal concerning the wife of the Secretary of War toppled Andrew Jackson's entire cabinet and paved the way for Martin Van Buren to become president. In the 1890s, a sex scandal between a married

senator and a student marked the beginning of the women's suffrage movement. After their organized protests cost the senator his
reelection, women were ready to fight for the right to vote.

Financial corruption and abuse of power have altered the
course of history, too. Just as voters responded to Jimmy Carter in
the post-Watergate era, honest Abraham Lincoln was elected as a
reaction to the widespread corruption of the Buchanan administration before him. But not all political scandals inspire a change in
the direction of government. Each scandal, no matter how great or
small, sets off a chain reaction of events which can influence the
course of history in many other ways. Sometimes the influence can
only be measured by a senate vote that is silenced or a bill that isn't
passed. The United States actually lost the opportunity to buy
Cuba for $30 million because Congress refused to appropriate
funding for fear President Buchanan would use the money as a
personal "slush fund."

Throughout history, politicians have made serious mistakes
in either their private or their public lives, or both. It is more the
media scrutiny of scandals that is cyclical in nature. For example,
in 1884, the womanizing of Grover Cleveland was a widely publicized campaign issue, but in 1906, the press virtually ignored the
curious friendship between Woodrow Wilson and Mrs. Mary
Hulbert Peck. In fact, from Woodrow Wilson's administration
through the 1960s, most personal scandals surfaced only after a
politician died. Today, however, the cycle for personal scrutiny
has returned in full bloom. But in reality, neither Gary Hart nor
Grover Cleveland suffered any worse than George Washington,
who died a broken man; Thomas Jefferson, whose seduction of his
best friend's wife made the front pages of *The New York Post*; or
Ben Franklin who endured the wide distribution of a 1764 campaign document that identified the real mother of his child not as
his wife but as her handmaiden. Today, television may spread the
news more quickly, but hardly less painfully.

The real difference in 1988, however, is that voters are now
asked to choose from a greater smorgasbord of misconduct. "I
made a mistake in my personal life," Gary Hart confessed in a

"Good Morning America" interview soon after his '88 campaign reentry. "I've also insisted, as I think I have a right to, that my mistake in my personal life be put against the mistakes of this administration . . . selling arms to terrorists, lying to Congress, shredding documents."

As history shows, Americans do understand the difference. California Democrat Robert Leggett was reelected despite the fact that his constituents knew he had bought separate houses for his wife and mistress. Gerry Studds (D-Mass.) was reelected in spite of his official censure by the House of Representatives after the congressman acknowledged an affair with a seventeen-year-old male page as "a mutually voluntary private relationship between adults." And Michigan Democrat Don Riegle survived as great a political and personal embarrassment as any when, in the middle of his 1976 campaign for Senate, the Detroit News printed transcripts of tape-recorded pillow talk between him and his mistress, "Dorothy." Riegle squared off with the press, called his behavior an aberration which "had occurred in a period of great personal difficulty during which I was breaking up with my wife of twelve years," and was elected to the Senate where he still serves today.

But as *Fall from Grace* will demonstrate, it's not always such keen public relations efforts on the part of politicians that make the difference. Americans can be a very forgiving people. But while we accept apologies and embrace candor, we loathe denials and cover-ups. And, ultimately, we draw the line at financial corruption and illegal activities. While Leggett, Studds, and Riegle were reelected, the congressmen who accepted ABSCAM bribes were not. They went to jail.

Still, the 1988 campaign seems to reflect a growing need for Americans to find their moral bearing. *Fall from Grace* is a response to that need, which was pointed up by the Gary Hart ordeal and the subsequent attention given the "character issue." For only through an examination of all the scandals in their context of history can one begin to judge, for example, if womanizing really matters, if a candidate has any right to privacy, which foibles are excusably human and which are not.

The information presented in the following pages has been painstakingly gathered from presidential papers, biographical works, academic theses, newspaper accounts, media studies, government documents, personal interviews, and more. A few less-than-earth-shattering scandals, such as George Washington's unrequited love for his next-door neighbor's wife, have been included to serve as a measure of distinction. A few more are included, admittedly, because of their irresistible human interest appeal. The amount of space given a particular scandal is in no way a reflection of its importance in history. Some scandals, of a more obscure or complicated nature, are given greater coverage, while some of the better-known scandals, such as JFK's romance with Marilyn Monroe, have been presented more succinctly because of the depth in which they have been covered elsewhere. In a few instances, some political scandals have been omitted entirely simply because they did not involve a moral stumbling. Such was the case with President Andrew Johnson, the only U. S. President to endure impeachment proceedings. While eleven articles of impeachment were brought against him, most were related to his firing of Secretary of War Edwin M. Stanton, an act which certain political opponents viewed as a violation of a law which required Senate approval for certain executive branch dismissals.

So, as we look towards our next administration, will America find its moral bearing? Probably so. Will we see more sex and corruption? Absolutely. As a journalist who has reported scandals for the past twelve years, I believe sex, scandal, and corruption in the political system are as American as apple pie. But, then again, so is the painful purging process that the American people are so willing to endure as so many of our leaders fall from grace.

FALL FROM GRACE

"We The People . . ."

Scandals of Colonial America

L ONG BEFORE THERE WAS a United States of America, there was sex, scandal, and corruption in American politics. In fact, some of the most notorious—and bizarre—of tales can be traced to our colonial leaders. Such was the case with Edward Hyde, the governor-general of New York, better known as Lord Cornbury.

When Cornbury first arrived at the shores of Manhattan Island on May 3, 1702, he was greeted warmly by the local aristocrats, who honored him with "the freedom of the city." To the English and Dutch settlers, there was much about Cornbury to inspire confidence. Besides having served for sixteen years in British Parliament, he was also the first cousin of Queen Anne, the thirty-seven-year-old British monarch who had succeeded the throne that year. But it wasn't long before his new subjects learned the awful truth. He was a thief, a bigot, a grafter, a drunk, and, strange as it was, a transvestite. The combination of public and private wrongdoings was so outrageous that Lord Cornbury fanned the fires of revolution and later served as an inspiration for the articles of impeachment in the United States Constitution. Never again would anyone have to endure such a despicable or corrupt leader without a legal recourse for removal from office.

The first signs of Cornbury's eccentricities emerged when he asked that a special allowance of two thousand pounds go with the "freedom of the city" distinction. The taxpayers agreed and His High Mightiness, as he preferred to be called, was presented with the money at a banquet in his honor. After the dining, dancing, and merriment, he took center stage to address his people. But instead of discussing his plans for the future of the colonies, Lord Cornbury delivered an embarrassing dissertation on the sensual beauty of his wife's ears. If that wasn't enough, he insisted that all attending the banquet touch Lady Cornbury's ears and see for themselves.

That was just the beginning. When Lord Cornbury opened the New York Assembly in 1702 he showed up in drag, clad in a hooped gown and elaborate headdress and carrying a fan, much in the style of the fashionable Queen Anne. When his choice of clothing was questioned, he replied, "You are all very stupid people not to see the propriety of it all. In this place, and on this occasion, I represent a woman, and in all respects I ought to represent her as faithfully as I can."

Few people accepted Lord Cornbury's excuse that he dressed like a woman to better represent Queen Anne. They knew he was, oddly enough, a colonial cross-dresser. At first, he wore women's clothing occasionally, mainly in the evening. One story was told by a night watchman who investigated what he thought was a drunken prostitute prowling the grounds of Fort Anne, where Lord Cornbury resided. The watchman, like others after him, discovered the trespasser to be none other than Lord Cornbury, who surprised the guard by giggling and pulling firmly on his ears. Eventually, Cornbury began appearing regularly in women's clothes, often for months at a time.

Lady Cornbury was good for a scandal or two herself. Although Cornbury had once claimed his wife's ears were the finest in the land, he soon lost interest in them. Before long Lady Cornbury was penniless, left with just a few dresses His High Mightiness had not "borrowed" for his own wardrobe. But Lady Cornbury learned to be as resourceful as her husband. Besides

Lord Cornbury wore women's clothing when he addressed the New York assembly.

kickbacks and payoffs, Lord Cornbury supplemented his income in other interesting ways—like inviting local aristocrats to his grand balls and billing them for admission. Whenever Lady Cornbury needed anything, she went on shopping sprees—in people's homes. Whatever she selected, whether it was home furnishings or ball gowns, she simply sent for the following day. It got so out of

hand that when the locals heard her carriage wheels turn towards
their houses, they would hide their favorite belongings.

More serious than the family's strange fetishes and bizarre
habits, however, were Cornbury's utterly unscrupulous political
activities, which served to undermine the authority of the British
rule. Cornbury "gave" many of his friends large—and illegal—
land grants in return for cash. Among the hundreds of thousands of
acres he gave away was one tract of land south of Albany, known
as the Hardenbergh tract, which was larger than the entire colony
of Connecticut. Another tract was given to a group of nine friends
that included his secretary. In return they named the land Hyde
Park after Cornbury's family. That land is remembered today not
as the estate which honored the much-despised Lord Cornbury, but
as the homestead of the beloved Franklin D. Roosevelt, whose
family bought the property two hundred years later.

When it came time to build his own home, Cornbury simply
conned the taxpayers. In early 1707, Cornbury claimed to have
received secret information that the French were going to attack
New York by sea and urged the assembly to finance the building of
protective batteries between Staten Island and Long Island. The
assembly agreed and taxed the citizens fifteen hundred pounds.
Not surprisingly, the French never attacked, and Cornbury built a
new house for himself with the funds.

His High Mightiness was also known for his religious oppression. His persecution of the Quakers ultimately helped to set the
stage for the American revolution. In 1704, Cornbury pushed an
unpopular militia bill through the assembly in New Jersey (where
he had also been serving as governor since 1703) by blocking the
votes of three newly elected Quakers. By questioning their property qualifications, he was able to block the Quakers' votes just long
enough for the measure to pass. Just two years later when the militia bill was up for renewal, the full assembly voted it down. Because of hatred for Cornbury, muster calls were ignored and
penalties were not collected.

The last straw for the colonists came in August 1707, when
Lady Cornbury died and His High Mightiness showed up at her

funeral in drag. At that point, even Queen Anne could no longer defend him. Besides his unconventional behavior, Cornbury's legislative record was appalling. During his five years in office, only nine laws were passed, and six of those were vetoed in England. Finally, in response to complaints from the assemblies of New York and New Jersey, the queen agreed to remove him, sending word that his kinship to her "should not Protect him in Oppressing her Subjects."

In December 1708, Cornbury's replacement arrived and His High Mightiness was thrown in a New York debtor's prison. He didn't stay for long, however, much to the dismay of his opponents. The following year, Cornbury's father died. Cornbury became Earl of Clarendon, which enabled him to cancel his debts. In 1723, he died in England with honors, leaving behind a heightened passion for the American Revolution.

In March 1774, on the eve of the American Revolution, officials of the British Crown formally inquired as to the "state and condition" of New Jersey's defenses. Governor William Franklin had no choice but to reply, "There are no Forts and Places of Defense within the colony." Ever since the Quaker vote had united against Cornbury's oppression, decades before, the assembly had never been able to allocate enough funds for a worthy militia. This weakened defense was a notable legacy of Lord Cornbury, as were the articles of impeachment, for which he helped to pave the way.

Had Cornbury been a fair and honest leader, had his transvestitism been his only character flaw, perhaps his subjects would have tolerated him. After all, the colonists certainly seemed to take other sex scandals in stride. William Franklin, for example, had become governor of New Jersey despite the fact that he was an illegitimate child. His father, the immortal Benjamin Franklin, politically survived many such scandals and was simply accepted as one of America's more colorful founding fathers.

★ ★ ★

The elder Franklin had first shocked the moralistic Quakers of Philadelphia on September 1, 1730, when he took Deborah Read as his common-law wife. The flamboyant twenty-four-year-old printer could not marry Deborah legally because she had already married once and had been abandoned by her husband. Under Pennsylvania law, remarrying without divorce or proof of the spouse's death was a felony, punishable with thirty-nine lashes at the public whipping post and life imprisonment at a hard labor camp. Their common-law marriage was the obvious alternative, but the one that provided the most fuel for the gossip mill.

Still, public response to Benjamin Franklin's common-law marriage was tame compared to reactions when six months later he brought home an illegitimate son by another woman. Deborah raised baby William with love and affection as if he was her own.

Interestingly, one of the mud-slinging pamphlets of the day provides a rare clue to the identity of a woman who might have been William Franklin's real mother. According to a 1764 document, written as a parody "epitaph" for Ben Franklin, William's mother was a lowly type who later moved into the Franklin home to work as a maid so that she could be closer to her child.

An Epitaph & c
To the much esteem'd memory of
B. . . . . F. . . . Esq. L.L.D.

Possessed of many lucrative
Offices
Procured to him by the Interest of men
Whom he infamously treated,
And receiving enormous Sums
from the Province,
For Services
He never performed
After betraying it to Party and Contention,
He lived, as to the Appearance of Wealth
In Moderate Circumstances.
His Principal Estate, seeming to consist
In his Hand Maid Barbara

A most valuable Slave,
The Foster Mother
of his last Offspring
Who did his dirty Work
And in two Angelic Females,
whom Barbara also served
As Kitchen Wench and Gold Finder,
But alas the Loss!
Providence for wise tho' secret Ends
Lately deprived him of the Mother
of Excellency [William's title as Governor].
His Fortune was not however impaired
For he piously withheld from her
Manes
The pitiful Stipend of Ten pounds per Annum
On which he had cruelly suffered her
To Starve;
Then stole her to the grave in Silence,
Without a Pall, the covering due to her dignity
Without a Tomb, or even
A Monumental Inscription.

The mere suggestion that the mother of William Franklin lived with the family was shocking. Most other unwed mothers were lashed in the market place, then left in the streets to die of disease and hunger.

There is no question that Ben Franklin was quite a womanizer—well into his seventies. His political opponents didn't have to chronicle his affairs, as Franklin wrote and published extensively about them himself! The older he got, the more philosophical he became, but he still kept on writing. One of his most entertaining pieces, dated June 25, 1745, lists eight reasons why old mistresses are preferable to younger ones:

1. Because as they have more Knowledge of the World and their Minds are better stor'd with Observations, their Conversation is more improving and more lastingly agreeable.

2. Because when Women cease to be handsome, they study to be good. To maintain their Influence over Men, they supply the Diminution of Beauty by an Augmentation of Utility. They learn to do 1000 Services small and great and are the most tender and useful of all Friends when you are sick. Thus they continue amiable. And hence there is hardly such a thing to be found as an old Woman who is not a good Woman.

3. Because there is no hazard of Children, which irregularly produc'd may be attended with much Inconvenience.

4. Because thro' more Experience, they are more prudent and discreet in conducting an Intrigue to prevent Suspicion. The commerce with them is therefore safer with regard to your Reputation. And with regard to theirs, if the Affair should happen to be known, considerate People might be rather inclin'd to excuse an old Woman who would kindly take care of a young Man, form his Manners by her good Counsels, and prevent his ruining his Health and Fortune among mercenary Prostitutes.

5. Because in every Animal that walks upright, the Deficiency of the Fluids that fill the Muscles appears first in the highest Part: The Face first grows land and wrinkled; then the Neck, then the Breast, and regarding only what is below the Girdle, it is impossible of two Women to know an old from a young one. And as in the dark all Cats are grey, the Pleasure of corporal Enjoyment with an old Woman is at least equal, and frequently superior, every Knack being by Practice capable of Improvement.

6. Because the Sin is less. The debauching a Virgin may be her Ruin, and make her for Life unhappy.

7. Because the Compunction is less. The having made a young Girl *miserable* may give you frequent bitter Reflections; none of which can attend the making an old Woman *happy*.

8. [thly and Lastly] They are so *grateful*! Thus much for my Paradox. But still I advise you to marry directly.

Franklin didn't always take his own advice, however. In March 1755, at the age of forty-nine, he had a May-December romance with twenty-four-year-old Catherine Ray. On another oc-

Artist Charles Willson Peale sketched this scene after accidentally barging in on Benjamin Franklin.

---

casion Charles Willson Peale, the well-known portrait artist then in residence at the Academy of Philadelphia, caught a glimpse of Franklin kissing and fondling a young girl on his lap. As Peale later told the story, he tiptoed downstairs, left the premises, and quickly sketched the scene before loudly banging on the door to announce his arrival.

Today many scholars generously view Ben Franklin's affairs as more naughty than lecherous. They might have been. But perhaps it was because he acknowledged his own indiscretions that neither historians nor his contemporaries were ever able to use them to inflict any serious political damage. If anything, Franklin's basic honesty and integrity did more to inspire trust than disgrace. His son William became the respected governor of New Jersey. And he, of course, became one of the original signers of the Constitution and Declaration of Independence.

"Pursuing Judgement Rather than Passion":

Scandals in the Life and Times of George Washington

THE DATE WAS SEPTEMBER 12, 1758, and young George Washington, homesick and tired of fighting the French from his spartan base at Fort Cumberland, sat down to write a letter to the woman he loved. Corresponding in wartime was not an easy task, but they managed to send each other letters as often as circumstances allowed. On a few occasions, the strapping, six-foot-tall soldier managed to sneak in a detour from the bleak battlefield to visit her overnight. And once she loaned him a horse after seeing that his was worn out. Little about this would have been terribly interesting, except for the small fact that the woman receiving all the young colonel's attention was not his faithful fiancée Martha Custis, but Mrs. Sally Fairfax, the wife of his close friend and next-door neighbor.

Washington's relationship with Sally Fairfax was probably the most important emotional bond of his adult life. There is no question that he loved her profoundly. But just how far Washington's passion for Sally developed is open for speculation. Their romance was played out against the backdrop of the Revolutionary War, and they behaved as if they sensed that their personal integrity would be scrutinized by posterity. Although deeply in love, they seem to have been above the kind of conduct more commonly associated with men of great power today.

12

Mrs. Sally Fairfax, George Washington's next-door neighbor—and wife of his close friend.

George first met Sally when he was sixteen years old and living with his half-brother Lawrence at Mount Vernon. A humble and shy teenager, George was awestruck by the estate next door called Belvoir. Belvoir was a two-story brick structure owned by William Fairfax, a well-educated nobleman. It had four rooms and a passageway on the lower floor, and five rooms with another passageway on the second floor. It also had a servants' hall, a cellar, nearby offices, stables, a coach house and an elaborate garden. The mahogany dining room furniture alone cost more than all of the Washingtons' furnishings together.

When Lawrence Washington married Fairfax's daughter, Anne, the doors of Belvoir suddenly opened to George and he became a regular visitor. Even after Lawrence Washington died of tuberculosis, George was still treated as part of the family. In particular, he struck up a close friendship with Fairfax's son George William who lived at Belvoir with his bride, Sally. Sally was nineteen years old, beautiful, well-educated, and well-bred. One of Sally's descendants later described Washington's initial reaction to her as ''spontaneous combustion.''

Sally Fairfax's influence on George Washington cannot be overstated. Until their relationship, George had no more than the equivalent of an elementary-school education. John Adams once noted, ''That Washington was not a scholar was certain. That he was too illiterate, unread, unlearned for his station and reputation is equally past dispute.'' Obviously John Adams was not aware of the extent of Washington's informal education at Belvoir. During his treasured moments there, Sally and her father-in-law introduced George to many ideological concepts through the reading of plays and literature. In particular, George felt himself drawn to the high-minded principles of Roman philosophy, which they frequently discussed. Among the lessons at Belvoir, George learned that the greatest of all achievements is to win the respect of one's countrymen through honorable deeds.

Little is officially documented regarding the depth of Sally's feelings for George. He destroyed all of the letters she wrote to him over the years. Most of what is known about Washington's relationship with Sally comes from his letters to her, which she saved. The correspondence ranges from a letter he wrote to Sally on the eve of his marriage to Martha, to the final letter he wrote to her, twenty-five years after they had last seen each other. Many passages of Washington's letters are cryptic, written as if he knew they might be discovered, but taken as a whole they reveal a deep and abiding passion.

Only one message from Sally to Washington exists today—a postscript she added to a letter her father-in-law wrote. In order to keep above suspicion, Sally had the postscript cosigned by two other women. It read: "Dear Sir: After thanking heaven for your safe return, I must accuse you of great unkindness in refusing us the pleasure of seeing you this night. I do assure you that nothing but our being satisfied that our company would be disagreeable should prevent us from trying if our legs would not carry us to Mount Vernon this night, but if you will not come to us tomorrow Morning very early we shall be at Mount Vernon." Although the letter appeared rather innocent, its real message was clear. Sally was angry that Washington had not visited her right away after returning from battle.

The most difficult period for Washington probably came when Sally's father-in-law died and George William sailed to England to settle his estate, leaving Sally alone at Belvoir. Although this was his big chance, Washington chose not to visit her at all. Instead, he withdrew to Mount Vernon where, lovesick, he convinced himself he was going to an early grave just like his brother Lawrence. In March 1758, after a doctor in Williamsburg assured him he wasn't dying, he apparently decided to force thoughts of Sally out of his mind and find a wife of his own.

Regardless of the feelings that had evolved between Sally and George Washington, it is highly unlikely that she ever would have left George William for him. Divorce in colonial times was both socially and financially devastating. In marriage, a woman's property became her husband's.

Resigned that he would never marry the woman he truly loved, Washington may have decided to marry for money. After two awkward and unsuccessful courtships, Washington finally proposed marriage to Martha Dandridge Custis, a pleasant, if plain, twenty-six-year-old widow who was one of the wealthiest women in Virginia. The $100,000 left Martha by her first husband would become Washington's upon their marriage.

Even as the wedding date approached, Sally was still well in the picture. She supervised the renovations Washington ordered at

Mount Vernon as he prepared to receive his new bride. Washington also continued to write to Sally from his camp at Fort Cumberland where he fought to drive the French from the territories. His most intriguing correspondence to her was the letter of September 12, 1758, a few months before the wedding. With all of Washington's spelling and punctuation intact, the excerpts from this letter best establish the depth of his feelings, even though he tries to disguise them.

Camp at Fort Cumberland 12.th Sept. 1758–

Dear Madam,
        Yesterday I was honourd with your short, but very agreable favour . . .
        If you allow that any honour can be derivd from opposition to our present System of management you destroy the merit of it entirely in me by attributing my anxiety to the annimating prospect of possessing Mrs. Custis.—When—I need not name it, –guess yourself. –Should not my own Honour and Country's welfare be the excitement? Tis true, I profess myself a Votary of Love—I acknowledge that a Lady is in the Case—and further I confess, that this Lady is known to you. –Yes Madam as well as she is to one who is too sensible of her Charms to deny the Power, whose Influence he feels and must ever Submit to. I feel the force of her amiable beauties in the recollection of a thousand tender passages that I could wish to obliterate, till I am bid to revive them. –but experience alas! sadly reminds me how impossible this is. –and evinces an Opinion which I have long entertained, that there is a Destiny, which has the Sovereign controul of our Actions –not to be resisted by the strongest efforts of Human Nature.–
        You have drawn me my dear Madam, or rather have I drawn myself, into an honest confession of a Simple Fact—miscontrue not my meaning—'tis obvious—doubt it not, nor expose it –the World has no business to know the object of my Love, –declared in this matter to—you when I want to conceal it—One thing above all

things in this World I wish to know, and only one person of your Acquaintance can solve me that or guess my meaning. –but adieu to this, till happier times, if I ever shall see them. –the hours at present are melancholy dull.

Be assured that I am D Madam, with the most unfeigned regard,

Yr most Obedient and Most Obligd Hble ServT

G. Washington

Unfortunately, Washington destroyed her reply, which arrived thirteen days later, but it appears to have disappointed him. In his next response he wrote to Sally, "Do we misunderstand the true meaning of each other's letters? I think it must appear so, though I would fain hope the contrary, as I cannot speak planer without–But I'll say no more leave you to guess the rest."

George and Martha were married on January 6, 1759. And despite the deep feelings he always harbored for Sally Fairfax, Washington created a happy home at Mount Vernon with Martha and the two children from her first marriage. Washington had been able to show tremendous self-restraint, perhaps because he believed in "pursuing judgement rather than passion," as he later instructed his step-granddaughter. A victim of an unhappy childhood, Washington viewed marriage as the most important event in a man's life. And, as he often said, he valued the tranquility of marriage above excitement.

The last time Washington ever saw Sally Fairfax was in 1773, when she and her husband sailed to England on what they hoped would be a short trip to settle a family estate matter. As they expected to return, there were no tearful goodbyes. The Fairfaxes left Washington in charge of renting out Belvoir. And as agreed, before he left to attend the First Continental Congress in Philadelphia in 1774, Washington arranged for an auction of their home furnishings, a colonial garage sale of sorts. Poignantly, Washington

George Washington relaxing at home with his family.

paid 169 pounds to buy a little something for himself—the bolster and pillows from Sally's bedroom. They would become his only tangible memory of her. Because of estate problems and the outbreak of the Revolutionary War, the Fairfaxes never returned.

On May 16, 1798, George Washington wrote his last letter to Sally Fairfax. He had not seen her for twenty-five years, yet his emotional recall was quite clear. He wrote:

> My Dear Madam:
>
> Five and twenty years have nearly passed away since I have considered myself as the permanent resident at this place, or have been in a situation to indulge myself in a familiar intercourse with my friends by letter or otherwise. During this period so many important events have occurred and such changes in men and things have taken place as the compass of a letter would give you but an inadequate idea of. None of which events, however, nor all of them together, have been able to eradicate from my mind the recollection of those happy moments, the happiest in my life, which I have enjoyed in your company. . . . [I]t is a matter of sore regret, when I

cast my eyes towards Belvoir, which I often do, to reflect, the
former inhabitants of it with whom we lived in such harmony and
friendship no longer reside there and that the ruins can only be
viewed as the memento of former pleasure. Permit me to add that I
have wondered often, your nearest relations being in this country,
that you should not prefer spending the evening of your life among
them, rather than close the sublunary scene in a foreign country,
numerous as your acquaintances may be and sincere as the friendships you may have formed.

   No friendship could have been more sincere than that of
George Washington and Sally Fairfax. But in spite of everything
he lived for, Washington died a broken man whose true integrity
was not to be appreciated for years to come. In his last year in
office, he was attacked on almost a daily basis for everything from
expense account violations to the national celebration of his birthday, which many felt was more fitting for an English monarch than
a revolutionary. His retirement to Mount Vernon, after two terms
as the nation's first president, was bittersweet and empty.
   Sally Fairfax died in 1811 at the age of eighty-one, without
the luxuries of Belvoir or the comfort of the company of the president who loved her. But perhaps, as some believe, she died with
the personal satisfaction of having molded, refined, and tested the
great moral values possessed by the father of our country.

"The Intercourse with Mrs. Reynolds, in the Meantime Continued"

Scandals in the Life and Times of Alexander Hamilton

ALTHOUGH THE FIRST president was above reproach, the first cabinet found itself knee-deep in scandals ranging from serious incidents of financial misconduct to torrid tales of sexual blackmail—most of it centered in the office of Treasury Secretary Alexander Hamilton.

After only six months in office, Hamilton's second-in-command at the Treasury Department, William Duer, resigned under the threat of a congressional investigation into suspicious financial activities. A disgrace to the new government, it was also a serious embarrassment to Hamilton, who was Duer's cousin by marriage and lifelong friend.

Questions of Duer's activities at the Treasury Department had surfaced as early as September 1789, just a month after he took office. At first, Hamilton had ignored the rumors and resisted the mounting pressure to fire Duer. But when Hamilton was presented with proof that Duer mixed personal funds with public investments, he insisted that his assistant resign. To make matters worse, when Hamilton's new assistant scrutinized the federal accounts, he found Duer had left office owing the government $200,000.

Hamilton's early support of Duer had been detrimental enough, but his neglect in collecting Duer's debt proved even worse. Duer eventually used the $200,000 to finance a scam which, in 1792, backfired and touched off the first financial panic in U.S. history.

Duer had hoped to depress the stock of the Bank of the United States so that his own investment group could take control. At the same time, he tried to corner the market on government bonds, a maneuver that seriously eroded America's young financial system. As a result, Hamilton was forced to use government funds to stabilize the economy. Despite his efforts, a crash was inevitable. Panic swept the country, security prices tumbled, and angry mobs stormed the banks. Finally, with the economy in turmoil, Hamilton called in Duer's $200,000 debt. But it was too late. Duer's money was gone and the troubled treasury secretary was forced into a face-saving action. Within three days of non-payment, Hamilton asked his new treasury assistant to file a lawsuit against Duer. Duer pleaded with Hamilton to intervene on his behalf, but Hamilton refused, condemning Duer to a debtor's prison, in total financial ruin.

Although Hamilton ultimately stabilized the economy, the crash badly weakened his once powerful political position. Now, the Republican opposition, led by Secretary of State Thomas Jefferson, threatened to drive him from office, as they had Duer.

Hamilton and Jefferson were almost destined to hate each other. Their conflicting points of view led to the development of America's first political parties, the Federalists and the Republicans. But from the beginning the two young cabinet secretaries behaved more like sibling rivals than political ones. Hamilton and Jefferson had both lost their fathers at an early age. Jefferson's father had died, while Hamilton's father, who had never married his mother, abandoned the family a few years after his birth. Even more so than the rest of the country, the two secretaries looked upon the president as a strong father figure and competed for his attention. As Jefferson later recalled, "Hamilton and myself were daily pitted in the cabinet like two cocks."

By January 1793, the Second Congress embarked on an exhaustive investigation of Secretary Hamilton, who was also leader of the Federalist party. Although they tried their best, the members of Congress found no evidence of fraud, speculation, or official misconduct. The most anyone could prove was that Hamilton had combined two loans in 1790 that Congress wanted to keep separate. Still, on February 27, 1793, nine resolutions in Congress condemned Hamilton's handling of the loans and his disrespect for Congress.

Hamilton took his medicine graciously. As politically embarrassing as the resolutions were, he was incredibly relieved to know that a much more damaging scandal would be kept under wraps for the remainder of his term in office. While he was busy balancing the federal budget he had somehow found time to fall into a sexual blackmail trap set by a conniving mistress.

The blackmail plot was staged by Maria Reynolds and her husband, James, a con artist who had managed to stay just out of the grasp of the law. Reynolds's earlier schemes included collecting the money owed to soldiers and officers of the Continental Army. Unbeknownst to Hamilton, he had access to the government accounts lists, which were supplied to him by a low-level clerk inside the Treasury Department. While Reynolds was fairly inept at conning old soldiers, he proved to be masterful at blackmailing the treasury secretary.

Hamilton was an easy mark. With his wife, Elizabeth, remaining in their Albany, New York, home, Hamilton must have felt lonely and vulnerable in Philadelphia, the seat of the new government. The separation from his wife also kept Hamilton apart from his sister-in-law Angelica, with whom he had an ongoing affair. All of this, no doubt, made Maria Reynolds's job all the more simple.

On one fateful day in 1791, Maria arrived at Hamilton's Chestnut Street office and appealed to the treasury secretary for "help." Her husband, she explained, had deserted her and she was willing to do anything to keep the creditors at bay. Lured by the promise of sexual favors, Hamilton met her that evening at her townhouse on Market Street. She led him into her bedroom where they had a sexual encounter for which he paid her a sum of money. With Hamilton in this compromising position, who should enter but the outraged husband, James Reynolds? As Reynolds later wrote in a letter to Hamilton, "You took advantage of a poor Broken harted woman. . . . You have acted the part of the most Cruelest man in existance. . . . [S]he ses there is no other man that she Care for in this world. Now Sire you have bin the Cause of Cooling her affections for me."

Even though Reynolds claimed his home had been wrecked, he was not an uncooperative man. He encouraged Hamilton to continue the affair, admitting man-to-man that his wife was much more pleasant after Hamilton's visits. Reynolds told Hamilton, "I find when ever you have been with her, she is Cheerful and kind, but when you have not in some time she is Quite the Reverse and wishes to be alone by her self." Besides, for one thousand dollars in cold cash, he could learn to live with a broken heart. Hamilton paid Reynolds in two lump sums, $600 and $400, and ever the businessman, he demanded a signed receipt.

Hamilton continued the affair with Maria along with the payments to her husband, for almost a year. When the passions of his mistress began to stretch his personal budget, he borrowed money. On June 15, 1791, he borrowed two hundred dollars from Robert Troup, a friend who warned him that he was about to be investigated over the fallout from Duer.

With the affair in full swing, the only thing Hamilton needed less than an investigation was a surprise visit from his wife. On August 9, he wrote to Elizabeth that it was in the interest of her own health that she not come to Philadelphia for the rest of the summer: "I cannot be happy without you. Yet I must not advise you to urge your return. The confirmation of your health is so essential to our happiness that I am willing to make as long a sacrifice as the season and your patience will permit."

Two days later, he reminded her to write well in advance of any decision to visit Philadelphia. With his wife safely tucked away in Albany, Hamilton continued his illicit affair with Maria. By the fall, when he could no longer convince Elizabeth to stay at home, he performed a remarkable juggling act in order to see Maria. "I had frequent meetings with her—most of them at my own house . . . ," he later confessed, adding, "The intercourse with Mrs. Reynolds, in the meantime continued. . . . [H]er conduct made it very difficult to disentangle myself."

Hamilton only considered ending his extramarital affair when Mrs. Hamilton became pregnant. He had hoped for a "gradual discontinuance," but the plan failed when Maria threatened to kill herself. He later explained, "A more frequent intercourse continued to be pressed upon me on the pretext of its being essential to the party. . . . The appearances of a violent attachment were played of a genuine extreme distress at the idea of an interruption of the connection. . . . "

In a rather bizarre twist, Maria's husband acted with disgust at the very thought that Hamilton would dump another man's wife, one of the many charades played out to keep the blackmail scheme going. Hamilton later recalled, "Reynolds would occasionally relapse into discontent at his situation, would treat her very ill, hint at the assassination of me, and more openly threaten, by way of revenge, to inform Mrs. Hamilton."

Despite all the threats, the extortion, and the possibility of being discovered, Hamilton might have continued his affair indefinitely—had James Reynolds not asked him for a job in the United States Treasury Department. Hamilton had had enough. He might be an adulterer, he might pay off a lowly scoundrel like Reynolds with his last dime, but Hamilton would not compromise the public trust by giving Reynolds a government job, even though there was a vacant clerk position available.

As the plot thickened, Reynolds's past caught up with him and he and his partner, Jacob Clingman, were arrested on charges of defrauding old soldiers. Reynolds, waiting in his Philadelphia prison cell, assumed his buddy Hamilton would pull a few strings to release him. After all, the scheme, if traced to the Treasury Department, would be another great embarrassment to Hamilton. But once again, he would not abuse the public trust. Whatever was between the two men would only be handled by Hamilton as a private citizen, not with public money or political influence.

It must have taken considerable courage to refuse Reynolds at that moment. The con man and his partner were not the types to stay in jail for long. If Hamilton wouldn't make a deal, Reynolds knew Jefferson and the Republican opposition would.

In December 1792, Clingman contacted Congressman Frederick Muhlenburg, a Republican from Pennsylvania, and said he and Reynolds had enough information "to hang the Secretary of the Treasury, that he [Hamilton] was deeply concerned in speculation, that he had frequently given money to him [Reynolds]." The Republicans were delighted at the thought of finally linking Hamilton with Duer, who was already in debtor's prison. To help with the investigation, Muhlenburg called on two other Republican congressmen—James Monroe and Abraham Venable. The trio brought their inquiry first to Reynolds in prison, then to Maria in her house on Market Street. The congressmen were stunned that some of her letters seemed to suggest that the secretary of the treasury was guilty of speculating in government securities.

Finally, on December 15, 1792, with the restraint of a lynch mob, the three congressmen paid a surprise visit to Hamilton in his offices. At first Hamilton was indignant. But when they told him of the purpose of their visit, he was instantly more accommodating. Emotionally shaken, he agreed to set up a meeting for later that evening.

Incredibly, Hamilton told the congressmen the vivid details of his affair with Mrs. Reynolds. Being branded an adulterer was one thing. But he was not going to let Reynolds destroy his integrity by linking him falsely with Duer. Hamilton went to great lengths to back up his story with letters, notes, and receipts. So pathetically convincing was Hamilton that halfway through his explanation, the congressmen pleaded with him to stop. But Hamilton hung in there until the bitter end, explaining every last detail. What resulted in that room afterward was a gentleman's code of honor unmatched by future politicians. The three Republican congressmen, convinced that Hamilton's integrity was intact, pledged never to repeat the tale they had just been told. The opposition placed a greater value on protecting the public's confidence in government than on partisan politics.

Jefferson was given a full account of the meeting and also chose to remain silent. But then again, he may have felt certain that Hamilton would be skewered by Congress on fraud charges. And just to make sure, the Republicans handed down the nine resolutions condemning Hamilton just two days before Congress went into recess for the summer. It was a strategy that left Hamilton with little chance to reply . . . or so they thought. Much to their surprise, the prolific politician prepared his response to the resolutions in record time, satisfying friends and foes alike.

Fair play in politics ruled the day—at least until 1796, when a copy of the transcript of Hamilton's confession was leaked to a local muckraker named James Thomson Callender. A strong ally of Thomas Jefferson, Callender published the sordid details of Hamilton's affair in a pamphlet called, "History for the Year 1796." As the details seemed to implicate his involvement in financial speculation, Hamilton quickly responded with the publication of his own confession. Not surprisingly, Hamilton's "Observations of Certain Documents contained in . . . the history of the United States for the Year 1796," was a bestseller.

Like so many other political wives of generations to come, Elizabeth Hamilton stuck by her man, inspiring the rest of the country to forgive him for his sins. To her, Hamilton gratefully said, "You are my good genius. . . . [Y]ou are all that is charming in my estimation and the more I see of your sex the more I become convinced of the judiciousness of my choice." In his pamphlet he more publicly confessed, "I can never cease to condemn myself for the pain which it may inflict in a bosom eminently entitled to all my gratitude, fidelity, and love."

During the six years Hamilton's scandal had been kept a secret, the soap opera continued. Maria divorced James Reynolds and married his business partner, Jacob Clingman, although Maria's attorney, Aaron Burr, unfortunately failed to notice that the marriage took place thirty minutes before the paperwork for the divorce was finalized.

Ultimately, Hamilton blamed James Monroe, who kept the only transcript of the meeting, for leaking the confession to the

OBSERVATIONS

ON

CERTAIN DOCUMENTS

CONTAINED IN NO. V & VI OF

" THE HISTORY OF THE UNITED STATES
FOR THE YEAR 1796,"

IN WHICH THE

CHARGE OF SPECULATION

AGAINST

ALEXANDER HAMILTON,

LATE SECRETARY OF THE TREASURY,

IS FULLY REFUTED.

WRITTEN BY HIMSELF.

PHILADELPHIA:
PRINTED FOR JOHN FENNO, BY JOHN BIOREN,
1797.

In 1797, Alexander Hamilton published his own account as a victim of sexual blackmail.

press. At one point, he even challenged Monroe to a duel. Monroe
called upon Aaron Burr to stand in for him, but Burr used diploma-
cy instead of pistols. Several years later, on July 11, 1804, during
his term as vice president under Thomas Jefferson, Burr killed
Hamilton in a duel over an unrelated challenge. This became a
scandal in its own right, as the Bergen County, New Jersey, grand
jury indicted Burr for murder. Burr, who was also president of the
Senate, returned to Washington, D.C., where the charges were
quickly forgotten.

Meanwhile, James Callender died of alcoholism—but only
after turning on his old friend Jefferson and dragging him through
the mud, just as he had Hamilton.

"My Head and My Heart"

Scandals in the Life and Times of Thomas Jefferson

ALMOST EVERY SEEDY scandal ever connected to Thomas Jefferson—and there were many—can be traced back to James Thomson Callender, the muckraker who routinely attacked politicians until his death from alcoholism in July 1803. At that time, some even suspected suicide when his body was discovered floating in three feet of water in the James River outside of Richmond, Virginia. Regardless of the disgrace in which he died, Callender's role in early American politics cannot be overlooked. Besides rocking the Federalist party and its leader Alexander Hamilton, he was the key that unlocked many of the secrets in the private world of Thomas Jefferson, the man who would become America's first secretary of state, its second vice president and finally, its third president.

John F. Kennedy once invited a group of Nobel laureates to a dinner in the Executive Mansion and marvelled at "the most extraordinary collection of talent . . . that has ever been gathered together at the White House—with the exception of when Thomas Jefferson dined alone." Jefferson's talent went beyond his achievements as a founding father and author of the Declaration of Independence. He was an inventor whose patents included the automatic door, the dumbwaiter, the thumbtack, and a copy machine that moved a second pen when he drafted correspondence. His experiments with rice-growing helped make the United States

Thomas Jefferson—architect, linguist, inventor, and philanderer.

a leading rice producer. As an architect, Jefferson designed build-ings for the University of Virginia and the seat of government in Richmond. As a linguist, he wrote a comparative vocabulary study of the American Indians. When the Library of Congress was burned by the British in 1814, Jefferson offered his personal libra-ry to replace it. In light of his vast accomplishments, it is almost impossible to imagine that he ever had time to get involved in so many romantic entanglements.

Jefferson went to great lengths to protect his privacy. While he kept copies of 18,000 letters he wrote, and filed 25,000 more he received, he destroyed all correspondence with his wife, Martha, and his mother. Today no picture of Martha Jefferson exists and little is known about Jefferson's marital life. James Callender, however, made sure the world would know about Jefferson's scan-dals from the early seduction of his neighbor's wife to his alleged black slave mistress and her children at Monticello.

Before delving into the juicy details of Jefferson's romantic affairs, it is important to take a look at what little is known about his ten-year marriage to Martha Wayles Skelton, which began on January 1, 1772. He was so devoted to his wife that it is doubtful he was ever unfaithful. Because of her poor health, Jefferson actually resigned from Congress on September 2, 1776, to take care of her. Martha had suffered through many difficult childbirths. Four out of their seven children did not survive. Four months after giving birth to their last child, Martha Jefferson died. During his bedside vigil, Jefferson vowed that he would never remarry. And he was true to his vow.

Documentation of the Jeffersons' last days together is enough to touch even the most callous heart. On one occasion, Martha copied a passage for Jefferson from *Tristram Shandy*, one of his favorite books. She wrote, "Time wastes too fast; every letter I trace tells me what rapidity life follows my pen. The days and hours of it are flying over our heads like clouds of windy day never to return—more everything presses on—." Jefferson finished writing the passage for her: "—and every time I kiss thy hand to bid adieu, every absence which follows it, are preludes to that

eternal separation which we are shortly to make!'' He later enclosed a lock of her hair and saved their notes in an envelope.

Eight weeks after his wife's death on September 6, 1782,
Jefferson returned to politics. It has been speculated that had Martha Jefferson lived a longer life, Thomas Jefferson would have
never become our third president.

★ ★ ★

Jefferson remained ''scandal-free'' in the press until 1802,
his second year as president, when James Callender began a series
of savage attacks. It was a surprise to many who were well aware
that Jefferson had supported Callender in his attacks on Alexander
Hamilton and, later, against John Adams, whom Jefferson served
as vice president. But Callender had become fickle and disloyal
towards the end of his life, which was a series of misfortunes he
brought upon himself.

Callender came to America from Scotland in 1793, fleeing
sedition charges which stemmed from his vitriolic press attacks
against the British government. But if he expected America to be
the land of golden opportunity, he would soon learn otherwise.

Although the 1796 Hamilton exposé was a great coup, the
notorious muckraker wound up moving aimlessly from newspaper
to newspaper. In one time of need he hinted that he wanted to stay
with Jefferson at Monticello. Jefferson ignored the hint, sent him
fifty dollars, and wished him well.

In 1799, Callender wrote ''The Prospect Before Us,'' a criticism of the federal government and President John Adams. In it he
said Americans had a choice, ''between Adams, war, and beg-
gary, and Jefferson, peace and competency.'' He called Adams,
''that strange compound of ignorance and ferocity, of deceit and
weakness,'' adding, ''[T]he people of the United States have a
million good reasons for wishing to see a peaceable, a constitutional, and a speedy termination of the reign of Mr. Adams.''

Callender sent the proofs of his pamphlet to Jefferson, then
vice president, an Adams opponent. Jefferson gave the work high
marks and wrote back, ''Such papers cannot fail to produce the
best efforts.'' The most the pamphlet produced, however, was

Callender's arrest and grand jury indictment for violation of the 1798 Sedition Act. Claiming the indictment was a clear violation of free speech, Jefferson provided a strong defense counsel for Callender. But the judge, who was counted among the anti- Jefferson forces, thought otherwise. Callender was found guilty, fined two hundred dollars, and given a nine-month sentence. A few years later, Jefferson, as president, would impeach the judge who made that ruling. But as of June 6, 1800, Callender landed in jail.

Just days after Jefferson was inaugurated president in March 1801, he ordered Callender set free. He promised to return the $200 fine, but Callender wanted more for his loyalty. He was after a $1,500-a-year job as postmaster of Richmond. When he was turned down by Secretary of State James Madison, who acted for the president, he vowed to take revenge. The following year, at his new job with the *Richmond Recorder*, Callender published the letter in which Jefferson had sent him the fifty dollars, claiming the payment was hush money. He also published other correspondence which revealed that as vice president, Jefferson had supported his attacks on Adams. Jefferson later wrote to James Monroe, "I am really mortified at the base ingratitude of Callender. It presents human nature in a hideous form." Hideous or not, the war was on between Jefferson and Callender.

Callender soon graduated from publishing bribery charges to writing about the sex scandals in Jefferson's life. The earliest scandal he uncovered was Jefferson's seduction of Betsey Walker, the wife of his close friend John. The seduction began with great subtlety in 1768 and built up to a bona fide advance during the summer of either 1769 or 1770 while John was at Fort Stanwix working on a treaty with the Indians. What made the situation particularly scandalous was that Jefferson had been an usher at their wedding. Under the circumstances, it seemed logical for Walker to ask Jefferson to look after his wife and child while he was away for four months. He also asked Jefferson to be the executor of his will in the event anything happened to him. According to the following account, detailed in an 1805 letter written by John Walker to a Jefferson enemy, Jefferson did a lot more: "[W]e went on a visit to Col. Coles a mutual acquaintance and distant neighbor. Mr. Jefferson was there. On the ladys retiring to bed he pretended to be sick, complained of a headache & left the gentlemen among whom I was. Instead of going to bed as his sickness authorized a belief he stole into my room where my wife was undressing or in bed."

John Walker and James Thomson Callender weren't the only ones to exploit the Betsey Walker affair. On April 5, 1805, the widely read *New York Evening Post* published the Betsey Walker story and brutally attacked the president's virtue. The smear article began with Jefferson's own words, taken from his second inaugural speech, in which he said, "I shall now enter on the duties which my fellow citizens have again called me, and shall proceed in the spirit of those principles which they have approved. I fear not that any motives of interest may lead me astray, I am sensible of no passion which could seduce me knowingly from the path of justice."

The paper continued with editorial comments almost more befitting the Gary Hart campaign 182 years later:

> Mr. Jefferson, indeed admits that the "weaknesses of human nature and the limits of his own understanding will produce errors of judgement, sometimes injurious to the interest" of the people, but as to "going astray from motives of interest" or being "seduced by passion from the path of justice" that he has no apprehension of; he denied that any such thing can happen to him. While therefore other mortals are constantly liable to wander from the path of rectitude, so that it has been pronounced by divine authority that there is "none righteous, no not one"—behold here comes one who if we may believe his own accounts of himself is exempted from the common frailties that beset the rest of mankind. . . .
>
> [He who has] corrupted the integrity of the nation, has demoralized the American people, for the purpose of promoting his personal aggrandizement, now boasts that no motives of interest can lead him astray.

Jefferson was called a "scoundrel," a "scourge," "the out-cast of America, without abilities and without virtue." The *Post*'s account of how Jefferson, "stole to the chamber of his absent friend at dead of night and attempted to violate his bed" made the charges all the more difficult to ignore. Finally, President Jefferson admitted his guilt to intimate friends. One better-known disclosure was to Robert Smith, the secretary of the navy, to whom he wrote, "You will perceive that I plead guilty to one of their charges, that when young and single, I offered love to a handsome lady. I acknolege its incorrectness. It is the only one founded in truth among all their allegations against me."

★ ★ ★

Sixteen years after the Betsey Walker affair, Jefferson, while serving as minister to France, rediscovered his soft spot for married women. Jefferson had accepted the foreign post in May 1774, after the long period of isolation that followed the death of his wife.

When Jefferson first arrived in Paris, he had a much lower profile than his predecessor, Benjamin Franklin, who had become a darling of the society ladies. Jefferson enrolled his eldest daughter, Patsy, in a convent school and rented a modest house on the Rue Têtebout. Before long, he moved to a more expensive one on the Champs Elysees, hired extra servants, became an avid collector of furniture and art, and made his debut on the social scene. One of his closest friends was John Trumbull, an American artist who stayed with Jefferson while designing a canvas for the Declaration of Independence. Trumbull ran with a fast arty crowd, and on one fateful Sunday in August 1786, he invited Jefferson to join some friends for an afternoon at the trendy Paris grain market, the Halle aux Bleds. There he met Richard Cosway, a well-known English miniaturist, and his wife, Maria.

Maria, twenty-seven, was beautiful, with blonde curls, deep blue eyes, and a coquettish Italian accent. The moment Jefferson first laid eyes on her, he fell in love with her, and the more he learned about her, the deeper his emotions ran. She sang, played

Mrs. Maria Cosway, one of the two married women with whom Thomas Jefferson had affairs.

the harpsichord, and was a respected painter in her own right, although her husband made it clear there would be only one famous artist in the family.

Born in Florence, Italy, Maria Louisa Catherine Cecilia Hadfield Cosway had once considered becoming a nun. Luckily for Jefferson, she moved to London instead and was introduced to society by none other than Angelica Church, the sexy sister-in-law of Alexander Hamilton. Maria fell into a crowd of eighteenth-century "jetsetters," an adventurous, ambitious crowd. She married Richard Cosway, a short, pretentious artist whose clientele included top socialites, such as the Prince of Wales and the prince's mistresses. Maria, in fact, was afraid of Richard, who, as letters discovered years later revealed, had been having his own extramarital affairs—with both women and men.

For Jefferson, age forty-three, the first afternoon he spent with Maria stirred strong emotions which he had thought buried along with his wife four years before. Disregarding the presence of her husband, Jefferson could not leave Maria's side. In order to prolong their encounter, he broke a dinner engagement with the Duchesse de la Rochefoucauld d'Anville and insisted that everyone else break their plans, too. When all was rearranged, the foursome traveled by carriage to the Parc de St. Cloud for dinner, took a stroll through a gallery, and went onto Paris to see a fireworks display.

The real fireworks, however, were between Jefferson and Mrs. Cosway. On August 9, less than a week after their first meeting, the once-solemn widower wrote to Abigail Adams: "Here we have singing, dancing, laugh and merriment. No assassinations, no treasons, rebellions nor other dark deeds. . . . [T]hey have as much happiness in one year as an Englishman has in ten."

During the following weeks he spent with Maria, Jefferson came out of his emotional shell. As minister of France, he was able to arrange his schedule around their meetings, taking afternoons off for sightseeing, gallery visits, and more. Jefferson later recalled their afternoons in a letter to her: "How beautiful was every object! the Port of Neuilly, the hills along the Seine, the rainbows of the machine of Marly, the terras of St. Germains, the chateaux, the gardens, the statues of Marly, the pavillion of Lucienne. Recollect too Madrid, Bagatelle, the King's garden, the Desert.'' Even Richard Cosway seemed to encourage the relationship. When Jefferson visited Maria in their home, Richard left them alone together.

By September 18, 1786, with only a few days left until the Cosways returned to London, Jefferson broke his right wrist. There are many versions of the story, but all suspect he was showing off for his new love. One tale has Jefferson jumping over a fence as they walked along the Seine; another has him jumping over a pool on the way to the carriage. Regardless of the way it happened, Jefferson never fully recovered from the break and was in pain for the rest of his life.

October 4 was planned as their last whirlwind day together. Despite the agony of his injured wrist, he rode with her in a carriage, which bounced over the cobblestones. As a result, Jefferson had to call for a surgeon late that evening. Even then, he wrote a love note to Maria with his other hand. The heartache of their separation was far more severe than the pain a broken bone could ever inflict.

When the Cosways postponed their departure an extra day, Jefferson went to their home on the outskirts of Paris to say his final goodbyes. Afterward, Jefferson described himself as feeling ''more dead than alive.'' That evening Jefferson returned home and wrote what has to be one of the most extraordinary love letters in the world. Still left-handed and clumsy, he wrote twelve pages of dialogue known as ''My Head and My Heart.'' It can still be debated which side won.

> HEAD: Thou art the most incorrigible of all the beings that ever sinned! I reminded you of the follies of the first day, intending to deduce from thence some useful lessons for you; but instead of listening to these, you kindle at the recollection, you retrace the whole series with a fondness which shows you want nothing but the opportunity to act it over again. I often told you during the course

that you were imprudently engaging your affections under circumstances that must cost you a great deal of pain: that the persons
indeed were of the greatest merit, possessing good sense, good
humor, honest hearts, honest manners, and eminence in a lovely
art: that the lady had moreover qualities and accomplishments be-
longing to her sex, which might form a chapter apart for her; such
as music, modesty, beauty, and that softness of disposition, which
is the ornament of her sex and charm of ours. But that all the considerations would increase the pang of separation; that their stay here
was to be short; that you rack our whole system when you are parted
from those you love, complaining that such a separation is worse
than death, inasmuch as this ends our sufferings, whereas that only
begins them: and that the separation would in this instance be the
more severe as you would probably never see them again.

HEART: But they told me they would come back again the
next year.

HEAD: But in the meantime see what you suffer: and their
return too depends on so many circumstances tht if you had a grain
of prudence you would not count upon it. Upon the whole it is
improbable and therefore you should abandon the idea of ever seeing them again.

HEART: May heaven abandon me if I do!

HEAD: Very well. Suppose then, they come back. They are to
stay two months, and when these are expired, what is to follow?
Perhaps you flatter yourself they may come to America?

HEART: God only knows what is to happen. I see nothing
impossible in that supposition. And I see things wonderfully contrived sometimes to make us happy.

The following August, Maria returned to Paris to visit Jefferson for four months—without her husband. By all accounts, the
anticipation of their reunion was much more exciting than the reality of it. When she left for London on December 8, she stood him
up for their farewell breakfast. Although they would continue to
write to each other for the rest of their lives, they never saw each
other again.

In the end, Jefferson's "Head" finally won. The same could not be said for Maria, who in June 1790, abandoned her husband and three-month-old daughter for Luigi Marchesi, an Italian opera singer. Some years later, she retired to a convent, where she established a girls' college through the Church of Santa Maria della Grazie. On January 5, 1838, her remains were interred near the nun's chapel there.

★ ★ ★

One theory as to why the Maria Cosway romance fizzled that second summer in Paris is perhaps the most scandalous of all those put forth by James Thomson Callender. He claimed that was the summer Thomas Jefferson began an affair with Sally Hemings, his seventeen-year-old mulatto slave. The controversy surrounding this relationship has been argued by biographers for years. Unfortunately, Jefferson remained silent on the subject.

Jefferson took Sally Hemings to Paris that summer to help him look after his daughter. Some say that when she returned to Virginia, more than two years later, she was pregnant by Jefferson. Others have argued there was no pregnancy at all. If she had a child, experts say, it would have been recorded in Jefferson's "Farm Book," his meticulous records of more than one hundred slaves. It was not.

One theory for Jefferson's silence on the subject of Sally Hemings is that he didn't want to reveal another embarrassing truth—that Sally was actually the half-sister of his dead wife, Martha. Jefferson's father-in-law had taken an African woman named Betty as his concubine after the death of his third wife. They had six children, including Sally, who were willed to Martha after her father's death. As Jefferson's "house slaves," they were afforded certain privileges.

In 1802, Callender wrote in the *Richmond Recorder* that Sally had become Jefferson's mistress. Callender was a hack, an alcoholic, and a scandalmonger, but he had been pretty accurate in his earlier exposés involving Maria Reynolds and Betsey Walker. Could the Sally Hemings story be true?

Callender was not the only one who thought so. It was even

immortalized in verses such as this one written by Joseph Dennie, editor of the *Port Folio* of Philadelphia:

> Of all the damsels on the green
> On mountain or in valley
> A lass so luscious ne'er was seen
> As Monticellian Sally.
>
> Yankee Doodle, whose the noodle?
> What wife were half so handy?
> To breed a flock of slaves to stock
> A blackamoors the dandy.

In the 1830s, the story surfaced again in antislavery newspapers and abolitionist literature. Dr. Levi Gaylord claimed to have seen, "the Daughter of Thomas Jefferson sold in New Orleans, for one thousand dollars."

In 1873 Sally's son, Madison Hemings, published a startling interview in the *Pike County* (Ohio) *Republican*, in which he stated that his mother was Jefferson's concubine, that she became pregnant by him in Paris, and that Jefferson was his father. It is suspected, however, that Madison's testimony might have been orchestrated, even written, by someone else. The main tip-off, scholars say, is Madison's use of the French word "*enceinte*" instead of "pregnant," a more likely term to be used by a former slave.

More recently, Madison Hemings's statements were revived by psycho-historian Fawn Brodie in her bestselling 1974 book, *Thomas Jefferson: An Intimate History*. Dr. Brodie made a case for a romance between Jefferson and his slave/mistress that lasted through thirty-eight years and six children. She presented various oral histories of five generations of a family claiming to be the unacknowledged Jefferson descendants. Much of her evidence is circumstantial, however. For instance, she notes that Jefferson spent over 200 francs on new clothes for Sally in Paris. But was this expense a courtesy extended a mistress, as Brodie implied, or did Jefferson simply want his daughter's governess to look more presentable on the streets of Paris?

On the other hand, it is conceivable that, just as Jefferson destroyed documentation and correspondence relating to his wife and mother, he might have done the same for Sally. In any event, whether the Hemings affair is true or not, it is incredible to think that the stories of this alleged liaison, based on one man's revenge, have survived so many years.

★ ★ ★

One of the most interesting scandals in the Jefferson Administration isn't a romantic interlude at all. It is an obscure covert military operation conducted in 1806, which shows that Lieutenant Colonel Oliver North has a historical counterpart.

North's forerunner was Colonel William S. Smith, the son-in-law of John Adams, the second president. A Revolutionary War hero, Colonel Smith set out to organize freedom fighters to help Francisco de Miranda resist Spanish occupation in Venezuela. He raised private funds, outfitted weapons, and enlisted soldiers of fortune. On February 2, 1806, some of his troops set sail aboard the *Leander*, a chartered merchant vessel. Among the recruits was Smith's son, William Steuben, who left Columbia College to help the cause. The American public became aware of the covert operation when the *Leander* was lost to the Spanish and William Steuben Smith was put on display much like the incident involving Eugene Hasenfus, the mercenary who was captured by the Sandinistas in Nicaragua in 1986 after his supply plane was shot down en route to delivering relief to the Contras.

Colonel Smith was indicted in New York for violating the Neutrality Act of 1794 which made it unlawful to "set on foot directly or indirectly within the United States any military expedition or enterprise to be carried on against the territory of a foreign . . . state with whom the United States is at peace." Until the trial began in July 1806, Smith and his wife, Abigail, lived together in a small house—on the grounds of a prison. Needless to say, it was an awkward situation for both President Jefferson and former President John Adams, Abigail's father.

Unlike his modern day counterpart, Colonel Smith claimed his orders came directly from President Jefferson and Secretary of State James Madison. Madison and other government leaders ignored their subpoenas and refused to appear in court, forcing a judge to decide whether or not executive approval was an essential element of the defense.

A fascinating aspect of the story is the issue of "original intent." While today experts often argue the original intent of the framers of the Constitution, in 1806 it was easy to determine. William Patterson, the judge who presided over Colonel Smith's case *was* one of the framers, having served as a key delegate to the Constitutional Convention.

The battle lines were drawn. The defense lawyer presented a case in which Colonel Smith was "a man more sinned against than sinning." He argued that his client was a subordinate agent of the president and should thus be acquitted. He also argued that the president was not forbidden to provide and prepare covert operations "while Congress are in actual and secret deliberation whether they shall declare war against a nation that is committing and provoking hostilities."

The prosecution argued that Congress, and only Congress, can declare war. Moreover, they said, the knowledge of the president does not justify the actions of the offender.

In the final analysis, Judge Patterson ruled for the prosecution, explaining that the President of the United States "cannot authorize a person to do what the law forbids." Colonel Smith was then ordered to stand trial for his covert operations without the benefit of testimony from Madison and the others.

According to the *Federal Case Reporter*, Volume 27, page 1245, "[T]he jury retired, and after an absence of two hours, they returned a verdict of not guilty."

The trial was over, but the story was not. Much like Oliver North, Colonel Smith had become a popular folk hero. If history does repeat itself, its interesting to note that in 1813, Colonel Smith ran for Congress and won.

"The World Is Tired of Us"

Scandals in the Life and Times of
the Adams Family

JOHN ADAMS AND JOHN Quincy Adams were the first and only father and son to become presidents of the United States. And with that historical distinction came another—they were the first first family to be put under the national microscope. It was a natural curiosity to wonder what qualities possessed by the Adams family produced two such leaders. Unfortunately, with their enviable political heritage came stories of manic depression, alcoholism, and self-destruction that spanned four generations. In many ways, they were the Kennedys of early American history.

Much like the Kennedys, the high expectations that came with the family name were behind many of the family scandals. And in each case, the "family myth," as it has been called, took its greatest toll on the third generation. Just as the drug bust of Robert Kennedy, Jr. and the fatal overdose of his brother David shocked the country, so did the suicide of the oldest son of John Quincy Adams in 1829. The Kennedy family will be examined more closely later in the context of modern times, but the similarity of the two political dynasties is uncanny.

Most of what is known about the Adamses comes from the papers that were retained by the family. On microfilm today, the documents run over five miles in length. The family's willingness to allow the public access to letters, diaries, and every scrap of

44

THE ADAMS FAMILY

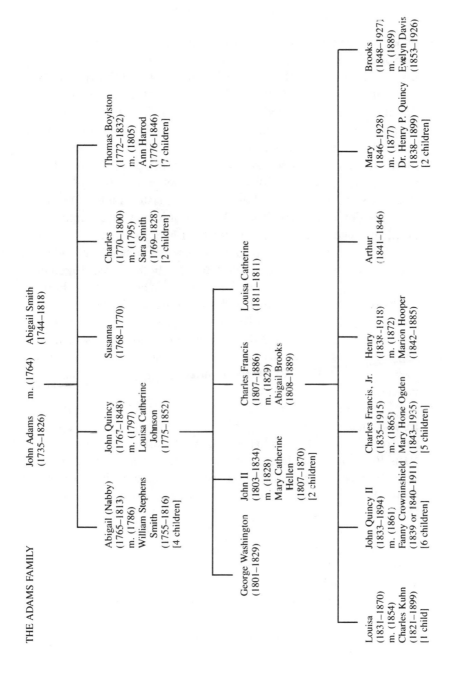

John Adams   m. (1764)   Abigail Smith
(1735–1826)   (1744–1818)

Abigail (Nabby)   John Quincy   Susanna   Charles   Thomas Boylston
(1765–1813)   (1767–1848)   (1768–1770) (1770–1800) (1772–1832)
m. (1786)   m. (1797)   m. (1795)   m. (1805)
William Stephens   Louisa Catherine   Sara Smith Ann Harrod
Smith   Johnson   (1769–1828) (1776–1846)
(1755–1816)   (1775–1852)   [2 children] [7 children]
[4 children]

George Washington   John II   Charles Francis   Louisa Catherine
(1801–1829)   (1803–1834)   (1807–1886)   (1811–1811)
                    m. (1828)   m. (1829)
                    Mary Catherine   Abigail Brooks
                    Hellen   (1808–1889)
                    (1807–1870)
                    [2 children]

Louisa   John Quincy II   Charles Francis, Jr. Henry   Arthur   Mary   Brooks
(1831–1870)   (1833–1894)   (1835–1915)   (1838–1918) (1841–1846) (1846–1928)   (1848–1927)
m. (1854)   m. (1861)   m. (1865)   m. (1872)   m. (1877)   m. (1889)
Charles Kuhn   Fanny Crowninshield Mary Hone Ogden   Marion Hooper   Dr. Henry P. Quincy Evelyn Davis
(1821–1899)   (1839 or 1840–1911) (1843–1935)   (1842–1885)   (1838–1899)   (1853–1926)
[1 child]   [6 children]   [5 children]   [2 children]

paper written on by them has been called an act of courage. It is also an act of public service, which was the prime motivating force instilled in every family member beginning with John Adams.

John Adams was born in 1735, the son of a Boston deacon. Although he was expected to go to Harvard College and study to become a clergyman, John struggled for his personal independence. But he maintained a strong moral fiber. In fact, until his marriage he was celibate. As he wrote in his diary, "No father, brother, son or friend ever had cause of grief or resentment for any intercourse between me and any daughter, sister, mother, or any other relation of the female sex. My children may be assured that no illegitimate brother or sister exists or ever existed."

In 1789, John Adams became America's first vice president and served under George Washington for both terms. Together Washington and Adams set the standards for both offices. Early on, Washington decided that nothing should dilute the power of the president, not even the office of vice president. It was a great vision, but one which left Adams with little to do. In a moment of candor, Adams dubbed his job "the most insignificant office that ever the invention of man contrived or his imagination conceived."

A short, stout, pompous, erudite man, Adams was difficult for Americans to embrace. In the Senate, where many had grown tired of Adams's attention to titles and protocol, he was nicknamed "His Rotundity." Although he became America's second president, he was never popular. When voters denied him a second term, Adams set out to recapture his early power through his children.

Adams and his wife, Abigail, had three sons—John Quincy, Charles, and Thomas. They had one daughter, Abigail (who later married colonel William Smith), who was nicknamed "Nabby." Two other daughters did not live to adulthood.

In the early years of marriage, John Adams's political commitments kept him away from home for long periods of time. As a delegate to the Continental Congress in Philadelphia from 1774 to 1777, Adams had only a few brief visits with the family, who remained in Braintree, Massachusetts. In 1778 he left for France, where he served with Benjamin Franklin as part of the American delegation. He returned from Europe in 1779 for only four months, during which time he drafted the Massachusetts constitution.

While Abigail found the long separations trying, she emerged as a strong matriarch, instilling in her children respect for their father's dedication to public service. From the start, the children were expected to build on his accomplishments.

The first to fall short of family expectations was Adams's second son, Charles. Charles's problems could be traced back to November 1779, when, at the age of eight, he and John Quincy sailed with their father to the Netherlands, where Adams had been appointed minister from the United States. Although the boys had looked forward to the journey, Charles became so homesick that Adams had no choice but to send him back to his mother. Because of the slowness of travel by ship, he did not reach her for six months. His father and brother, meanwhile, remained in Europe for almost nine years, during which time Adams also served as the first U.S. minister to Great Britain. In 1788, when Adams requested his own recall to America, he acknowledged the neglect of his wife. In a letter to a friend, he wrote, "I hope to be married once more myself in a few months to a very amiable lady whom I have inhumanely left a widow in America for nine years with the exception of a few weeks only." But the greatest toll of the separation, he would later learn, was on Charles.

By the time Charles was sent to Harvard (as was the second generation of Kennedys nearly two centuries later), he was a full-fledged alcoholic. The remedy his mother prescribed was a good stabilizing marriage. Charles agreed, and, conveniently, he married the sister of his brother-in-law, Colonel Smith. Unfortunately, it was a family association not meant for the faint-hearted.

Before he dabbled in covert operations, Colonel Smith was involved in risky land speculations that went bust in the financial panic of 1797. Charles, hoping to save his brother-in-law from jail, secretly loaned him some money that belonged to John Quincy. If Colonel Smith had been able to repay it quickly, no one would have ever known about it. But Smith couldn't pay it back at all. When the Adamses discovered what had happened, Charles was formally disowned from the family and sent off in disgrace. In November 1800, he died alone and drunk in a seedy New York apartment, having never visited with John Adams during his entire presidency.

The "family myth" also took its toll on the president's youngest son, Thomas. Having served as a lawyer and a judge, Thomas's career had great promise. But his drinking binges ruined it all. After many years fighting "to keep off the Blue devils" of depression, he followed in his brother Charles's footsteps, dying an alcoholic.

Although his two youngest sons failed him, John Adams's eldest son, John Quincy, kept the "family myth" alive. When he was sworn in as the country's sixth president in 1825, he fulfilled his aging father's ambition to return an Adams to the presidency. Unfortunately, like his father, John Quincy Adams was also not a strong leader. By June 1827, it was apparent that he had failed to implement most of his presidential plans. The more public criticism he was dealt, the further he lapsed into manic depression. Both John Quincy and his father, in fact, had severe persecution complexes. In addition, John Quincy suffered from such psychosomatic illnesses as cramps, constipation, loss of appetite, and indigestion. At one time he admitted having "an imaginary wish that [life] were terminated."

Still, John Quincy and Louisa Adams had high hopes for their children's futures. George Washington Adams, the first-born, was expected to become president. Charles and John, Jr. were encouraged to enter public service, too, although John was also chosen to run the family mills in the hope of ensuring financial security for all.

During his term in the White House, the entire John Quincy Adams family seemed burdened with problems. His wife, Louisa, took off periodically to various spas, their son Charles fled to New York, and George complained of various nervous disorders after losing an election in the Massachusetts legislature. George, in fact, had severe emotional problems and was abusing snuff, alcohol, and opium.

As early as 1816, John Quincy wrote to George, "I fear that too many of my hopes are built upon you." George indeed carried a tremendous burden for he felt an intense pressure at being the first adult son of a president. And living down the name "George Washington Adams" was no easy task—especially for someone who was groomed to be president from the day he was born.

As a child, George once ran home to his mother after he had "been thrown out of a swing as high as the poplar by the Otis boys." The next day his swollen shoulder had to be reset. John Adams, brimming with pride over his grandson's bravery at the "bone setter's," gave him a quarter. George caught up with a friend and "told him to run and spend it all on Gingerbread for the boys, and when HE was PRESIDENT, HE would make HIM Secretary of State." George Washington Adams was only six.

For all the bragging, George never even made it into the local legislature. On April 29, 1829, about two weeks after his twenty-eighth birthday, he committed suicide aboard the *Benjamin Franklin*, a passenger steamship bound for New York. Earlier that evening, he had suffered a full-blown anxiety attack, where he believed other passengers were conspiring against him while the engine formed a voice repeating "Let it be, let it be. Let it be, let it be." He accused a passenger of spreading gossip about him and finally, at three a.m., he asked the captain to return to shore. About 3:30 in the morning, he plunged into the sea, an incident John Quincy preferred to believe was an accident.

Early in June, his bloated body washed ashore at East Chester, seventeen miles from New York City. John Quincy traveled there and collected his son's watch, pen knife, silver pencil case, comb, seal, pocketbook, and the key to his trunk. Afterwards, Charles was sent to sort out the rest of his brother's affairs. And affairs there were. George had left a letter for Charles in which he requested, in the event he died in 1828, that he pay off his debts and give the balance to Eliza Dolph, a chambermaid who was pregnant with his child.

If there were more surprises, they went up in flames, as Charles burned most of George's papers. One of the few manuscripts to survive, however, gave the world some shocking insights into how tragic George's life had been. The manuscript, titled "A Review of the Year 1825," was never completed, but what was there was wretched. In it George revealed how he thought chance, his parents, and bad schoolmasters were all responsible for his failure by the age of twenty-four. He recalled the six months of tutoring it took just so he could pass his college entrance exam. And he spoke of his frustration that his keen interest in poetry and literature didn't fit into his parents' master plan. In general, he felt ill-prepared for Harvard, indeed for life.

The "family myth" fell apart with George's brother, John, too. John had served as his father's personal secretary in the White House and was later chosen to manage the family flour mills. But one by one the mills went bankrupt, and John began to drink heavily. His health deteriorated so quickly that he lost his eyesight. Although his problems were likely alcohol-related, his mother believed his illness was related to the dampness of the mills. Whatever the cause, in 1834, John, Jr. lapsed into a coma and died with his father at his bedside.

If the loss of a second son wasn't enough, the family also endured terrible financial setbacks. Luckily, they were able to borrow thousands of dollars from an old servant, Antoine Guista. The money enabled them to renew their bank loans and keep their business afloat.

Despite his private tragedies, John Quincy Adams was first and foremost a public servant. A few years after his second-term defeat by Andrew Jackson, former President John Quincy Adams ran for a seat in congress. He won and served in the House of Representatives for the next seventeen years.

In the fourth generation of Adamses, depression bouts also plagued Henry and Brooks, two of the sons of Charles, the only one of his generation to carry the "family myth" forward. Henry and Brooks extended the family prominence into the twentieth century by successfully serving the family as historians. Henry became a professor of history at Harvard University and wrote scholarly books that included nine volumes of U.S. history under the Jefferson and Madison administrations and his highly acclaimed 1906 autobiography, *The Education of Henry Adams*. His wife, Marion, committed suicide in 1885.

Brooks was respected for his works, in which he warned of the "unchecked evils of capitalism" and predicted that the U.S. and Soviet would emerge as superpowers. With his death in 1927, the Adams political dynasty came to an end. Of his family, Brooks Adams wrote, "It is now full four generations since John Adams wrote the constitution of Massachusetts. It is time that we perished. The world is tired of us."

"God Help the Women who Must Live in Washington"

Scandals in the Life and Times of Andrew Jackson

W HEN ANDREW JACK-
son beat John Quincy Adams in the 1828 presidential race, it
marked the end of one of the most bitter and vicious campaigns of
all time. Most of the attacks centered around Jackson's wife, Rachel, who, as it turned out, had not legally divorced her first husband before she married Jackson almost forty years before. The
headlines screamed "ADULTERESS!," "BIGAMIST," and
more. One pamphlet read, "Anyone approving of Andrew Jackson must therefore declare in favor of the philosophy that any man
wanting anyone else's pretty wife has nothing to do but take his
pistol in one hand and a horsewhip in another and possess her."

Jackson's victory in the 1828 presidential election was an
empty one. Although his wife of thirty-seven years was by his side
on election night, she never lived to see him take the oath of office.
Rachel, whose heart condition was aggravated by the stress of the
campaign, died nine weeks before Jackson's March inauguration.
She was buried in the satin gown which she had planned to wear to
his inaugural ball. The black armband he wore to his swearing-in
ceremony to symbolize his mourning also served as a clear remind-
er that Jackson blamed his political opponents for her untimely
death. Rachel's death, even more than her life, would influence
the new president throughout his entire administration.

Andrew Jackson took his personal sorrow to the White House.

Andrew Jackson first met Rachel Donelson Robards in Nashville, Tennessee, in 1788, when, as a young prosecuting attorney, he was referred by a friend to a boarding house owned by her mother. From the moment he met her, according to his roommate John Overton, Jackson never had eyes for another woman. That very first night, he pumped Overton for all the information he had about this beautiful, witty woman who puffed on a pipe and tugged on his heartstrings.

*Rachel Jackson, wife of the president-elect, died just weeks before
the inauguration.*

Rachel's background intrigued Jackson. Her father, Colonel
John Donelson, had led a group of 120 settlers including his family
(his wife, Rachel, and ten more brothers and sisters) across Virginia, through one thousand miles of bad weather and Indian attacks
to the Cumberland. In 1785, a few months before her eighteenth
birthday, Rachel married Captain Lewis Robards and moved in
with his mother in Harrodsburg. What began as a storybook mar-

riage for Rachel turned into a nightmare fueled by Robards's insane jealousy. In one jealous rage, he accused her of having an affair with a man to whom she had only given a glass of water. After hurling abusive language at her, he sent his wife back to her mother, on the horse Mrs. Donelson had included in Rachel's dowry. A while later, however, they reconciled.

Jackson could not understand how a woman as lovely as Rachel could be treated so poorly. But in no time, he, too, bore the brunt of Captain Robards's jealous rage. In fact, Robards was so aggressive towards him, Jackson moved several miles away to help keep peace in the household.

Jackson's separation from the entire Donelson family proved difficult. His own father had died before his birth and his mother died when he was fourteen. His relationship with the Donelsons was the closest he had felt to a real family in a long time. But he wasn't away for long. His move did nothing to ease Rachel's husband's jealousy. Soon after, Robards denounced Jackson and Rachel and took off for Kentucky. He soon returned, only to fly into yet another jealous rage. This was the last straw for Rachel. In July 1790, she sent word to her family asking to be rescued. Andrew Jackson showed up and did just that.

By the end of the month, Captain Robards filed a complaint in the Harrodsburg Court that his wife, Rachel, had "eloped . . . with another man." The complaint was fully unwarranted. Jackson had actually returned Rachel to her mother.

By the winter, Captain Robards was threatening to force Rachel to come back to Kentucky with him. The family decided the only way to protect her was to spirit her away to Natchez, Mississippi, where friends of the family could hide her on their plantation. Since the 2,000-mile river trek was dangerous, Andrew Jackson volunteered to protect her against Indian attacks and pirates. John Overton took over Jackson's legal practice for three months, until his return in April 1791.

A few weeks later, Overton heard that Captain Robards had been granted a divorce from Rachel by the General Assembly of Virginia on the grounds that Rachel had "lived in adultery with another man.'' When Jackson heard this, he was furious over the slur against Rachel—and then ran to ask Mrs. Donelson for her daughter's hand in marriage. Rachel's mother asked him, ''Would you sacrifice your life to save my child's good name?'' He replied, ''Ten thousand lives, Madam, if I had them!''

Andrew and Rachel were married in Natchez, Mississippi, in August 1791, and spent their honeymoon in a log cabin on a bluff overlooking the meeting of the Bayou Pierre and Mississippi Rivers. They were young (both twenty-four) and in love, with a wonderful future ahead. Jackson and his bride returned to Tennessee, where he established a booming law practice. In 1793, he appeared in 206 out of 435 litigations of record in Nashville. Everything was perfect—until December 1793, when Jackson learned from Overton that the Virginia Assembly had not granted Captain Robards a divorce, but only the right to sue for one.

Robards's divorce had not been granted until two years after Andrew and Rachel had married. Jackson cringed as he read the document, which stated, ''On the 27th day of September, 1793, this day came the plaintiff by his attorney, and thereupon came also a jury . . . who being duly sworn well and truly to inquire into the allegation in the plaintiff's declaration . . . do say, that the defendant, Rachel Robards, hath deserted the plaintiff, Lewis Robards, and hath, and doth, still live in adultery with another man. It is therefore considered by the court that the marriage between the plaintiff and the defendant be dissolved.''

One of the worst moments in Jackson's life was telling Rachel they were not legally married. In a quiet, solemn ceremony on January 17, 1794, the couple was remarried in Nashville, Tennessee. Still, one can only wonder, as the voters later would, why a lawyer such as Jackson never checked out the documents with the Virginia Assembly himself. Whatever the rationale, the oversight would haunt him for the rest of his life and Rachel's.

Jackson went to great lengths to protect Rachel's honor. On one occasion, he actually challenged one Charles Dickinson to a duel and killed him for uttering a slur regarding Rachel's ''adultery.'' Jackson chose the weapons, and at five a.m. both men charged the nine-inch barrels with seventy-caliber balls. Jackson and Dickinson paced off the ground and took their places. John Overton was referee.

"Gentlemen, are you ready?" asked Overton.

"Ready," said Dickinson.

"Yes, sir," said Jackson.

"FIRE!"

As a puff of smoke arose from Jackson's dark-blue frock coat, it was apparent that Dickinson had nailed him with the first shot. Almost instantly, Jackson grabbed his chest but he didn't fall to the ground.

"My God! Have I missed him?" Dickinson asked in amazement as Jackson aimed, fired back and scored a direct hit.

Actually, Dickinson hadn't missed at all. In fact, his aim had been perfectly centered to the heart. What he did not know was that Jackson was much thinner than he appeared in his oversized coat, which threw off the position. By all standards, Jackson should have died in the duel. But at ten o'clock that evening, while a surgeon examined Jackson's flesh wound to the chest, Dickinson died instead.

By the time Jackson ascended to national prominence, his reputation preceded him. Stories of Jackson's marriage scandal and subsequent duel were circulated widely throughout the 1824 presidential election, which Jackson lost to John Quincy Adams. His defeat was bitter enough without these slurs. Jackson had received more electoral votes than his opponents, who also included Henry Clay, the Whig candidate, and William C. Crawford, a U.S. senator who had held various cabinet positions in the Madison and Monroe administration. Jackson led with 43 percent followed by Adams with 31 percent and Clay and Crawford with 13 percent each. Jackson's total electoral votes unfortunately did not constitute a majority and the vote was thrown to the House of Representatives. At that time, Adams is alleged to have struck a deal with Clay by promising to appoint him secretary of state in return for his electoral votes. What became known as the "Corrupt Bargain" squeezed Jackson out and sealed the election for Adams.

Today deals in which one candidate trades off his support to another are acceptable, but in 1824 this was scandalous.

It is hard to say how much Rachel Jackson contributed to his 1824 defeat, but everyone was well aware of her personal history. One newspaper editorial pleaded with voters not to "place such a woman as Mrs. Jackson at the head of the female society of the United States." But these few stinging commentaries were nothing compared to the serious mudslinging that accompanied Jackson's second run for the presidency four years later.

When the whispers about Rachel began to darken Jackson's second campaign against John Quincy Adams, Jackson wrote to a friend in Virginia, "I can assure you that whenever my enemies think it worth while to investigate the character of M. J. [Mrs. Jackson] I fear not . . . as I know how to defend her."

Even the threat of his dueling pistols could not protect Rachel from the cruel gossip she endured. In Washington, the grand debate centered around whether the ladies would even visit her. The answer to that question was unequivocal. Rachel Jackson was snubbed. There were no tickets to balls or parties and few dinner invitations, only their visits to church. Although Jackson tried to keep the slanderous newspaper articles from her, she somehow learned their content.

Rachel slipped into a deep depression during the campaign, and her health began to fail. She hung on long enough to see Jackson win the election, but after that, she appeared to give up. By mid-December, doctors were called in and they bled her as was the common medical practice of the day. On December 22, she died with the president-elect at her bedside.

Refusing to believe that she was dead, Jackson demanded that blankets be brought to her in case "she does come to." He stayed alone with her body through the next morning. Two days later, ten thousand people—twice as many as lived in Nashville—attended her funeral. As Jackson had protected her honor in life, he would also protect it in death. Her gravestone read, "A being so gentle, so virtuous, slander might wound but could not dishonor."

★ ★ ★

Andrew Jackson was sworn in as the seventh president of the United States on March 4, 1829, before a record crowd, who had come to see the Tennessee frontiersman. They came by horse, mule, and foot, with their coonskin caps and whiskey. Jackson's election had marked the end of political control by such eastern aristocrats as Thomas Jefferson and John Quincy Adams. Wigs and ruffles were out, buckskin pants were in. For a great part of the country, it was a new beginning, but for the powdered and per- fumed group roped off behind Jackson on the inaugural stand, there was one last social battle to wage. Vice President and Mrs. John C. Calhoun, along with the cabinet members and their wives, refused to accept Secretary of War John Eaton and Peggy, his twenty-nine-year-old bride of three months. Apparently, Peggy's reputation wasn't "pure" enough for them, a moral judgment that would ultimately bring down the entire cabinet.

Peggy O'Neal Eaton was the daughter of a Washington, D.C., tavern owner and proprietor of an inn called the Franklin House. She was raised there during a time when travel was diffi- cult and the local inns served as the center for community news and politics, and there she developed certain character traits that were considered appealing to men and shocking to women.

It was said that one boy committed suicide over her, two oth- ers fought a duel, and another would have eloped with her if she hadn't kicked over a flower pot while climbing out the window. That was all before the age of sixteen, when she married Navy Lieutenant John Timberlake. Timberlake was a heavy drinker who spent long stretches of time at sea. During his long absences, Peg- gy remained at Franklin House, where one of the regular boarders was John H. Eaton, a young senator from Tennessee and a friend of Andrew Jackson's. Eaton was a tall, wealthy widower who had helped the O'Neal family during their times of financial trouble. Eaton enjoyed Franklin House so much he had recommended it to Andrew Jackson. During one of Jackson's stays with the O'Neals, he wrote to Rachel, "I can with truth say I never was in a more

Satirical drawing of scandalous Peggy Eaton dancing before Andrew Jackson and his cabinet.

agreeable and worthy family.'' He called Peggy ''the smartest little woman in America.''

The Washington wives didn't quite see her in the same light. From the beginning, they kept their husbands away. Former President James Monroe and his wife barred Peggy from social functions even though her husband's rank entitled her to invitations. The fact that John Eaton began escorting her to balls didn't endear her any more to them.

In April 1828, Peggy received the news that her husband had died at sea. The Washington wives chose to believe he drank himself to death over his wife's affair with Eaton. Jackson, who wanted Eaton to be a member of his cabinet, advised his friend, ''If you love Margaret Timberlake, go and marry her at once and shut their mouths.''

Eaton did marry Peggy, but it didn't stop the gossip. When a delegation of congressmen suggested that Jackson drop Eaton from the cabinet, Jackson snapped, ''I did not come here to make a Cabinet for the ladies of this place, but for the nation.''

President Jackson was not about to let the evil tongues that had destroyed his beloved Rachel claim his friend's wife, too. But when Peggy was snubbed at the inauguration and later that evening at the ball, it appeared that she would be forced to endure the same cruel treatment as had his wife. Jackson's first solution was to delay the traditional formal dinner for the cabinet members until the scandal blew over. It never did, and as tensions mounted, the secretary of the Navy warned Jackson that he would have "less difficulty in fighting over again the battle of New Orleans."

Finally, the president called an unprecedented cabinet meeting for all members except for Eaton. The purpose was to end the "petticoat war." To signal the end of the issue, he declared Peggy to have been "chaste as a virgin" when she married Eaton. No one dared to remind the president that Peggy was the mother of two at the time. When Jackson gave his formal cabinet dinner, he seated Peggy right next to him. The redoubtable Mrs. Eaton arrived dressed in a low-cut, one-shouldered gown that left little to the imagination. This only further outraged the Washington wives, and whenever she appeared on the dance floor they cleared out in protest.

What had begun as a petty social feud now developed into a full-fledged power struggle—especially between the two cabinet members who vied to succeed the president. On one side there was Vice President Calhoun, who refused to invite the Eatons to his home because of the strong feelings of his wife, Floride. On the other side was Secretary of State Martin Van Buren, who led the pro-Peggy faction and threw a party in her honor. He even convinced all his bachelor friends, including the British and Russian ministers, to do the same. Ultimately, cabinet members, congressmen, and Washington diplomats found themselves forced to choose sides on the Eaton issue. Many were no longer on speaking terms with each other. The discord even crept under the roof of the White House. When Emily Donelson, the president's niece and White House social hostess, refused to invite Peggy to dinner, Jackson sent her and her husband home to Tennessee.

In short order, Jackson's cabinet had become the laughing stock of the country. Recognizing Jackson's own intransigence in the matter, probably due in large part to his own fresh memories of his wife's treatment, and feeling an obligation to return the government to working order, Van Buren finally moved to resolve the impasse. His solution was to resign along with Eaton, and to ask the president to demand the other cabinet secretaries to follow suit. As the entire cabinet was dissolved, the toast heard in political circles was, "To the next Cabinet—may they all be bachelors—or leave their wives at home."

Van Buren's loyalty was so appreciated that Jackson chose him as his running mate for his 1832 reelection campaign. Following the resolution of the Peggy Eaton affair, the president had written to Van Buren, "You may rest assured . . . [Vice President] Calhoun & Co. are politically dead." As a bit of extra insurance at the nominating convention, the president imposed a "two-thirds rule" that he was certain no candidate other than Van Buren could survive. They didn't. Van Buren became vice president and the "two-thirds rule" remained in effect until 1936.

★ ★ ★

Peggy Eaton's life ended in scandal just as it had begun. At the age of sixty, Peggy married Antonio Buchignani, a nineteen-year-old private dancing instructor she had hired to help prepare her granddaughter Emily for her debut. In the end, sadly, Peggy was beaten. Five years after their marriage, Peggy's young husband took all of her money, and her granddaughter, to Italy. Peggy Eaton died lonely and penniless in 1879. Although President and Mrs. Rutherford Hayes sent a wreath of white roses to her grave, a more fitting memorial might have been Peggy's own words, "God help the women who must live in Washington."

When all was said and done, Jackson finished his presidency more popular in the polls than he started, a remarkable accomplishment for any president. Although many other factors also influenced his presidency, his political power was strengthened by his handling of the Eaton affair. Jackson's influence continued long after his presidency. He not only hand-picked Van Buren as his successor, he is considered the single most important influence in the nomination and election of James K. Polk. Later, the presidential campaigns of Franklin Pierce and James Buchanan, Jackson's Minister to Russia, also greatly benefitted from his early support. And, just as he wrote to Van Buren, John C. Calhoun & Co. were politically dead. While the scandals had hurt his opponents, they ultimately bolstered Andrew Jackson.

A Heartbeat Away

Scandals in the Lives and Times of Martin Van Buren and John Tyler

THROUGHOUT THE EATON affair, Jackson's cabinet was so closely scrutinized by the press that by the time Martin Van Buren ran for president in 1836, there was literally nothing left to tell. He had been called an opportunist, a corseted, aristocratic dandy, and even the illegitimate child of Aaron Burr. But when those old rumors wouldn't fly anymore, the press found another target for their attacks: Kentuckian Richard Johnson, the man Van Buren had selected to run as his vice president. What a field day reporters must have had after learning that Johnson, who had never married, had kept a mistress and fathered two children by her. Under Kentucky law they were actually forbidden to marry because Johnson's mistress, Julia, was black!

★ ★ ★

Richard M. Johnson had been selected as the vice presidential candidate based on his reputation as a hero of the War of 1812. He was known far and wide as the killer of the legendary Indian leader Tecumseh. A representative from Kentucky since 1807, Johnson advocated military measures against Britain and France whom he warned were no longer honoring America's commitment to neutrality. After the War Department approved his plan to organize a volunteer army, he led a regiment of riflemen from

64

Richard Johnson, Vice President in 1836, was the father of two children by a black mistress.

Richard Johnson's war heroics were exaggerated.

Kentucky to Detroit and then on to Canada as part of a larger U.S. force under the command of future President William Henry Harrison. On October 5, 1813, they caught up with a combined force of British troops and 1,500 Indian warriors led by General Henry Procter and Tecumseh.

No one really knew who actually fired the fatal shot at Tecumseh, but since Johnson personally led the attack, he was forever after credited with the deed. Everyone seemed anxious to create a war hero. One of his captains wrote an "eyewitness" account of the fatal encounter, relating how Johnson, though wounded in the thigh, hip, hand, and arm, kept on fighting. A playwright created a five-act play, *The Warrior Sage,* which immortalized the moment and made Johnson a household name.

After Johnson returned to his seat in Congress, President James Monroe presented him with a commemorative sword "as testimony of the high sense entertained by Congress of the daring and distinguished valor displayed by himself [Johnson] and the regiment of volunteers under his command, in charging the enemy on the Thames, in Upper Canada, on the 5th of October, 1813." Senator James Barbour of Virginia added his voice to the chorus of accolades: "Colonel Johnson, early in the combat, received two severe wounds, attended with the loss of much blood. In this trying crisis any ordinary courage would have retired him from the combat; on him it had a different effect. It seemed to impart to him new courage, which manifested itself in a prodigy of valor, which loses nothing in comparison with the most splendid achievement."

From 1819 to 1829, Johnson served in the Senate and then returned to the House where his record of achievement was fairly unspectacular. His two most passionate issues were abolishing prison terms for debtors and keeping mail delivery on Sunday. He probably would not have been considered as Van Buren's running mate had it not been for the timely publication of the *Authentic Biography of Colonel Richard M. Johnson* by William Emmons. Suddenly his war heroics grew to Herculean proportions. In this latest account, he was outnumbered three to one and was shot twenty-five times. He rode his horse through the battle carnage to seek out Tecumseh, who heard his horse stumble and emptied his rifle into the colonel. Johnson still went after the Indian chief, who was dressed in savage costume and war paint "till he came so near that the Indian was raising a tomahawk to strike him down."

Emmons might as well have written a script for a Hollywood western with his description of how, with the tomahawk poised above his head, "the Colonel raised his pistol, and discharging its contents into the breast of the Indian chief, laid him dead upon the spot." Emmons gushed, "This was one of the most glorious victories of the war."

Johnson never bothered to set the record straight, perpetuating what may be one of the first "Biden-ized" résumés. Despite its obvious exaggeration, the biography worked wonders on his fellow Democrats at the Baltimore convention, who nominated Johnson for vice president.

Once Johnson was selected as Van Buren's official running mate, however, his opponents began to question the authenticity—and relevance—of some of the heroic accounts. John Catron, chief justice of the Tennessee Supreme Court, asked whether a "lucky random shot, even if it did hit Tecumseh, qualifies a man for Vice President." The *Ohio State Journal* editorialized that "the killing of Tecumseh appears to be the principal recommendation of Colonel Johnson for the Vice Presidency."

As difficult as it was for Johnson to answer these charges, he certainly preferred to face them than to endure the attacks that were now leveled against him and his black mistress, Julia Chinn, and their children. John Catron had warned President Jackson, "The very moment Col. J. [Johnson] is announced, the newspapers will open upon him with facts." And they did, describing how "he has endeavored often to force his daughter into society, that the mother in her life time, and they now, rode in carriages, and claimed equality. The idea of voting for him is loathed beyond anything that has occurred with us."

Julia Chinn had died several years earlier, but their mulatto children, whom Johnson continued to support, were living reminders of his controversial relationship. The romance apparently began after Johnson's mother destroyed another relationship he had with an impoverished seamstress. In defiance, he became involved with Julia, a slave he had inherited from his father.

The press quickly transformed him from "The Hero of the Thames" to "The Great Amalgamator." The *United States Telegraph* made its first exception to the newspaper's policy to "abstain from meddling with the private life of any candidate for office.'' They called Johnson's nomination a ''crisis'' led by misguided fanatics who were ''endeavoring to disturb the harmony which exists between the north and south, and in defiance of the Constitution and the most sacred institution of the social system, and preaching the immediate abolition of *Slavery* and *amalgamation* of White and Black—the *Free* and *Slave* population of the Country—the placing in nomination for office a man who is to receive the support of these fanatics.''

The editor added, ''It may be a matter of no importance to mere political automatons whether RICHARD M. JOHNSON is a *White* or a *Black* man—whether he is *free* or a *slave*—or whether he is married to, or has been in connection with a jet-black, thick-lipped, odoriferous negro wench, by whom he has reared a family of children whom he has endeavored to force upon society as every way worthy of being considered the equals . . . of his free white fellow citizens; it matters not, we say, with MR. VAN BUREN and his followers what may be the color of either Johnson, his wife, or his children.''

Although Johnson's personal life had become a central issue in the 1836 presidential campaign, Van Buren stood firmly behind his selection for a running mate. In doing so, he avoided the kind of political fallout that occurred in the 1972 presidential elections after Democratic candidate George McGovern dropped Thomas Eagleton from the ticket amid a scandal regarding his mental health history. Perhaps McGovern might have taken a cue from Van Buren, who actually turned the political tides in his favor by the strength of his personal commitment, which inspired others to jump on the band wagon of support.

For one, Thomas Henderson, a clergyman who had been Johnson's next-door neighbor in Kentucky for ten years, conducted his own campaign to balance the bad press. On July 7, 1835, he published a letter in the *Washington Daily Globe*, in which he wrote, ''If he [Johnson] stands charged with keeping a disorderly house, I have, as a constant visitor for twenty-three years, and living for the last ten nearly in the yard, never been able to discover it.'' He also pointed out that Julia Chinn was a member of the

Baptist church and "sustained a good character as pious, humble christian, to the day of her death."

Finally, the day of reckoning at the polls arrived. Martin Van Buren swept the majority vote in the electoral college. Richard Johnson, however, fell only one vote short, and for the first and only time in history, the Senate was called upon to determine the outcome of a vice-presidential election. On February 6, 1837, they voted thirty-three to sixteen in his favor, and Richard M. Johnson became vice president.

As vice president, Johnson created another furor when he took his second black mistress. When she ran off and eloped with an Indian, he took yet another, who accompanied him to social gatherings, much to the dismay of Washington society. Needless to say, his behavior was not about to help him realize his dreams of becoming president. By 1839, Johnson had thrown in the towel and took an extended leave of absence to manage a hotel and spa that he owned in White Sulphur Springs, Virginia. In Van Buren's second presidential campaign, the Democratic party was so disgusted that they refused to renominate Johnson, or any other vice president for that matter.

★ ★ ★

Although Van Buren was a good president—he is credited with establishing free banking and energizing the economy to expand free enterprise—the voters were in need of a change. On March 4, 1841, William Henry Harrison was sworn in as the ninth president of the United States. John Tyler was his vice president.

No one at the time realized how critical the choice of vice president would be. One month to the day after taking the oath of office, the sixty-eight-year-old president died as a result of a cold he caught while delivering a one-hour-and-forty-minute inaugural address in the chilly outdoors without a hat, coat, or gloves. For the first time in history, the vice president acceded to the highest office.

Having succeeded the first U. S. president to die in office, John Tyler was in for a rough ride from both Congress and the cabinet that he had inherited from William Henry Harrison. He faced an uphill battle at every twist and turn of his administration. Even the new president's plan to mop up corruption in government led to a call for his impeachment. His subsequent use of executive privilege caused a confrontation between government branches, the likes of which would not be seen again until Richard Nixon challenged the Watergate prosecutors over 130 years later.

Executive privilege was first invoked by Thomas Jefferson when he refused to respond to a subpoena to appear in court and present documents relating to Aaron Burr's treason trial. Burr, formerly Jefferson's vice president, was charged with treason after his business partner, General James Wilkinson, blew the whistle on a scheme to set up a new country from parts of Mexico and some western territories. In declining to testify or hand over related papers, Thomas Jefferson set the precedent for executive privilege. President Tyler tested its limits.

Within months of assuming office, Tyler broke with the Whig party that Harrison had led, and vetoed two of their key economic bills. Calling him "Traitor Tyler," the entire cabinet resigned in protest except for Secretary of State Daniel Webster, who was in the midst of delicate negotiations with Great Britain over the Maine boundary dispute. Tyler quickly appointed a new cabinet filled with loyal supporters and took firm control of the presidency.

One of Tyler's top priorities was to establish a corruption-free government. In May 1841, he appointed a commission made up of three private citizens headed by George Poindexter, a former U. S. senator and governor of Mississippi. When the Whig-controlled House got wind of the investigation, two separate issues disturbed them—the president's authority to pay private citizens with public funds, and the president's authority to keep information about such investigations from the Congress. They demanded to see the Poindexter Commission's report and to know how much and from what source the commission members were paid.

Tyler responded, but only after he wrote a secret letter to Poindexter ordering him not to show his report to anyone but the President. Then he explained to Congress that his actions were legal under his constitutional duty to enforce laws. He made no mention of salaries or funding.

Poindexter's report revealed massive fraud in the office of Democrat Jesse D. Hoyt, the New York collector appointed by Van Buren. This was distressing news as Hoyt had been hired to replace Samuel Swartwort, a Jackson appointee who became the first to embezzle more than a million dollars from the United States government. He had fled to Europe with $2,250,000. It was only when the president learned that the commission's report also contained information embarrassing to the Whigs that he released it to Congress.

In turn, Congress, feeling goaded by Tyler, passed a law that forbid the president to pay agents or commissioners appointed to conduct investigations until Congress specifically appropriated funds for such payments. Their argument was that all activities paid for by tax dollars should be made accountable to the public. While their reasoning was valid, the action only served to make Tyler more adversarial towards Congress. When they asked for information regarding job requests from his political supporters, he refused, calling their actions "dangerous, impolitic and unconstitutional." When they asked the secretary of war, John C. Spencer, to reveal information about army fraud against the Cherokees, Tyler directed him not to cooperate.

In the midst of all the executive privilege debates, Tyler vetoed yet another Whig bill. That was the last straw for his opponents. A House select committee, led by former President John Quincy Adams, now a congressman from Massachusetts, and John Minor Botts of Virginia, charged that Tyler had committed impeachable offenses in his actions as president. On August 30, 1842, the president challenged the House to move forward with formal impeachment charges so that he could defend his record. His opponents took him up on the suggestion, and in January, Bott presented nine articles of impeachment: six abuses of power and three charges of misconduct of office, which included lying and withholding information from the representatives of the people. The House, however, ultimately voted down Bott's articles of impeachment and Tyler never had his day in court.

Tyler finished his term in office without any further major attacks from congress. The legislature, however, was not yet ready to give up entirely its attacks on Tyler or its investigation of the use of executive privilege, even after the end of his term. Several years later, during the term of James Polk, Tyler's successor, more allegations of abuse of executive privilege during Tyler's term surfaced. This time the focus of the charges was Tyler's secretary of state, Daniel Webster.

Webster, who had been handling the volatile Maine boundary controversy with Britain, had been authorized by Tyler to pay off local newspaper editors and politicians to support his upcoming talks with Lord Ashburton. The money came from a secret fund that Congress had established in 1810 to deal with delicate problems abroad. When the House asked President Polk to turn over Tyler's record of all payments made from the secret fund to Webster, he refused. Webster was cleared of all charges, and the new Democratic congress decided to honor President Polk's view of executive privilege.

"Corruption Beyond Example"

Scandals in the Life and Times of
James Buchanan

T HE 1850s WAS A POLITICAL
era marked by violence, corruption, and decadence. A senator was
brutally beaten by a congressman after delivering an anti-slavery
speech. Another congressman was tried for murdering his wife's
lover. Endless charges of corruption and fraud were aired on the
floor of Congress in session after session, and a United States
president was quietly acknowledged to be homosexual. In all, it
was quite a decade for scandal in American politics.

The 1850s had been ushered in by President Zachary Taylor,
who died suddenly on July 9, 1850, from gastrointestinal upset
most likely caused by eating unsanitary raw fruit. Despite his brief
time in office (he served only sixteen months), his administration
was not without a few embarrassing incidents. George W. Crawford, the secretary of war, was investigated by Congress after it
was discovered he earned $95,000 as a result of a questionable
cabinet-level decision handed down by two other cabinet members. George Galphin, a former client in Crawford's law practice,
had filed a pre-Revolutionary War claim against the government,
which amounted to $235,000 with interest. The treasury secretary
and attorney general both agreed to pay his heirs the full amount
which included Crawford's healthy fee. As other cabinet members
called for his resignation, the term "Galphinism" was coined.

74

Much like the term "Watergate" today, "Galphinism" was synonymous with corruption in the executive branch. The president took most of the heat for refusing to fire his controversial secretary of war.

When a second scandal emerged involving Thomas Ewing, the secretary of the interior, Taylor finally agreed to restructure the entire cabinet. Secretary Ewing had been charged with hiring and making illegal payments to large numbers of government clerks without authorization from Congress. Although Taylor died before he could clean house, the task was completed by his successor, Millard Fillmore, who demanded the resignations of the entire tainted group.

★ ★ ★

The emotionally-charged 1850s was a particularly violent time for legislators whose passions ran high, particularly over the issue of slavery. From the beginning of American history, sporadic scuffles had always occurred between adversary lawmakers. In 1798, Federalist Roger Griswold insulted Representative Matthew Lyon in the House of Representatives and Lyon spat in his face. Two weeks later Griswold, brandishing his cane, and Lyon, wielding a pair of fireplace tongs, began the first reorded brawl in Congress.

In 1856, it was a different story. The brutal beating of Massachusetts Senator Charles Sumner by a political foe turned the Senate into "the Chamber of Assassins." Sumner was a highly educated, cultured egomaniac. While his personality was not the most congenial, his oratory was certainly the most commanding. At one o'clock on May 19, 1856, he delivered one of the most extraordinary speeches of his career. If it had been up to his political enemies, it would have been his last.

The focus of the speech was the Kansas territory, where he claimed judges had been bullied and ballot boxes stuffed to illegally impose a pro-slavery legislation. His target was South Carolina Senator Andrew Pickens Butler. Using a plethora of sexual metaphors, Sumner spoke of Butler's "Mistress Slavery," the "rape of a virgin territory" and more. But while some arguments were

SOUTHERN CHIVALRY — ARGUMENT versus CLUB'S.

The near-fatal beating of Charles Sumner turned the Senate into a "Chamber of Assassins."

powerful and visionary, other comments were personal and vicious. One cruel barb was aimed at Butler's speech impediment, which had been caused by a stroke. Sumner said, "With incoherent phrases, discharged the loose expectoration of his speech . . . with error, sometimes of principle, sometimes of fact . . . [H]e cannot ope his mouth but out there flies a blunder." He called Butler's "shameful imbecility" a blot on the nation.

His speech, which soon became known as the "Crime Against Kansas" speech, ignited near hysteria in the thirty-fourth Congress. The reactions on both sides of the issue were highly charged. Pro-slavery Senator Lewis Cass labeled the speech "the most un-American and unpatriotic that ever grated on the ears of the members of this body." On the other hand, abolitionist William Lloyd Garrison thought the speech one "worth dying for."

While Senator Butler wasn't present to hear the insults hurled, his nephew, Representative Preston S. Brooks of South Carolina, was. Three days later, in a premeditated surprise attack, he set out to avenge his uncle's honor. The Senate had adjourned at noon, following a touching eulogy to a fellow representative.

Brooks entered and found Sumner at his desk in the senate chamber. Calmly, Brooks said, "I have read your speech twice over carefully. It is a libel on South Carolina and Mr. Butler who is a relative of mine." He then beat Sumner with his cane until it was reduced to splinters and the Senator from Massachusetts fell to the floor, covered in blood. As Sumner later testified,

> Other persons were about me, offering friendly assistance; but I did not recognize any of them, others were at a distance, looking on, and offering no assistance, of whom I recognized only Mr. Douglas, of Illinois, Mr. Toombs, of Georgia, and I thought also my assailant standing between them. I was helped from the floor, and conducted to the lobby of the Senate where I was placed upon a sofa. Of those who helped me there I have no recollection. As I entered the lobby I recognized Mr. Slidell, of Louisiana, who retreated; but I recognized no one else until I felt a friendly grasp of the hand which seemed to come from Mr. Campbell, of Ohio.

Representatives Douglas, Toombs, and Slidell gave their own versions to the House Select Committee. All denied abetting the assailant, although Toombs confessed he approved of the attack.

Reaction to the beating was split right along the lines of the slavery issue. Northerners were sympathetic to Sumner. Henry Wadsworth Longfellow wrote to Sumner, "I have no words to write you about this savage atrocity, only enough to express our sorrow and sympathy." Ralph Waldo Emerson and Oliver Wendell Holmes gave speeches in Sumner's defense. But in the South, Brooks was an instant hero. His constituents sent him commemorative canes engraved with slogans such as "Hit him again." One admirer even sent him a silver pitcher with the inscription: "Preston S. Brooks, May 22, 1856."

The day after the attack, the Senate agreed to investigate the incident, but by the end of the week they decided that jurisdiction over Brooks belonged to the House. Three days later, they began their investigation. The first testimony was from the victim. Appearing before the House covered with bandages, Sumner described how he had been beaten with great force at least one dozen times in the short span of only a minute. All sorts of expert witnesses and doctors were called before the committee. Even a cane expert testified on the strength of different woods. On June 2, 1856, the majority report of the House Select Committee concluded that Preston Brooks's attack against Charles Sumner was a breach of congressional privilege. It said, "The act cannot be regarded by the committee otherwise than as an aggravated assault upon the inestimable right of freedom of speech guaranteed by the Constitution . . . and, if carried to its ultimate consequences, must result in anarchy and bring in its train all the evils of a reign of terror."

The majority report was one thing. Getting a majority vote to expel Brooks from Congress was another. As high-spirited debates continued over the next month, nearly a million copies of the "Crimes Against Kansas" speech were distributed outside Congress.

Finally, on July 14, 1856, Brooks decided to let Congress get on with the business of running the country. He addressed the speaker of the House and resigned from his seat in the thirty-fourth Congress. But he wasn't away for long. He ran for office again in South Carolina and was sworn in that August 1. His victory was short-lived, however, as he died five months later of a liver disease.

Although five doctors reported that his attack wasn't all that serious, Charles Sumner lived with intense pain and could barely walk, read, or write for two years. It was three full years before he resumed his Senate duties. During his absence, his empty seat became a symbol of the antislavery movement he had so passionately endorsed. While some of his colleagues believed his lengthy convalescence was just a ploy to further his cause and his career, historians today believe he probably suffered from a post-traumatic stress syndrome as a result of the attack.

Daniel Sickles killed his wife's lover, the son of Francis Scott Key.

* * *

During the unprecedented debates in the House and Senate that stemmed from the Charles Sumner attack, one U.S. representative sat in Congress, distracted more by his personal problems at home. Representative Daniel S. Sickles, a Democrat from New York, was consumed by his suspicion that his young wife, Teresa, was having an affair with the U.S. attorney for the District of Columbia. Day after day, he was driven to the brink of madness by his suspicions. Finally, when he learned those suspicions were well-founded, he gunned down his wife's lover in the street, fatally wounding Phillip Barton Key, the son of Francis Scott Key, composer of "The Star-Spangled Banner."

Daniel Sickles had married Teresa Bagioli in 1852, when she was just sixteen years old and he was thirty-two. He was a fairly unscrupulous attorney who had been charged three times with embezzlement, although he was exonerated each time. His private life was also hardly pristine—he kept a prostitute as his mistress.

Soon after his marriage, Sickles was appointed first secretary of the American legation in London, where James Buchanan, a powerful Democrat, served as the U.S. ambassador. In the years that followed, the two men became good friends and worked together on Buchanan's 1856 bid for the presidency. At the time Buchanan won the election, Sickles was also elected to Congress, clearly giving him an inside track to the White House. His new-found political clout would lead to the unravelling of his marriage.

At Buchanan's Inaugural Ball in 1857, Sickles was treated like the man of the hour, with many of the guests stopping by between waltzes to ask for political favors. One of them was Phillip Barton Key, who needed Sickles to put in a good word for him so that Buchanan would reappoint him U.S. Attorney in Washington, D.C. Sickles knew a good opportunity when he saw one. Key, with his prestigious family ties, could help open doors to the inner circles of "old society" and boost Sickles's fading respectability. It was a match made only in politics. The only person who found it more enthralling was Sickles's wife, Teresa. Unbeknownst to the new representative, she was quite taken with Key. While her husband passed the night politicking, she enjoyed dance after dance with her husband's new ally.

Sickles worked hard at positioning himself among the aristocratic families that had been prominent since before the Revolutionary War. He rented a mansion on Lafayette Square, just in front of the White House, and entertained lavishly. While Sickles helped reappoint Key, the well-connected U.S. Attorney provided Sickles with party guests drawn from the "A" list of Washington. Everything seemed to be running smoothly, except that Key was falling madly in love with the congressman's wife.

Key was then thirty-nine years old, a widower with four children. By the spring of 1858, in the throes of mid-life crisis, he began an affair with twenty-two-year-old Teresa. Although Sickles would later try to portray him as a notorious adulterer, Key was quite amateurish in his style. When he wanted to see Teresa, he would walk through Lafayette Square and signal her by waving a white handkerchief. He might as well have worn a sign around his neck—half the town knew what he was up to. When a friend suggested he try a little more discretion, Key rented a house a few blocks away on 15th Street in the poorer section of town. Key and Teresa were so obviously out of place, that the other half of the town also figured it out. One Friday in February 1859, an anonymous "do-gooder" sent separate letters to both Teresa and her husband, outlining the affair and warning them to stop.

Sickles was devastated. The following day, he took Teresa into the guest house and forced her to write the confession of her adultery with Key in front of a servant who acted as a witness. Sobbing, she wrote, "I have been at the house of 15th St. with Mr. Key. . . . I did what is usual for a wicked woman to do . . . an intimacy of an improper kind. . . . I undressed myself. Mr. Key undressed also. . . . [We] went to bed together."

Sickles demanded his wedding ring back, forced Teresa to sleep on the floor of the guest room that night, and told her to return to her mother. The next morning, insult was added to Sickles's injury when he spotted Key in front of the window, twirling his handkerchief to signal Teresa. In a total fit of rage, Sickles grabbed a loaded revolver, ran out to the street and shouted, "Key, you scoundrel, you have dishonored my bed—you must die!" Then he cocked the gun, aimed, and fired. Key reached into the breast pocket of his coat and pulled out the only thing he had to protect himself with—a pair of opera glasses—which he threw into Sickles's face. Sickles then pulled out another gun and fired, and then drew out a third gun and shot at pointblank range. As a crowd gathered at the scene, Sickles went back to his house, told Teresa, "I've killed him," and waited for the police.

The shooting made the most sensational capital news copy since the Charles Sumner attack. Interestingly, the public perceived Teresa as the victim and her husband the villain. Dredging up Sickles's weak reputation, one paper wrote, "The man who makes no scruple to invade and destroy the domestic peace of others—he who, in his own practice, regards adultery as a joke, and the matrimonial bond as no barrier against the utmost capricious licentiousness—has little right to complain when the mischief which he carries without scruple into other families enters his own.''

To help plead his case in the press, Sickles leaked Teresa's confession. Now the public clearly believed Key was the villain, which was just the sentiment Sickles needed going into his murder trial. The one other element Sickles required was a sympathetic prosecuting attorney. That wasn't too much of a problem; President Buchanan would take care of the appointment, which would ironically fill the job recently vacated by Phillip Barton Key.

Sickles, who pleaded temporary mental aberration as his defense, was acquitted. And while the sympathetic public waited to read the next installment, ''The Divorce,'' they were never quite satisfied. Unbeknownst to all, the congressman and his wife had secretly rekindled their courtship while he awaited his trial, and three months later they were officially reunited. Ironically, his murder charge, his own infidelities, and his early days as an embezzler had not damaged his career. But his reconciliation with Teresa signaled the beginning of the end of it. Sickles eventually returned to his own womanizing ways. Teresa died of tuberculosis at the age of thirty-one.

★ ★ ★

When James Buchanan was sworn in as the fifteenth president of the United States in 1857, his inaugural address contained a strong warning against political corruption:

> Next in importance to the maintenance of the Constitution and the Union is the duty of preserving the government free from the taint, or even the suspicion, of corruption. Public virtue is the vital spirit of republics; and history shows that when this has decayed, and the love of money has usurped its place, although the forms of free government may remain for a season, the substance has departed forever.

This was an ironic choice for Buchanan's first official statement. As one group of New Jersey Republicans would later declare, by the end of his administration, corruption was ''beyond

James Buchanan—swore against corruption—yet lived by it.

example and to a degree under which no nation can lone exist.''

The corruption began even before he was elected. Buchanan had condoned unethical, perhaps illegal, tactics to nail down blocks of votes. Buchanan promised his close personal friend, George Plitt of Philadelphia, naval contracts in return for campaign contributions. And in Indiana and Pennsylvania (Buchanan's home state) aliens were fraudulently naturalized and taken to the polls by the Democrats. In crucial states where votes could make a difference for his opponents, John C. Frémont and Millard Fillmore, immigrant voters were relocated.

Once Buchanan was elected, it was a real free-for-all. First, political supporters were taken care of. In one instance, the secretary of the navy, Isaac Toucey, arranged deadlines for certain government contracts in such a way that they could only be met by W. C. N. Swift of New Bedford, Massachusetts, who had given $16,000 to Buchanan's campaign.

By the first session of the thirty-fifth Congress, a House committee discovered that the military reservation at Fort Snelling, Minnesota, had been sold privately to a group which included Secretary of War John B. Floyd's personal banker and the brother of the customs collector for the port of New York, another Buchanan appointee. While other investigations were underway in the House, the doorkeeper (another Democrat) had to resign when it was discovered he falsified accounts.

How much, if any, of the corruption could be traced directly to the president was the question—until a letter surfaced that was written by W. C. Patterson to Buchanan. In it, Patterson urged the president to give a lucrative contract to a Philadelphia firm that promised to influence the 1858 reelection of Buchanan's close friend, Congressman Thomas Florence. Buchanan had initialed the letter and sent it to the Navy Department, which awarded the contract to the firm without question. Ten days later, Florence was reelected.

Buchanan and his appointees had endless innovations to keep the political wheels greased. Some of their most lucrative schemes involved the public printing contracts. Until Congress established a government printing office in 1869 (most likely a result of Buchanan's abuses), all government documents were printed by the private sector. Those contracts, since Andrew Jackson's administration, had gone to political friends of the president.

As investigations revealed, Cornelius Wendell made millions of dollars from printing contracts between 1853 and 1860. Two ranking Republicans, Preston King and John Covode, uncovered graft, kickbacks, and overpayments by the superintendent of public printing, and had him sent directly to jail. New laws were passed, a new superintendent was hired, and Buchanan came up smelling like a rose—almost.

With no more contracts coming his way, Cornelius Wendell, financial manager of the pro-administration *Washington Union*, became a star witness for King's Senate committee and told the inside story on how the "slush funds" worked. He testified that, at the direction of the president, he had given contracts to two Philadelphia newspapers who had contributed $100,000 to Buchanan's political causes over a period of four years. Wendell explained that in one session of Congress alone, his printing profits were $166,000. He was paid $40,000 per contract and jobbed out the work at half the price.

Wendell's most damaging testimony related to the Lecompton constitution, which called for the admission of Kansas to the Union as a slave state. Wendell had spent nearly $40,000 to bribe various congressmen to vote in favor of it. One stubborn congressman was offered, but refused, $80,000 (through a printing contract) to throw his vote.

This disclosure was most shocking to the many voters who had elected Buchanan because of his neutrality on the "Bleeding Kansas" issue. Buchanan had been living in England when the controversy began brewing and, unlike the other candidates, he had no position to defend. Under the circumstances, it was shocking to learn that Buchanan's men had orchestrated secret bribes.

The corruption didn't end there, either. On May 15, Isaac V. Fowler, the postmaster of New York, fled the country with $155,000 of government funds. And on December 29, 1860, Secretary of War Floyd resigned after endorsing $5,000,000 in phony bills, which a New York contracting firm used as collateral for bank loans.

★ ★ ★

Unfortunately, Buchanan's myriad scandals had a destructive effect on much of Buchanan's legislation, regardless of its overall merit. One vital bill, which would have authorized the purchase of Cuba from Spain for $30,000,000, was withdrawn when the senator who introduced it feared Buchanan would divert the money to his own slush fund.

Buchanan's personal scandals were just as outrageous as his public ones. Having the distinction of being America's only bachelor president, his sexual preference has remained a point of debate. Today there is evidence that President James Buchanan was a homosexual. He is known to have had one serious heterosexual relationship, but a great mystery surrounds it.

Buchanan was engaged to Anne C. Coleman during the summer of 1819. After a quarrel, she broke off the engagement, and died December 9 under mysterious circumstances—most likely suicide. Buchanan wrote her obituary notice for the Lancaster newspaper and sent the following letter to Anne's father. It is the only piece of Buchanan correspondence about the incident which exists today.

[James Buchanan to Robert Coleman, Esq.]
Lancaster, December 10, 1819

MY DEAR SIR:
     You have lost a child, a dear, dear child. I have lost the only earthly object of my affections, without whom life now presents to me a dreary blank. My prospects are all cut off, and I feel that my happiness will be buried with her in the grave. It is now no time for explanation, but the time will come when you will discover that she, as well as I, have been much abused. God forgive the authors of it. My feelings of resentment against them, whoever they may be, are buried in the dust. I have now one request to make, and, for

the love of God and of your dear departed daughter whom I loved infinitely more than any other human being could love, deny me not. Afford me the melancholy pleasure of seeing her body before its internment. I would not for the world be denied this request.

I might make another, but from the misrepresentations which must have been made to you, I am almost afraid. I would like to follow her remains to the grave as a mourner. I would like to convince the world, and I hope yet to convince you, that she was infinitely dearer to me than life. I may sustain the shock of her death, but I feel that happiness has fled from me forever. The prayer which I make to God without ceasing is, that I yet may be able to show my veneration for the memory of my dear departed saint, by my respect and attachment for her surviving friends.

May Heaven bless you, and enable you to bear the shock with the fortitude of a Christian. I am, forever, your sincere and grateful friend,

JAMES BUCHANAN

Anne's father returned the letter unopened, creating even more intrigue about the couple's breakup. It was clear Robert Coleman blamed Buchanan for his daughter's death. The true story, however, followed Buchanan to the grave. At one time, it appeared Buchanan was going to reveal the circumstances. When he was in his seventies, he revealed to a friend that he had placed sealed documents on deposit in the city of New York, which some day would explain the breakup. Buchanan had sent this package, along with others, to a bank in New York during the Civil War to protect them from Confederate troops. After he died, the executors of his will found the papers, sealed separately from the others, with a note in his handwriting that they be destroyed without being read. The executors honored his wish, and burned the package without breaking the seal.

Perhaps Buchanan's dark secret was that he was a homosexual, a notion that has crept through historical literature for decades. In particular, Buchanan's intimate friendship with Senator Wil-

Sen. William R. King, from Alabama—considered too "close" a friend of Buchanan's.

liam Rufus De Vane King of Alabama stirred a fair share of curiosity. King had entered Congress in 1819, two years before Buchanan. In 1834, when Buchanan moved from the House to the Senate, he and King became inseparable and piqued the interests of local gossips. As one historian noted, King's "fastidious habits and conspicuous intimacy with the bachelor Buchanan gave rise to some cruel jibes."

Buchanan and King shared rooms over a twenty-three-year friendship. Andrew Jackson called King "Miss Nancy" and

Aaron Brown, a Tennessee Democrat who was James K. Polk's former law partner, called him Buchanan's "better half" and "Aunt Fancy."

At one point, in 1844, Buchanan wanted to run for president with King as his running mate. While his own ambitions were temporarily thwarted, he still urged King to run for vice president. On January 14, in a letter to Sarah Polk marked "Confidential," Aaron Brown wrote, "Mr. Buchanan looks gloomy & dissatisfied & so did *his better half* until a little private flattery & a certain newspaper puff which you doubtless noticed, excited hopes that by getting *a divorce* she might set up again in the world to some tolerable advantage . . . *Aunt Fancy* may now be seen every day, triged out in her best clothes and smirking about in hopes of securing better terms than with her former companion." Brown's confidential letter makes other derogatory references such as "Mr. Buchanan & *his wife*" and "Mrs. B."

Another suggestion of a homosexual relationship comes from King's own correspondence to Buchanan. In 1844, after President Tyler appointed him Minister to France, King wrote to Buchanan: "I am selfish enough to hope you will not be able to procure an associate who will cause you to feel no regret at our separation. For myself, I shall feel lonely in the midst of Paris, for here I shall no Friend with whom I can commune as with my own thoughts." In another letter, King complained that he hadn't heard from Buchanan—"this verifying the old adage, out of sight, out of mind." He also suggested the United States would be better represented in Paris "by someone who has more the spirit of a man." The French ministry had come a long way since the scandals of Benjamin Franklin and Thomas Jefferson.

King was elected vice president in 1853 under Franklin Pierce, but he died of tuberculosis one month after he was sworn in. He was so ill at the time of the inauguration that he was allowed to take the oath of office in Cuba where he had gone for a rest. Interestingly, King is the only bachelor vice president in U.S. history.

Buchanan's failings, both private and public, finally caught

Washington
January 14th 1844

Confidential

Dear Madam

you see that after the manner of one of
our friends with whom you are intimately acquainted I have
headed this letter with the usual precaution — Not that there
is any thing really secret in it, but it gives an air of
mystery & interest to one's correspondence. Washington
the theatre of so many of your younger but I hope not
happier days is excruciatingly dull this Winter. Congress
is dull, the public assemblies of the city are dull — The
select private parties are dull. What the matter may
be I cannot tell you. It may be that those who are
now in patronage & you know every body here lives
on patronage, are sure that their days are numbered & &
those who are looking forward for their places are
not sure that they can ever attain them. Among the
Magnates there is evident uneasiness. Mr. Buchannan
looks gloomy & dissatisfied & so did his better half until
a little private flattery & a certain newspaper puff
which you doubtless noticed, made her hopes that by getting
a divorce she might set up again in the world to
some tolerable advantage. Since which casual events,
which she has taken for real and permanent overtures, Aunt

Nancy may be now seen every day, trigged
out in her best clothes & smirking about in hopes of seeing
better times than with her former companion.
You will however see in the Globe of tomorrow that
she is presented to the world "as no better than she
should be". This however is what every prude deserves
who sets herself up for more than she is worth.
But I have done with metaphor & innuendo.

Aaron Brown's 1844 letter to Sarah Polk made derogatory remarks about Buchanan's "relationship."

up with him during his final year in office. On June 13, 1860, President Buchanan was formally censured by Congress in perhaps the strongest show of Republican solidarity ever. For the upcoming presidential convention, the Republican National Committee sent out invitations addressed to those opposed to "federal corruption and usurpation."

As a reaction to the corruption within the Buchanan administration, candidates with the slightest hint of questionable connections were passed over for the nomination and the Republicans offered "Honest Abe" Lincoln as their candidate. While it's been the popular belief that Lincoln was elected primarily for his antislavery platform, his victory had just as much to do with the voters' need to purge the government of corruption. Senator James W. Grimes of Iowa wrote, "Our triumph was achieved more because of Lincoln's . . . honesty and the known corruption of the Democrats, than because of the negro question." William B. Stokes of Tennessee agreed, declaring before Congress that "the corruptions of the present administration" caused "thousands of people of the country" to vote for Lincoln, who might not have otherwise.

Buchanan, meanwhile, decided one presidential term was enough and retired to his estate, Wheatland, near Lancaster, Pennsylvania. To his successor, Abraham Lincoln, he wrote, "My dear sir, if you are as happy on entering the White House as I on leaving, you are a very happy man indeed."

"It Would Stink in the Nostrils of the American People"

Scandals in the Life and Times of Abraham Lincoln

A1971 POLL OF OVER one thousand leading historians ranked Abraham Lincoln as America's greatest president. As a young candidate for the Senate, he had promised to put an end to the volatile slavery issue with his famous speech in which he warned, "A house divided against itself cannot stand." Inaugurated president in 1861, Lincoln was able to fulfill that dream and many others. Through his first term, he led the country through the darkest moments of "the war to save the Union" and he helped put an end to slavery forever. But his leadership during these unprecedented times was not without major compromise. Lincoln suspended freedom of speech, freedom of the press, and the writ of habeas corpus, the law that protects against illegal imprisonment by requiring anyone who is arrested to be brought before a judge or court.

Despite Lincoln's disregard for constitutional guarantees, it was his wife who was at the center of most of the Presidential scandals. First Lady Mary Todd Lincoln was attacked for everything from her jealous nature to her penchant for lavish parties and spending sprees, which were flaunted in the face of a bleak civil war.

Nicknamed "The Hellcat," Mrs. Lincoln was destined to be an unpopular first lady. Northerners hated her because she came

Mary Todd Lincoln came under fire for extravagent spending during the Civil War.

from a prominent Southern family who were slaveholders. Southerners hated her because she deserted their cause. Neither side trusted her. Despite her unwavering loyalty to the Union, she was accused of being a Confederate spy and investigated for treason. Her enemies believed she was working on behalf of her three half-brothers who were fighting for the Confederate side, as was the husband of Mary Todd's sister. Eventually, a joint committee held a clandestine meeting to formalize charges.

As the committee secretly debated the merits of an indictment against the first lady, its deliberations were unexpectedly interrupted by the appearance of a surprise witness—the president. Lincoln had heard about the meeting and invited himself in. He pulled up a chair and read a brief but very direct statement: "I, Abraham Lincoln, President of the United States, appear of my own volition before this Committee of the Senate to say that I, of my own knowledge, know that it is untrue that any of my family hold treasonable communication with the enemy." The members of the committee were left speechless as Lincoln stood up and departed from the room as quickly as he had entered. Immediately afterwards, the committee, sobered by his bold response, unanimously decided to drop the treason issue. According to one member, the committee was "so greatly affected" they had to adjourn for the rest of the day.

While the president had nipped the treason scandal in the bud, there was little he could do about the other problems with his wife. Mary Todd Lincoln's extravagant spending made her the Imelda Marcos of her day. In one four-month period alone, she purchased 300 pairs of kid gloves. She had trunks full of clothing she never took out of the department-store packaging.

Most of Mary Todd Lincoln's astronomical personal bills remained unpaid throughout Lincoln's first term, as the more fashionable stores were happy to extend credit to a first lady. The bills she incurred at the White House, however, were a completely different story. She exceeded her $20,000 White House decorating budget, which had been approved by Congress, by $6,700. Although she enlisted the support of others to help her convince the president to ask Congress to cover the difference, this was wartime and Lincoln was not in an indulgent spirit. "I'll pay it out of my own pocket first," he fumed, "It would stink in the nostrils of the American people to have it said the President of the United States had approved a bill over-running an appropriation of $20,000 for *flub dubs* for this damned old house, when the soldiers cannot have blankets."

The first lady's extravagant wartime parties didn't fare too well with the public, either. While the rest of the country tightened its belt, stoically enduring the wartime pinch, she spent small fortunes perfecting the fine art of entertaining which at times included splurges such as sugar centerpieces reenacting great Civil War battles. Despite his wife's embarrassing excesses, Lincoln was reelected to a second term in 1864. Those who feared a change in leadership during the war breathed a sigh of relief. So did Mary Todd Lincoln, although her reasons were not as high-minded.

She needed his presidental income to pay off enormous department-store bills she had incurred. Mrs. Lincoln had confided to her seamstress, Elizabeth Keckley, who had been a slave for thirty years and spent four years in the White House: "If he should be defeated I do not know what would become of us all. To me, to him, there is more at stake in this election than he dreams of." When the seamstress asked what she meant, the first lady replied, "Simply this, I have contracted large debts of which he knows nothing and which he will be unable to pay if he is defeated. . . . I owe altogether about $27,000—the principal portion at Stewarts [Department Store] in New York. You understand, Elizabeth, that Mr. Lincoln has but little idea of the expense of a woman's wardrobe."

The sad truth was that Mary Todd Lincoln was mentally ill. Her extravagant spending sprees were usually followed by extreme fits of miserliness, as she was also consumed by an irrational fear of losing her money. Lincoln had a form of mental illness himself, suffering from bouts of manic depression throughout his life. Together, they made quite a team.

★ ★ ★

Mary Todd met Abraham Lincoln in 1839 when he was a thirty-year-old lawyer and Illinois state legislator and she was twenty-one. From the start, Lincoln was quite taken with her and within a year they were engaged, but on the morning of their wedding, "that fatal first of January [1841]," as Lincoln called it, he went into a panic and left her at the altar. Accounts vary greatly as to how, when, and why. As to the how and when, some have reported that he broke off the nuptial plans close to the wedding date, while others claim it was on the very day, forcing the last minute cancellation of the minister and dinner guests.

As for the why, others have suggested that a house guest of the Todd family, Matilda Edwards, had stolen Lincoln's affections. However, Mary's sister, Elizabeth, contended, "Mr. Lincoln loved Mary, he went crazy in my own opinion, not because he loved Miss Edwards as said, but because he wanted to marry and doubted his ability and capacity to please and support a wife. Lincoln and Mary were engaged, everything was ready and prepared for the marriage, even to the supper, etc. Mr. L. failed to meet his engagement, cause: insanity. In his lunacy he declared he hated Mary and loved Miss Edwards. This is true, yet it was not his real feelings. A crazy man hates those he loves when not himself, often, often is this the case."

Lincoln and Mary finally married on November 4, 1842—on two hours' notice. They had been meeting in secret for almost a year to avoid town gossip. Although their marriage has been portrayed in an unfavorable light, there is every reason to believe they were, indeed, in love. That doesn't mean, however, they lived happily ever after.

Much of their sadness stemmed from the fact that the Lincolns buried two of their four children. (A third died after Lincoln was assassinated.) Eddie died of tuberculosis at the age of three and Willie died of complications of a cold at the age of twelve, during Lincoln's first term. He was the first (and only) child to die in the White House. His death, in particular, was a terrible blow to the Lincolns. Three years later, at the time of Lincoln's assassination, the first lady insisted that Willie's body be removed from the Oak Hill Cemetery, laid in a new black walnut coffin, and placed on the presidential funeral train so father and son could make the slow trip home to Springfield, Illinois, together.

Mrs. Lincoln's spiritualism made matters even worse. The first lady entertained psychics and mediums regularly in the White House and had strong beliefs in the paranormal. She even held seances in the Red Room. Not long before Lincoln's death, she told him of a dream she had in which he was murdered; this premonition contributed to her eventual unravelling.

★ ★ ★

On April 14, 1865, Lincoln was fatally shot by John Wilkes Booth in the Ford Theater. With her face next to her dying husband's, Mary Todd Lincoln whispered, "Love, live but one moment to speak to our children. Oh, oh, that our little Tad might see his father before he died." She begged the doctors to kill her so that she could join him. Having already shown some mental instability, she never recovered from the shock of her husband's death.

Although he died without a will, Lincoln left a healthy $83,000 estate to be divided amongst his wife and two surviving sons. Under the keen financial management of Judge David Davies, it increased to $110,000 by 1868. In addition, Congress voted to pay Mrs. Lincoln her husband's salary for a year, which came to about $22,000 with deductions. Public donations to her added another $10,000. Still, the former first lady slipped into an irrational panic about money. Under the alias of "Mrs. Clarke," she went to New York to sell her clothing, a scheme which would become known as "the old-clothes scandal."

A consignment broker named W. H. Brady at 609 Broadway agreed to take Mary Todd Lincoln's account, which attracted a lot of curiosity seekers, but not many buyers. The unsympathetic public knew that Mrs. Lincoln was far from destitute. The *New York Evening Express* described, in humiliating detail, every item up for sale, including the dresses with stains under the arms and in the lining. The unsold items were invoiced and returned.

Invoice of articles sent to Mrs. A. Lincoln:

1 Trunk	1 Set of furs
1 Lace dress	2 Paisley shawls
1 Lace dress flounced	2 Gold bracelets
5 Lace shawls	16 Dresses
3 Camelhair shawls	2 Opera cloaks
1 Lace parasol cover	1 Purple shawl

1 Lace handkerchief	1 Feather cape
1 Sable boa	28 Yds. silk
1 White boa	

Articles sold:

1 Diamond Ring	2 Dresses
3 Small Diamond Rings	1 Child's shawl
1 Camelhair shawl	1 Lace Chantilly shawl
1 Red Camelhair shawl	1 Set of furs

To escape the embarrassment of the "old-clothes scandal," Mary Todd Lincoln decided to go abroad. Following her son Robert's marriage in September 1868, she set sail for Frankfurt with her youngest son, Tad. It was not long, however, before tragedy struck again. Soon after they returned in 1871, Tad died from a lingering cold. Mary Todd was by his side when he took his last breath and slumped forward in his chair.

Following Tad's death, Mrs. Lincoln endured yet another trial of her already fragile sanity. William H. Herndon, Lincoln's law partner for seventeen years, had embarked on a lecture tour across the country. In his talks, he revealed the most intimate details of the life of the martyred president. If there was one final event to help push Mary Todd Lincoln off the deep end, this was it.

After the assassination, Herndon had dedicated his life to gathering as much information about Lincoln as he could find. He wrote to everybody who ever knew Lincoln or his parents and published his own biographies. In his lectures he told many stories which upset Mrs. Lincoln, including the tale of the "fatal first of January [1841]" and another about a woman Lincoln was supposed to have loved named Ann Rutledge (which has since been discounted as pure fabrication). He lectured on the illegitimacy of Lincoln's mother (the president had long acknowledged this fact) and insinuated that Lincoln, too, was a bastard. Herndon discovered that Lincoln's father had been castrated, but could not pinpoint the date. So, he substituted a theory that Lincoln might have been fathered by his mother's close friend, Abraham Enloe.

Mrs. Lincoln drifted slowly and inexorably toward madness. Finally, in March 1875, while on an extended vacation in Florida, she succumbed totally. She suddenly became consumed with the belief that her last son, Robert, was also dying, and that someone was trying to poison her and had stolen her pocketbook. When she returned to Chicago on March 15, and checked into the Grand Pacific Hotel, Robert hired Pinkerton detectives to watch her. What they saw was disturbing. Mrs. Lincoln carried $57,000 in government securities and cash sewn into pockets in her petticoat because she was sure there was a plot to get her money. She would leave the hotel once and sometimes twice a day on reckless shopping sprees: $600 on lace curtains, $200 on soaps and perfumes, $450 for three watches. She also told the hotel manager that a man was communicating to her through her hotel-room wall and insisted the South Side of Chicago was in flames. Left with no recourse, Robert started proceedings to have his mother committed.

On May 19, 1875, the Cook County Court in Chicago began Mary Lincoln's insanity hearing. Doctors, salesmen, and other assorted witnesses testified about her conversations with imaginary people and her paranoid delusion that someone was trying to kill her. Not surprisingly, the twelve-man jury returned the verdict of insanity and the name, "Mary Lincoln," was entered on page 596 of the "Lunatic Record" of the Cook County Court.

Later that night, Mary Todd Lincoln returned to her hotel room and tried to commit suicide by swallowing what she thought was a mixture of camphor and laudanum. In reality, it was only sugar-water given to her by a perceptive pharmacist. The next day, she was taken to a state mental asylum in Batavia, Illinois, called "Bellevue Retreat." Mercifully, her stay lasted only a year, as in June 1876, she was declared sane and released. When she died on July 16, 1882, her autopsy showed she had a brain tumor.

"Letters Delivered All Right"

Scandals in the Life and Times of
Ulysses S. Grant

W HEN ULYSSES S. GRANT
first ran for president in 1868, he decided not to campaign or make
any promises to voters. His reputation as a Civil War hero was
enough to seal the victory. Although personally incorruptible, his
poor judgment of character and lack of political acumen set the
stage for one of the most corrupt eras in American politics. His
vice president, his personal secretary, and many members of his
cabinet dragged his reputation through the mud by their illegal and
unethical actions. Even his brother-in-law lured him into a scandal. When all was said and done, Ulysses S. Grant had to respond
to more charges of financial corruption than any other president,
either before or after his administration.

In his personal life, however, Grant was indeed above reproach, even if he had been a bit strange as a young man. He had no
girlfriends before meeting Julia Dent, the homely, crosseyed sister
of his fourth-year roommate at West Point. Grant later said that he
liked her eyes crossed. He must have. He proposed to her the moment he met her. They were married after a four-year engagement
during which they saw each other only once.

Another aspect of Grant's life, which is perhaps even more
surprising than his unusual courtship, was his initial failure as a
soldier. The sight of blood gave him a weak stomach. He was
horrified by hunting and found bullfights ''sickening.'' While a

young soldier at Fort Vancouver, he developed a severe case of homesickness, which led to a drinking problem. In April 1854, he was discovered drunk in public by his superior officer, Robert Buchanan, who demanded that he resign or stand trial. He resigned his post and left the military. He did not return to uniform until April 15, 1861, when President Lincoln asked for 75,000 volunteers to fight for the Union. The Civil War quickly hardened Grant to the terrors and rigors of war.

Although Grant went on to become a great war hero, he quickly proved that ability on the field of battle did not necessarily translate into ability in the executive office. As president, many of Grant's problems stemmed from his assembling one of the most unimpressive and undistinguished cabinets in U.S. political history. Most were personal friends about whom even he had reservations. He appointed Congressman Elihu Washburn secretary of state, only to replace him eleven days later with Hamilton Fish. He appointed General John Schofield secretary of war, but one week later changed his mind and appointed General John A. Rawlins, an old Civil War confidant. After he appointed Alexander T. Stewart, a wealthy New York businessman, secretary of the treasury, Congress put its foot down and passed a law forbidding anyone with such financial ties to head the Treasury Department. Stewart was out and George S. Boutwell was in.

Even with the end of musical cabinet chairs, Grant continued to display an abysmal lack of judgment in filling a number of other posts. He appointed Adolph E. Borie secretary of the navy, even though the wealthy Philadelphia businessman had no apparent qualifications for the job. If that wasn't enough to shake the public confidence, President Grant nominated a livery stable supervisor to become minister to Belgium.

★ ★ ★

One of the first major scandals of the Grant administration triggered Black Friday, the day that marked the beginning of the Gold Panic of 1869. It started when two speculators, James Fisk and Jay Gould, set out to corner the gold market. They enlisted the president's brother-in-law, Abel R. Corbin, to help them with their scheme. In return for an opportunity to cash in on their market manipulation, Corbin arranged a yachting party where Fisk and Gould could meet the president and pump him for information about future Treasury Department plans. It was critical for them to know whether the government was planning to sell any of its gold. In the event the Treasury Department made government gold more available, their speculation scheme would backfire and blow up in their faces.

On June 15, in a party aboard one of Fisk's steamers, President Grant became an unwitting accomplice in their gold scheme. As the speculators fished for information in the relaxed social environment, they discovered that Grant was indeed leaning toward selling more government gold. They were able to subtly influence him not to take that course of action. Later, the president's brother-in-law joined in, as planned, and presented Grant with a concocted theory of how selling gold would have a bad economic effect on the American agriculture market. The plan, so far, was working perfectly.

Assured they could now corner the market, Fisk and Gould soon began buying large amounts of gold at $140 an ounce which drove the price up to over $160. But on September 14, a glitch in the plan appeared. Although Grant was against government intervention, rumors began to circulate that Treasury Secretary Boutwell was about to step in and sell off some government gold reserves to stabilize the market. Three days later, Fisk and Gould were so nervous about the rumors they had the president's brother-in-law send a letter to Grant, suggesting the Treasury Department avoid involvement. But even then, some signals were crossed. After hand-delivering the letter, the messenger wired back, "Letters delivered all right." Ever the optimists, Fisk and Gould interpreted the wire to mean that Grant had agreed with Corbin's suggestion, and fueled by that news, the price of gold soared even higher—until September 24. On that day, forever known as Black Friday, Grant realized he had been duped and ordered Treasury Secretary Boutwell to sell off four million dollars in gold reserves. It was a necessary measure, but one which ignited panic selling and ruined many investors as the gold market began to plunge.

A congressional investigation into the scandals surrounding the Gold Panic, led by Representative James A. Garfield, exonerated Grant, although some question remained as to whether or not his wife, Julia, was involved. Fisk had asserted that out of Grant's brother-in-law's $1,500,000 account, $500,000 was earmarked for the first lady. Gould, on the other hand, denied it. As Grant thought it improper for his wife to testify, and many chivalrous congressmen agreed, she kept silent and the investigation was dropped. The spotlight then shifted to the other acknowledged guilty parties, in particular, Assistant Treasurer General Daniel Butterfield. Butterfield admitted to borrowing more than a million dollars so that he could speculate in the gold market for a profit of $25,000. After confessing that he had perjured himself, too, Butterfield was fired by the president.

Having successfully steered the economy through the Gold Panic, Secretary Boutwell left the Treasury Department to enter the Senate. His replacement, William A. Richardson, didn't fare quite as well. He was forced to resign after it was discovered he allowed a tax collector to keep 50 percent of the delinquent taxes he tracked down. The commission, as discovered by a congressional investigation, totaled $213,500. Finally, a new treasury secretary with impeccable credentials and the highest standard of integrity was brought in, Benjamin Helm Bristow. Unfortunately, Bristow not only kept the Treasury Department in order, but he also exposed the Whiskey Frauds—the scandal that was closest to the president's office and probably embarrassed Grant the most.

Millions of dollars in liquor taxes had been skimmed by the notorious "Whiskey Ring" headed by General John McDonald, supervisor of the Internal Revenue Bureau in St. Louis. In partnership with distillers, the IRS agents filed falsified production reports to avoid paying taxes. Although there had been slight pressure on Grant to clean up the timeworn practices that began in the Lincoln Administration, he took little action. Perhaps the reason Grant dragged his feet was that McDonald had once given him a team of expensive horses. But it is more likely the President's inaction was caused by the influence of General Orville E. Babcock, his personal secretary. Babcock, it was later discovered, had taken a direct bribe from McDonald to stop the investigations.

Treasury Secretary Bristow, on the other hand, was very aggressive in his pursuit of the Whiskey Ring scandals. On May 13, 1875, he had 350 men arrested, from Galveston to Boston. After the round-up, Bristow discussed the matter with the president, only to find him surprisingly naive. In advising Bristow on his next step, Grant recommended, "Well, Mr. Bristow, there is at least one honest man in St. Louis on whom we can rely—John McDonald." "Mr. President," Bristow sheepishly replied, "McDonald is the head and center of all the frauds. He is at this very time in New York ready to take a steamer on the first indication of any effort to arrest him."

Once the prosecution was underway, however, Grant took a very tough stance, opposing all grants of immunity in exchange for testimony. While it appeared to be a positive hard line, his opponents argued that denying immunity would only make the cases harder to prove. Maybe it did for some, but McDonald, for one, was found guilty and sent to jail where he wrote a book on the Whiskey Frauds. Babcock, who benefitted from the support of the president, was exonerated by the jury. His acquittal was, in part, due to the deposition Grant submitted, which defended him. Regardless of his courtroom loyalty, Grant fired him as his secretary soon after.

As embarrassing as the Whiskey Ring scandals had already been for Grant, they would soon become even more so, as subsequent press reports began to implicate his family in the affair. Several newspapers suggested that Frederick Dent Grant, the President's oldest son, and Orvil Grant, the President's brother, were somehow involved. In response, Grant insisted the attorney general ask the reporters to bring their evidence before a grand jury, but nothing ever came of the reports.

★ ★ ★

Probably the most notorious of the Grant administration scandals is that involving Crédit Mobilier. A construction company established by leaders of Union Pacific, it was set up, primarily, to profit from the extensive government financial support of railroad expansion. Crédit Mobilier officers made enormous profits for themselves by padding construction budgets and charging the Union Pacific exorbitant fees. Even more distressing, Crédit Mobilier was run by Oliver Ames and his brother, Oakes Ames—a congressman from Massachussetts who actively voted on most of the railroad bills. By the time the Crédit Mobilier Corporation completed its railroad construction, the Ames brothers' personal profits were estimated at $20 million.

Eventually, Congress got wind of their cozy and lucrative setup. To forestall any investigations, Congressman Ames then distributed Crédit Mobilier stock among selected officials at below market value and, in some cases, with deferred payments. Stock dividends were as high as 340 percent. The total stock distributed was estimated at $33 million, although no one person gained profits of more than a few hundred dollars.

When the Crédit Mobilier scandal first became public during Grant's reelection campaign in 1872, key administration figures were implicated—including Vice President Schuyler Colfax, who was quickly dropped from the ticket. Impeachment proceedings against him were considered, but dropped because Colfax had accepted the stock in 1867-68 while serving as speaker of the House. It was also discovered the wife of Grant's new vice president, Henry Wilson, had bought $2,000 worth of discounted stock. But when Wilson discovered legislative favors were expected of him, he asked that the investment be refunded and refused the $814 profit his wife was due. (Curiously, while the scandal rocked Capitol Hill and tainted the careers of many, it had little effect on one congressman—James A. Garfield. In spite of a small investment in Crédit Mobilier, he went on to become president.)

★ ★ ★

If Crédit Mobilier was the best known, the Belknap Scandal became the most intriguing of all the Grant Administration stories of corruption. None piqued the nation's curiosity more and for a good reason—it was a classic "juicy" scandal, involving high society, two sisters who married the same cabinet secretary, illegal kickbacks, suicide rumors, and an impeachment proceeding. It was so titillating and popular that newspapers published extra editions.

The scandal began to unfold on February 29, 1876, after Caleb P. Marsh gave a dramatic testimony before the House Committee on Expenditures in the War Department. Marsh, who held a War Department post-tradership at Fort Sill in the Indian Territory, admitted that for the past six years he had sent a total of $25,000 to Carrie and Puss Belknap, two sisters who were, respectively, the first and second wives of Secretary of War William W. Belknap. If Marsh's charges were true, Belknap was in violation of the law which states: "Every member of Congress, or any officer or agent of the government, who, directly or indirectly takes, receives, or agrees to receive, any money, property or other valuable consideration, whatever, from any person, for procuring or aiding to procure, any contract, office or place from the government or any department thereof . . . shall be imprisoned not more than two years, and fined not more than $10,000."

The day after Marsh's testimony, Belknap was informed of the accusation by Hiester Clymer, a Democratic congressman from Pennsylvania, who had been his college roommate at Princeton. After seeking legal counsel, Belknap read his response to the committee: "I have heard the charges read. Some things are true, some things are not true, and some things I know nothing about. But make your charge and put anything in it you may please, it makes no difference what, as to my guilt, which I will acknowledge without reserve. Only grant my wish that this investigation shall be pursued of further as affecting any member of my family."

William Belknap first met the Tomlinson sisters, Carita (Carrie) and Amanda (Puss) during the Civil War in Georgia where he was a provost marshal general for the Union army. The two girls had traveled from Kentucky to seek the parole of their two brothers, who had fought for the Confederates. They wound up in the offices of General Belknap, who was immediately charmed by the girls. Although there was little he could do to gain their brothers' release, he promised to look after them. In the meantime, he began wooing the eldest of the sisters, Carrie.

At the end of the Civil War, Belknap married Carrie and settled in Keokuk, Iowa, where he worked as a collector for the Internal Revenue Service. But when President Ulysses S. Grant asked him to become secretary of war in 1869, Belknap and his beautiful young wife quickly abandoned the quiet of Keokuk for the excitement of Washington. Carrie, in fact, was the social hit of the season. The *Washington Star* called her "the most brilliant of the Cabinet family," although given Grant's cabinet, it may have been a dubious honor.

Belknap was first introduced to Caleb Marsh in the summer of 1870 by Carrie's sister, Puss. Puss had come to visit the Belknaps at Long Branch, a part of the Jersey shore where many Washington politicians escaped the oppressive heat of the capital. The members of the group soon became fast friends, and at summer's end, the Marshes invited Carrie and Puss to visit their home in New York. The New York visit, however, was a traumatic one. Carrie, who was pregnant with her first child, became very ill. For almost a month, Mrs. Marsh nursed her around the clock. When Carrie was back on her feet, she was very grateful—grateful enough to seek the lucrative post-tradership at Fort Sill for Mrs. Marsh's husband.

On August 16, 1870, Marsh filled out an application form and was given the job, replacing a man named John Evans, who didn't want to relinquish the post. In order to keep the lucrative tradership, Evans agreed to pay a $3,000 quarterly fee to Marsh, who, in turn, split the money with Carrie. Apparently, all of this took place unbeknownst to Secretary Belknap, who once kicked a man out of his office for offering him a $10,000 bribe for another tradership.

The kickbacks continued until December when, just a few months after the baby was born, Carrie Belknap died suddenly. Puss and the Marshes rushed to Washington for the funeral and services, after which Puss insisted on moving into the Belknap house to look after the baby. Caleb Marsh, seeing Puss and the baby in the Belknap nursery, promised, "This child will have money coming to it before a great while." Puss told him, "Yes, the mother gave the child to me and told me that the money coming from you I must take and keep for it."

After a brief period of mourning, Puss, who was even prettier than her sister, quickly assumed her sister's place in Washington social circles. She adapted to her new life easily, enjoying official parties and gala balls on the arm of her handsome, sympathetic, forty-year-old cabinet secretary. Belknap, for his part, was glad for her company following the death of Carrie. The death of the infant in June 1871, however, temporarily ended her Washington whirlwind. Without a legitimate reason to live in the house, she was forced to return to Cincinnati.

Still, the $6,000 annual payments from Marsh kept coming, enabling Puss to travel to Europe and buy expensive furniture and couturier clothes. On one trip to Paris alone, she bought forty pairs of shoes. Her absence, however, was excruciating for Belknap who, after much anguish, wanted her back badly enough to face the Washington gossip-mongers. Finally, in December 1874, they were married in Harrodsburg, Kentucky. The bride wore a gown designed by Worth of Paris, a top name in European fashion.

Back in Washington, Puss Tomlinson Bower Belknap was irrepressible. She insisted Belknap move into a more luxurious three-story house, brought in an English maid and a French chef, and ordered an extensive hostess wardrobe from Paris. But just as Mary Todd Lincoln had learned. becoming the toast of the town was an expensive proposition. Just one year after the wedding, Puss asked Caleb Marsh for a $750 advance. Two months later, when a congressional investigation led right to his door, the money trail led to Puss Belknap.

Puss Belknap quickly became the most publicized woman in America, with daily accounts on the front pages chronicling every dirty detail. But she was her own best P. R. agent. Accepting just a few interview requests, from female reporters only, she presented herself as someone in mourning. One reporter described her as, "plainly dressed in heavy black silk; a simple knot of cherry ribbon fastened the ruche at her throat; the soft dark hair was simply parted, and a dainty little cap of French muslin, with cherry ribbons, covered her head. Not a bit of jewelry was visible.''

Meanwhile, the panic-stricken Caleb Marsh fled to Canada. In fear that Secretary Belknap might do the same, Grant stationed secret service men outside his home. Belknap was so distraught over the affront to his honor that he broke down crying and invited two officers to continue their surveillance from inside the house. The press quickly descended upon the beleaguered Belknap. With all the commotion around the secretary's G Street residence, they reported everything, including a few fictitious accounts as well, from an escape down the Potomac to an attempted suicide.

The following day an army officer went to visit Belknap on unrelated War Department business. Upon leaving, he described the condition of the secretary to the hungry press. ''Words fail to express how this man has suffered and aged during the last few days. His flowing silky beard was knotted and tangled, his hair was unkempt, great rings were under his eyes, and his sunken cheeks make up a picture of woe and despair that would have touched a heart of stone. I was so moved that I sprang forward with a word of comfort. . . . Belknap caught me by the hand and burst into tears. He was completely unmanned. He choked and sobbed: 'I am going to prove it to the people of this country that I am an honest man before this business'.''

Belknap resigned from his cabinet post, but the Senate began impeachment proceedings anyway. The question was then raised as to whether or not they could impeach someone who had already resigned. By a thirty-seven to twenty-seven vote, the Senate declared that they could, and the impeachment trial began. By the end of July, Belknap was acquitted and Puss went with their daughter to Europe for two years. After her return, Puss Belknap remained a darling of the Washington press. She made one of her greatest splashes when she appeared in a sleeveless, red-and-white French bathing suit with a short skirt and sheer stockings.

Belknap eventually went into private law practice, spending the rest of his life trying to keep up with family expenses. Although

Only 20 Cts. a month. No. 3, for March—ready at all News Depots—of "Frank Leslie's POPULAR MONTHLY," a new illustrated Magazine of 128 quarto pages—nearly double the size of the largest magazine—brimful of choice literature, and illustrated with over One Hundred fine engravings. Buy a copy and judge of its merits.

THE DAYS' DOINGS.

Illustrating Extraordinary Events of the Day.

Entered according to the Act of Congress, in the year 1876, by the Publisher of THE DAYS' DOINGS, in the office of the Librarian of Congress, at Washington.

No. 408.—VOL. XVI.   NEW YORK, MARCH 18, 1876.   {52 Weeks, $5.00} {24 Weeks}   PRICE, 10 CENTS.

THE NATIONAL DISGRACE.

AN AFFECTING EPISODE OF THE EXPOSÉ OF THE CRIME OF SECRETARY BELKNAP.—THE WIFE OF THE RUINED SECRETARY GOES, WITH HER INFANT, THROUGH THE STORMY NIGHT TO THE RESIDENCE OF MR. BLACKBURN, AND MAKES A PITEOUS APPEAL IN BEHALF OF HER HUSBAND.—See Next Page.

Newspapers such as The Day's Doings *published extra editions of the popular Belknap scandal.*

acquitted by the Senate, he lived out his life a man disgraced. His supporters only came to his defense after his death. On the day of his funeral, President Harrison ordered the War Department closed in his honor. In his obituaries, he was remembered as a victim of circumstances.

Although terribly embarrassed by all the scandals of his administration, and considered a presidential failure by most historians, Ulysses S. Grant was not a corrupt president. In fact, some believe the reason so much corruption was exposed during Grant's administration was not because it was any more abundant, but because Grant wanted it exposed. President Grant was reelected in 1872, but when he tried for a third term, the country had had enough.

"Bulldozing" and "The Fire of Lawless Passion"

Scandals in the Lives and Times of Rutherford B. Hayes and James A. Garfield

THE 1875 PRESIDENTIAL campaign found a large slate of candidates promising to end "Grantism," a term then synonymous with political corruption. In the top Democratic seat was Samuel Tilden who, as chairman of the New York Democratic committee from 1866 to 1874, had successfully broken the much-feared corruption ring of William March "Boss" Tweed, the leader of New York's infamous Tammany Hall. Since the time it was founded in 1789, Tammany Hall had been transformed from a simple social society that helped widows and orphans of the Revolutionary War to a powerful and corrupt political machine. Its notorious leader, Boss Tweed, controlled every political appointment, along with the funding of every government project in New York that passed the Board of Supervisors. His kickbacks were estimated at $200 million. Through Tweed's greedy manipulations, the bill for an $800,000 courthouse eventually topped $8,000,000! Forty chairs and three tables cost $170,729.60; repairs on fixtures for an unfinished building were $1,149,874.50; thermometers were billed at $7,500; the cost for brooms was listed at $41,190.95; and a plasterer charged $138,187.50—for two days work!

When Tweed was finally taken on, and beaten, Samuel Tilden led the attack. Tweed got twelve years in prison, where he

Political cartoon from The Wasp *shows Rutherford Hayes being pushed through a "side entrance," while Samuel Tilden is restrained from entering the White House.*

died, and Tilden easily won the Democratic presidential nomination at the St. Louis convention, beating his closest competitor 535 to 60.

The fight for the Republican nomination was not as clear cut. To begin with, the field was much more competitive, with candidates such as James G. Blaine of Maine, the leading contender, Oliver P. Morton of Indiana, Benjamin H. Bristow of Kentucky (who exposed the Whiskey Ring corruption under Grant), Roscoe Conkling of New York, and Rutherford B. Hayes of Ohio.

Through the first four ballots, Hayes trailed the pack. But, miraculously, he picked up momentum when delegates began to voice objections to ties with corruption that tainted Blaine, Morton, and Conkling. Although not as powerful as Tweed, "Boss" Conkling was just as legendary. A powerful and unscrupulous senator from New York, he was having a scandalous affair with Kate Chase Sprague, the wife of a Rhode Island senator and daughter of the Supreme Court Chief Justice, Salmon P. Chase. Like other political bosses of the day, he was in control of appointments to key offices, such as those in New York Customs, which were frequently investigated for bribery and extortion. It was doubtful such a candidate, in spite of his power, would gain the nomination.

Of all the Republican candidates, Bristow had the strongest reform record, but even he had to acknowledge the country wasn't quite ready for a Southern president. So in the spirit of good party politics, Bristow withdrew from the race and threw his support to Hayes, who had the cleanest reputation of the lot. On the fifth ballot, Hayes moved to third place, but still lagged far behind Blaine, 308 to 113. As the evening wore on, the delegates painstakingly assessed and reassessed all of the candidates, becoming increasingly aware that Hayes had no political enemies, no opposition. One by one, New York, North Carolina, Texas, and Vermont all swung their votes over to Hayes. By the seventh ballot, some reporters discovered that the candidate from Ohio finally had the majority by six votes. Tired delegates threw up their hats and shouted "Hayes! Hayes!"

If the nominating process in 1876 gave the public faith that corruption was over and reform ahead, the actual election was certain to destroy it. In fact, the presidential election of 1876 turned out to be the dirtiest in American history.

On election night, Hayes went to bed after conceding to a reporter that Tilden had won. Tilden had swept the popular vote and seemed certain to get the 185 electoral votes he needed. But James C. Reid, editor of the staunchly Republican *New York Times*, was not ready to throw in the towel. He stayed up through the wee hours of the night and, along with key Republican party leaders, plotted to get the election for Hayes. Their hopes centered on three states—Florida, Louisiana, and South Carolina. Without them, Tilden would have only 184 electoral votes, one vote short of the majority. If Hayes, on the other hand, won those electoral votes, he would be president.

Great confusion followed as they fired off telegrams to the Republican bosses in the three key states which read, "Can you hold your state? Answer at once." When Hayes woke up the next morning, he learned that the key states were still in question and "election night" continued through the next four months. The Republican bosses dug up evidence that blacks had been denied their right to vote and the electorate was turned upside down. Tilden majorities were magically turned into Hayes majorities and Congress was called upon to resolve the issue. But who in Congress would count the votes? All agreed it should be an electoral commission composed of five senators (three Republicans, two Democrats), five representatives (three Democrats, two Republicans), and five justices of the Supreme Court (two Republicans, two Democrats, and one Independent who would be selected by the four other justices).

Justice David Davis, the only Independent vote on the court, was actually ready to cast the key swing vote to Tilden. But right before the commission was formally in place, the Illinois State legislature elected him to the Senate, and he resigned from the court. Since only two Democrats sat on the Court, it was inevitable that Davis would be replaced by a Republican. Meanwhile, other behind-the-scenes deals were struck and compromises made on behalf of Hayes. In return for votes, the new administration, if elected, agreed to end military occupation in the South and begin true Reconstruction with transportation and education plans. In February 1877, the commission voted eight to seven to give all the disputed states to Hayes. The final count: Hayes 185, Tilden 184.

In 1878, the Potter Committee, a partisan committee investigating election fraud, made one last effort to claim the presidency for Tilden. But the more they searched for irregularities, the more they found in their own Democratic camp. The investigation took its most embarrassing turn when coded telegrams from Tilden headquarters revealed key campaigners had discussed bribe money with Southern canvassing boards.

Dubbed "Rutherfraud" and "His Fraudulency," Rutherford B. Hayes entered the White House as the nineteenth president of the United States under a cloud of suspicion. Samuel Tilden, on the other hand, happily retired to private life "with the consciousness that I shall receive from posterity the credit of having been elected to the highest position in the gift of the people, without any of the cares and responsibilities of the office."

In spite of his questionable start, Hayes, in fact, turned out to be a true reformer. Having vowed to only serve one term, thus avoiding the temptation to exchange jobs in return for favors and votes, he began to break down much of the corrupt political machinery around the country. He demanded that federal office holders refrain from political activity and fired two of Conkling's men in New York who did not adhere to his policy. Bravely, he challenged Conkling's power even further by nominating his own candidates to the vacated posts without consulting the boss. It was a noble attempt at reform, but the Senate, still strongly under Conkling's influence, voted down Hayes's appointments. It wasn't until the presidency of James Garfield that the Senate approved a federal appointment in New York without the consent of Boss Conkling. When it finally happened, and his grip on the Senate was broken, Conkling resigned his seat.

★ ★ ★

As the twentieth president of the United States, James A. Garfield earned few distinctions. The second president to be assassinated, he accomplished little in his few short months in office. In history books, it is often noted that he survived the Crédit Mobilier scandal and edged out former President Ulysses S. Grant and James Blaine of Maine for the 1880 Republican nomination. Only recently has it surfaced that Garfield has yet another distinction—he is the first U.S. President known to have had an extramarital affair. (Washington and Jefferson were bachelors who became involved with married women.)

Not much is known about "Mrs. Calhoun," but in 1978 biographer Allan Peskin uncovered references to the affair in Garfield's papers. The actual date of the affair has never been confirmed, but it most likely took place in October 1862, when, as Civil War general, Garfield had both the time and motivation. In fact, Garfield was despondent at that point in his life over not having his own command. He said, "I am thoroughly ashamed to be seen on the streets in uniform."

Garfield had a history of prolonged mental depression, which he would later call his ''years of darkness.'' To help cope with this particular crisis, Garfield took two trips to New York. During the first he visited Rebecca Selleck, his old college flame. But that left him even more depressed. During the second trip he had a happier rendezvous with Mrs. Calhoun.

Somehow Garfield's wife, Lucretia, discovered that her husband had been burned by ''the fire of lawless passion.'' Devastated, she wrote to him, ''James, I should not blame my own heart if it lost all faith in you. I hope it may not . . . but I shall not be forever telling you I love when there is evidently no more desire for it on your part that present manifestations indicate.'' Garfield wrote back, ''I should consider it wrong for us to continue any other than a business correspondence.'' Not long after this cool exchange, Garfield had a change of heart and begged her forgiveness.

The Garfield marriage had never been on very solid footing. Even their early courtship had all the markings of doom. Garfield and Lucretia Rudolph became engaged while he was teaching at Eclectic Institute in Hiram, Ohio, a college cofounded by her father. From the moment they decided to marry, he had second thoughts. When he visited his family in Ohio, ''a most dark and gloomy cloud'' hung over him. And when he returned to see Lucretia, he found their relationship more strained than ever. They probably would have called off the wedding plans had it not been for a bold move by Lucretia. She showed him her diary in which she was able to express her feelings in a way that moved him deeply. He said, ''Never before did I see such depths of suffering and such entire devotion of heart . . . From that journal I read depths of affection that I had never before known that she possessed.''

From that moment on, Garfield felt he was in love with Lucretia, but even that didn't stop him from almost abandoning the relationship again. While visiting a religious retreat, as he often did, he met Rebecca N. Selleck. Even though he was engaged to Lucretia, he began a regular correspondence that delighted his ''wild, passionate heart.'' Foolishly, he told Lucretia all about

Rebecca. No one was surprised when Lucretia lost her patience with the whole arrangement. She and Garfield had been engaged for over four years!

Garfield hated the whole subject of marriage, writing in his diary, "I will not at this time go down into the depths of all my thoughts on this sorrowful theme." When he reluctantly agreed to set a wedding date, November 11, 1858, he told his fiancée, "I don't want much parade about our marriage. Arrange that as you think best." There was no honeymoon.

Once married, Garfield insisted that his wife not join him on business trips. Once, he even expressed to her that marriage was "a great mistake." These were "the dark years," as he called them, the times of "sadness almost bordering on despair." He was having a nervous breakdown.

The Civil War meant yet another long separation for the Garfields. He joined the Union army in August 1861, and quickly rose through the ranks. After the Battle of Shiloh in April 1862, his health began to deteriorate. His skin was jaundiced, and he had dropped forty-three pounds. Sent home to convalesce, he was taken by Lucretia to a secluded farmhouse near Howland Springs to regain his strength. There, she nursed him back to health and rekindled their romance.

One day, after they were back home in Hiram, Lucretia passed her husband a note. She had jotted down how much time they had spent together since they were married. Out of four years and nine months of marriage, they had only been together twenty weeks. From that moment on, he vowed they would live together no matter what.

It was with this marital history that Garfield had his affair with Mrs. Calhoun. But like many political wives, Lucretia forgave him just the same. By January, the Garfields proclaimed a "truce to sadness" and it was all over—until 1867 when Garfield went to see Mrs. Calhoun again. Apparently, he was worried about the love letters he had written to her. With permission from his wife, he went to New York to take possession of what he feared could leave him vulnerable to political blackmail. The mission was accomplished without incident. Garfield got the letters (which he presumably destroyed since they have never been discovered), Mrs. Calhoun married a New York lawyer, and the chapter was closed.

Garfield's instincts were right. In 1880, when he secured the Republican presidential nomination over Ulysses S. Grant and James Blaine, it was largely on the basis of personal integrity. He was able to diminish his role in the Crédit Mobilier scandal by claiming he had refused the ten shares of stock offered to him. The $300 in question from the company, he said, was a personal loan. Whether it was or not was insignificant. He was able to produce evidence that he turned down much more lucrative opportunities that had come his way in the House of Representatives.

As a presidential candidate, Garfield was able to defend his honor vigorously. Certainly, his ability to cover the tracks of his extramarital affair also helped him become President, as short-lived as that honor was to be. President Garfield was shot by a disgruntled job seeker on July 2, 1881, in the Baltimore and Potomac railroad station in Washington, D.C., where he was waiting to board a train to see his wife, who was recovering from malaria in Elberon, New Jersey. As a tragic side-note, the president did not have to die. His two wounds, one that grazed his arm and another that penetrated some muscles in his back, were not fatal. Actually protective cysts had formed around the bullet, which was lodged in his back. However, he contracted blood poisoning when doctors probed for the bullet with bare fingers and unsterilized instruments. Seventy-nine days later, he died. If treated today, the bullet would have been left in place and Garfield would have been encouraged to be up and around within a few days.

"Tell the Truth"

Scandals in the Life and Times of Grover Cleveland

IF EVER THERE WAS A question as to which political vice Americans were more tolerant of—sexual philandering or financial corruption—the presidential election of 1884 presented a clear choice. Since there were no real pressing political issues of the day, the campaign was based solely on personal integrity—or lack of it. On the Democratic side, it was alleged that Grover Cleveland had seduced a widow, fathered her child, refused to marry her, and paid her off. On the Republican front, James Blaine was said to have personally profited from his seat in Congress. He had twisted laws and, as speaker of the House, pushed through legislation for his own financial gain. At one time, he was even charged with selling railroad bonds while working on related legislation. Ultimately, the choice for president was between the private immoralist and the public immoralist.

The years between 1870 and 1898 were known as the gilded age, a time of rapid industrial expansion and the rise of a ruling class of unprecedented wealth. And, as had been the case since the Civil War, most politicians viewed government as a branch of business. Grover Cleveland was an exception. The son of a Presbyterian minister, he was a champion of clean government. In his first years as mayor of Buffalo, he saved the city one million dollars by vetoing fraudulent sewage and street-cleaning contracts. As governor of New York, he won many more battles against corruption, preventing John Kelly, Boss Tweed's successor at Tammany Hall, from appointing his disreputable and incompetent friends to public office. This was a bold move for someone with Cleveland's presidential aspirations. Even with the demise of Tweed, it was generally accepted that no politician could ever be elected president without the support of Tammany Hall, which still controlled much of the New York vote. But as events would show, Cleveland's strength lay in his independence from the Tammany machine. When General Edward S. Bragg of Wisconsin nominated Cleveland for president at the 1884 convention, he said, "We love him most for the enemies he has made."

Blaine, on the other hand, was universally distrusted. Even Boss Conkling kept him at arm's distance. When asked why he refused to campaign for his fellow Republican, the still-influential Conkling quipped, "I do not engage in criminal practice." Newspapers also had a field day with Blaine, running charts and illustrations of how Blaine had grown rich in office. One full-page pictorial compared his humble home in Augusta, 1862, to his mansion in Washington, 1884. What's more, the $30,000 mortgage on the impressive estate was rumored to be held by a railroad magnate for whom he had done legislative favors.

Blaine had engaged in many questionable business deals. Now that he was a presidential candidate, these deals were scrutinized under the harshest light. Not only had Blaine accepted honorariums from businessmen he helped in Congress, he was unable to understand why anyone objected to the practice. It appeared his most profitable venture came in 1869 when, as speaker of the House, he handed down a decision that benefited the Little Rock & Fort Smith Railroad. The company showed their gratitude by letting Blaine sell bonds at an astronomical commission estimated to be close to $200,000. Beyond that, Blaine made money from nearly every railroad that was organized during his twelve years in the House.

With Blaine's record so full of ethical breaches, Grover Cleveland was the odds-on favorite in the presidential election—until July 21, 1884. On that day, the *Buffalo Evening Telegraph*

HOW BLAINE GREW RICH IN OFFICE.

BLAINE'S HOUSE IN AUGUSTA, 1862.

BLAINE'S MANSION IN WASHINGTON.
(See the Other Side.)

James Blaine personally profitted from his seat in Congress.

carried a front-page exposé called "A Terrible Tale." The article charged that Cleveland had fathered an illegitimate child. It was, perhaps, one of the worst allegations ever made against a presidential candidate. Worse yet, it was true.

In 1871, while sheriff of Buffalo, Grover Cleveland had become involved with Mrs. Maria C. Halpin, director of the cloak and lace department of a Buffalo store. She actually had been seeing several men, but when she had a son in 1874, she claimed Cleveland was the father. Neither she nor Cleveland were certain, but since the other men with whom she was involved were married, Cleveland willingly accepted responsibility. Although Maria demanded marriage, Cleveland consented only to child support.

As soon as the story broke, Cleveland's campaign manager and assorted supporters called an emergency meeting to discuss the problem and draw up a response. In his infinite wisdom, Cleveland, who was still a bachelor, decided on the bold step of admitting his part in the affair. "Tell the truth," he insisted. And they did.

Meanwhile, a similarly embarrassing story about Blaine's private life made its way to the Cleveland camp. Mrs. Blaine had given birth to their first child only three months after their wedding date. The news was certain to help even the morality score. But much to the surprise of his aides, Cleveland read the evidence, paid the informer, tore up the papers and burned them in the fireplace. "The other side can have a monopoly on all the dirt in this campaign," he proclaimed.

Despite Cleveland's honorable intentions, news of Blaine's shotgun wedding soon leaked out. Having kept a copy of the report, the informer had sold the story to the *Democratic Sentinel*. It hit like a bombshell, but, unlike Cleveland, Blaine wasn't prepared to address the truth. Instead, he claimed that he had TWO marriage ceremonies, six months apart, which had something to do with the death of his father. The details were vague, no witnesses were provided, no records were available and no one believed it.

The scandal probably would have stayed a front-page campaign issue had it not been overshadowed by more serious charges of Blaine's profiteering. Mid-campaign it was revealed that Blaine had lied to an 1876 House investigating committee regarding his railroad activities and had solicited false testimony. A damaging letter surfaced which Blaine had written to a railroad executive named Warren Fisher. In the correspondence, Blaine suggested Fisher release the following statement on his behalf: "The transaction was perfectly open, and there was no secrecy in regard to it than if you had been buying flour or sugar . . . your action in the whole matter was as open and fair as the day." Blaine's salutation was most damning of all. It read: "Regard this letter as strictly confidential. Do not show it to anyone. Kind regards to Mrs. Fisher. Burn this letter." Unfortunately for Blaine, Fisher had not been a strict follower of orders. Throughout the campaign, Blaine's own words would torment him, as the Democrats took to the streets chanting, "Blaine, Blaine, James G. Blaine, The Continental liar from the State of Maine, Burn this letter!"

In their own street demonstrations, however, the Republicans countered, "Ma! Ma! Where's my pa?"

But the Democrats would reply, "Gone to the White House, Ha, ha, ha."

As election day approached, Cleveland and Blaine were locked in a tight battle. The Maria Halpin scandal had done a lot of damage to Cleveland's campaign, but it had not been fatal. The timing of the scandal actually worked in his favor. If the story had broken at the time of the nomination, Cleveland's name would have certainly been withdrawn. If it had come out closer to election day, he would not have had enough time to answer the charges. But with three months to repair the damage, Cleveland had actually been able to turn it to his advantage. The more details that came out, the nobler he looked.

Cleveland, it was revealed, had dutifully watched over the child and had always acted in his best interest. Somewhere along the line, Maria had started drinking heavily. Concerned for the child's safety, Cleveland arranged for Maria to be sent to a mental institution and the boy to an orphanage. After a short while, she

Another   voice   for   Cleveland.

Grover Cleveland was elected president despite the scandal of an illegitimate child.

escaped and kidnapped the child. The crisis escalated until Cleveland found a prominent New York family to formally adopt him. (The child grew up to become a respected physician.)

Despite all this, going into the home stretch of the 1884 election, it looked like Blaine still had the edge. The pivotal state was New York, where there was a strong Irish Catholic vote. The fact that Blaine's mother was an Irish Catholic and his sister a mother superior in a Catholic convent didn't hurt. But with one week left before election day, the Blaine campaign stumbled. On the morning of October 29, Blaine met with 500 members of the local clergy in New York for one last public airing of Cleveland's illegitimate child scandal. But Reverend S. D. Burchard, pastor of the Murray Hill Presbyterian Church, did more harm than good when he called Cleveland's Democratic Party, the party of "Rum, Romanism, and Rebellion." The slur against Roman Catholics somehow went over Blaine's head, but not over that of Cleveland's campaign strategist who spread the story throughout the press. Cleveland subsequently carried New York state and captured 219 electoral votes to Blaine's 182.

One unidentified Chicago reformer best summed up the public's pulse in the 1884 election when he noted: "We are told that Mr. Blaine has been delinquent in office but blameless in private life, while Mr. Cleveland has been a model of official integrity, but culpable in his personal relations. We should therefore elect Mr. Cleveland to the public office which he is so well qualified to fill and remand Mr. Blaine to the private station which he is admirably fitted to adorn."

★ ★ ★

Even after Cleveland moved into the White House, gossip about the forty-nine-year-old bachelor president continued. His marriage to twenty-one-year-old Frances Folsom on June 2, 1886, fueled the public's appetite for intimate White House news. The fact that Cleveland announced their engagement only five days before the wedding drove the press wild. Overnight Frances became the "Princess Di" of her time, the focus of a massive investigation by curious reporters. Everyone knew that the president was old enough to be her father. Soon, however, they were also treated to stories of how Cleveland, a close friend of her father's, had bought Frances her first baby carriage and had served as the administrator of her father's estate following his tragic death in an accident.

A flock of reporters even trailed the newlyweds to their honeymoon retreat at Deer Park in the Cumberland Mountains of Maryland, camping out near their cottage and spying on them with long telescopes. There was no lack of interest in the youngest first lady ever, the first and only to be married in the White House. Not surprisingly, Cleveland began to chafe under this constant scrutiny, accusing the press of being "professional gossips" and "doing their utmost to make American journalism contemptible."

★ ★ ★

If the press had irritated Cleveland during his first term as president, he got them back in 1893, after he was elected for his second (non-consecutive) term. Having been diagnosed as having malignant mouth cancer, the president slipped away for a secret operation aboard a yacht, which cruised down the East River off Manhattan. The operation remained a secret until 1917, when one of the surgeons published the whole account in the *Saturday Evening Post*. Cleveland must have been pleased at denying the press such a good story, but in reality, his motives arose more from his own sense of duty and responsibility toward the country than from a desire to retaliate against the press.

★ ★ ★

On May 5, 1893, two months after his inauguration, Cleveland had noticed a rough area about the size of a quarter on top of his mouth. On June 18, White House physician Robert Maitland O'Reilly examined the growth and, along with Dr. Joseph D. Bryant, biopsied the tissue. They then sent it under a pseudonym to a pathologist at Johns Hopkins Hospital in Maryland. Diagnosis: malignancy.

For Cleveland, the timing couldn't have been worse. The country was caught in the throes of a dire financial panic. More than $100 million in silver notes, which were redeemable in gold, had been issued despite a gold reserve of only $101 million. The Treasury Department was being kept afloat only by not spending appropriations voted by Congress. Six hundred and forty-two banks were going under and masses of Americans were going hungry. Even the stable old Reading Railroad went into receivership. Such a fragile country, Cleveland believed, should not know about his cancer. An announcement of his illness would cause a loss in confidence in the leadership and further weaken the nation's economy.

On June 30, President Cleveland called for a special session of Congress to convene on August 7, to save the economy. A few minutes after the announcement, he set out with Dr. Bryant and Secretary of War Dan Lamont on his secret surgery mission. At 1:20 p.m., the group boarded a northbound train, carefully evading the press.

At dusk, the president and Dr. Bryant left the train station in New York and traveled by carriage to meet Commodore Elias C. Benedict, an eastern banker. Under the cover of darkness, they ferried out to his private yacht, the Oneida. Earlier that afternoon, at casually spaced intervals, the yacht had been boarded by Lamont's wife, Juliet; Dr. O'Reilly; Dr. Edward G. Janeway, the country's foremost physiologist; Dr. William W. Keen, a Philadelphia oral surgeon; Dr. Bryant's assistant, Dr. John F. Erdmann; and Dr. Ferdinand Hasbrouck, a young dentist who had expertise with nitrous oxide, the new ''laughing gas.''

The main salon on the yacht had been transformed into a surgery room. A straight-back chair for the patient was tied to the mast. Surgical instruments were on tables nearby, as were other various pieces of equipment to help check blood pressure, respiration and other vital signs.

Shortly before noon the following morning, the president, in his pajamas, was strapped into the surgery chair. Meanwhile up on deck, Dan Lamont and Dr. Bryant sunbathed to give the illusion of a pleasure cruise as the yacht sailed up Long Island Sound. Although Lamont could offer no medical expertise, Bryant had insisted on having a cabinet member present. He knew in the event that the president died during surgery, a trusted cabinet officer would be needed to verify the facts. Lamont, who had served as Cleveland's private secretary in his first administration, was the closest to the president and the logical choice.

Finally, Dr. Bryant went below and signalled Dr. Hasbrouck to start the gas. Nitrous oxide was a terrific breakthrough for the president since his 250-pound frame would have made him vulnerable to choking to death under heavy ether. Still, the surgery was risky—especially on a moving yacht with only basic emergency equipment.

First, two bicuspids were extracted to make room for Dr. Bryant to remove the cancerous area, which was cut out with an elec-
tric knife. The delicate part was cutting around the orbital palate,
better known as the eye socket. The entire upper left jaw was also
removed. Because the incision was inside the mouth, no external
scars would result.

By 2 p.m., the surgery was finished, the lethal sarcoma removed and the cavity stuffed with gauze. When the president started coming to, he was given a dose of morphine. While the
president slept, everyone took a stiff drink and called the operation
a success. After a few days of convalescing, Cleveland returned to
Buzzard's Bay where his pregnant wife was waiting. On July fifth,
the country was informed that the president had been treated for
two ulcerated teeth and a recurrence of some old rheumatism.

Five days later, an orthodontist arrived at Buzzard's Bay and
crafted a hard rubber plug for the hole in Cleveland's mouth. The
president was also fitted with a prosthetic jaw. Although the recu-
peration was progressing nicely when Cleveland began working
on his August 7 speech to Congress, a follow-up examination
showed more cancer. The patient and surgery team returned for
another performance aboard the Oneida, except for Dr. Hasbrouck, the anesthesiologist, who had other surgical obligations.
At this time, Hasbrouck actually tried to leak the story but the
Philadelphia Press reporter failed to corroborate the information.
As a result, a watered-down version ran, virtually unnoticed.

On August 7, just six weeks after his secret surgery, President
Cleveland gave his uncompromising message to Congress to help
stabilize the economy. In a climate where the press wrote about
even the most insignificant first family details, undergoing secret
surgery on a private yacht was an extraordinary feat, to say the
least. How wise it was to do so, without even informing the vice
president, was another story. Any type of surgery in the nineteenth
century carried great risks. The possibility of the president suffering serious complications or perhaps even dying was very real.
What was intended as a secret mission to protect the national interest could have been just the opposite. It wasn't until the twenty-

fifth amendment of the Constitution was passed in 1967 that a systematic framework was established for the temporary or permanent transfer of power from the president to the vice president in the event of death or incapacity. Cleveland's case could certainly have been an early inspiration for the amendment.

In his own way, the reporter who missed the scoop of a lifetime left a legacy, too. Ever since Cleveland's secret surgery was revealed, reporters have never let a president so much as sneeze without a full disclosure. From newspaper photos of Lyndon Johnson's gall bladder scar to the television road maps of Ronald Reagan's intestines, the public now learns everything about the president's health, even if it's sometimes more than they'd really like to know.

"Exposed and Confessed Unchastity"

More Scandals in the Gilded Age

W HY DOES ONE POLITI-
cian survive a sex scandal while another is ruined by it? Even in
Grover Cleveland's day it came down to the basic issue of character. Cleveland's political success, in spite of the Maria Halpin affair, was a direct result of his intrinsic honesty and acceptance of
responsibility. No matter what else he was guilty of, he wasn't a
liar or a hypocrite. The same cannot be said of a number of his
contemporaries, who were unable to survive their own scandals.

A good case in point is William Campbell Preston Breckinridge, a Kentucky congressman who once dreamed of running for
president. Breckinridge could boast of a distinguished political lin-
eage. His grandfather was a U.S. senator; his uncle John C. Breckinridge had served as vice president under Buchanan; another
cousin was also in Congress; and his first wife was the granddaughter of Henry Clay. Like Cleveland, Breckinridge was the son
of a minister. He was a father of five; he seldom drank, smoked,
played cards, or bet horses. His only vice, his constituents would
learn, was keeping a teenage mistress.

To say that the disclosure of Breckinridge's affair with
Madeline Pollard was shocking would be an understatement. The
apparently happily married congressman had built much of his ca-

MADELINE BREAKS DOWN IN COURT.

Madeline Pollard sues W.C.P. Breckinridge, Kentucky congressman, for breach of promise.

reer on morality issues. Nationally known as the "silver-tongued orator from Kentucky," Breckinridge lectured regularly on the evils of sex. In one address at Sayre Institute, a prestigious girls' school in his hometown, he warned the students to avoid "useless handshaking, promiscuous kissing, needless touches, and all exposures.'' To the students at Bourbon County (Kentucky) Female College, he preached, ''Chastity is the foundation, the cornerstone of human society. . . . [P]ure homes make pure government.''

His lectures certainly came back to haunt him in 1893 when Madeline Pollard sued him for $50,000 for his breach of promise to marry her. She claimed she had been his mistress since April 1, 1884, when at the age of seventeen she was seduced by him. She decided to go public after his second wife died. Madeline expected to marry the congressman as he had promised, but he secretly married his cousin instead. Worse yet, at the time Madeline realized she had been conned, she miscarried what would have been their third child together.

From the start, Breckinridge was convinced he could survive the scandal as Cleveland had his. After all, Cleveland didn't marry Maria Halpin either. After a weak attempt to buy Madeline's silence, Breckinridge's strategy was to square off in court, where he believed he could prove that it takes two to make a seduction.

The congressman's first mistake was to select six high-powered attorneys to help him present his case. In stark contrast, Madeline showed up in court escorted only by a nun. Dressed in dramatic black, Madeline looked plain and anything but sexy. Her voice was soft and vulnerable as, from the witness stand, she described the details of the seduction in a closed carriage on a hot summer night by the ''silver-tongued orator.'' Soon after their encounter, Madeline explained, she enrolled in Sayre Institute to be closer to him. At Sayre, where he had lectured against ''useless handshaking,'' they had at least fifty meetings until he moved her to Washington in September 1887. She had her first child in Kentucky, the second in Washington. Before the judge, jury, and spectators, Madeline fainted on the witness stand as she told of the tragic death of their second baby.

Madeline garnered even more sympathy and support as Breckinridge's defense attorneys began their attack on her reputation, another strategic error by the congressman. The attorneys presented statements from witnesses who claimed she was ''fast,'' ''forward,'' and had once been caught in a ''compromising position'' with a man on a bridge. But the evidence was hearsay and the judge dismissed most of it. Besides, he added, it was "too filthy and obscene" to introduce anyway.

Still, little by little, Breckinridge began to change Madeline's image from the poor, innocent, inexperienced young maiden to an experienced woman who knew exactly what she was doing. He actually might have succeeded in exonerating himself if only he had followed Cleveland's example just a little. His ultimate blunder was denying any knowledge of the children, except for the last pregnancy. Certainly, he admitted, he had visited Madeline up to seven times a day in Washington, certainly he had recommended her for a government job, and certainly he had given her large amounts of money. Yet he insisted he had never known she had borne any children from their affair. The jury found his testimony unlikely and awarded Madeline $15,000—three years' salary for a congressman.

One historian wrote, "The fall of Breckinridge was like that of an archangel." Breckinridge, however, didn't believe it was over and decided to run for reelection to Congress. On May 4, 1894, he gave one of the most impassioned speeches of his career. With tears in his eyes he confessed, "I knew the secret sin; I tried to atone for it," adding that he had been "entangled by weakness, by passion, by sin, in coils which it was almost impossible to break." As he brushed away a tear, the effect was magnificent, enough to make Breckinridge feel he might even win the election.

The one stubborn political force he hadn't anticipated, however, was that of the Kentucky women who rallied in opposition. Their response to the Breckinridge scandal would become a milestone in the creation of the woman's suffrage movement. As the *Kentucky Gazette* reported, "Women who never took the slightest interest in politics in their lives have become active politicians." A protest meeting at the Opera House, where Breckinridge had delivered his tearful apology, drew one thousand women. A barbecue in Owens drew even more. Susan B. Anthony, then president of the National American Woman Suffrage Association, emerged as their leader, insisting that "exposed and confessed unchastity" must not win.

JUDGE BRADLEY.
· CLEARING THE COURT OF WOMEN ·

Madeline Pollard's "palimony" trial sparked the women's suffrage movement.

As the election neared, reporters came from all parts of the country to record the influence of Kentucky women. As expected, Breckinridge was badly beaten at the polls. Breckinridge had lost not only the battle, but also the war. Women, who for the first time tasted political clout in an election, would remain involved in the process forever—only from that point forward, they chose to turn their influence to fighting for their own right to vote.

★ ★ ★

While Breckinridge's scandal had cost him a career, fellow Kentucky congressman William Preston Taulbee lost not only his career but also his wife, and finally, his life, in a bizarre twist of fate surrounding the news coverage of his fling with a patent office secretary.

By the age of thirty-seven, William Taulbee, a former Methodist minister and son of a Kentucky state senator, had become one of the more respected members of Congress—until a Louisville newspaper published the lurid details of his lunchtime escapades, which included sex on the office stairwells. One paper wrote how the love scenes "were rather warmer than they were proper." Another described the woman as "bright as a sunbeam and saucy as a bowl of jelly." Immediately after the scandal broke, Taulbee's wife of seventeen years left him. Faced with the facts, Taulbee recognized that the scandal had also ruined his career and chose not to run for reelection.

With his life in ruins, an angry, broken Taulbee withdrew from public life into his own private, bitter world, where he remained in a terrible state of mind. Less than a year later, he ran into Charley Kinkaid, the *Louisville Times* reporter who had broken the first story. The mere sight of the reporter made him lose control, and the excongressman shouted at Kincaid and attacked him. He yanked on his ears and called him a liar. As onlookers separated them, the fearful reporter cried out, "I am a small man and unarmed." In a rage, Taulbee suggested he remedy that.

Two hours later, as Kincaid was walking down the steps into a basement restaurant, he bumped into Taulbee again. Those inside the restaurant heard a shot ring out. Taulbee walked a few steps and then collapsed. Kincaid told onlookers, "I did it."

Taulbee remained in critical condition for six days before he finally succumbed on March 11, 1890. Soon after, Louisville police charged Kincaid with first-degree murder. Oddly enough, the public rushed to defend Kincaid. In Kentucky the public regarded the incident as one of self defense, or at least defense of honor which they deemed equally justifiable. The jury agreed and Kincaid was acquitted.

★ ★ ★

One of the longest-running sex scandals of the 1880s involved the love affair between California Senator William Sharon and Althea Hill. Their affair not only caused a major political scandal, but it also led to three separate Supreme Court decisions! The beginning of the story seemed simple enough—senator meets girl, senator cavorts with girl, senator dumps girl. But when it was all over, Althea Hill sued him for "palimony," drew a pistol in one courtroom, ran off with her attorney, and at the very least helped put the senator in an early grave.

Senator Sharon was a widower who had accumulated his enormous wealth through real estate development and silver speculation. When he was elected to the Senate in 1875, his fortune was estimated at $15 million. Although he represented the people of Nevada, he lived in San Francisco, where he owned an extravagant home along with the most luxurious hotel in the west, The Palace. There, his favorite pastimes included money, poker, and beautiful women.

Sharon met Sarah Althea Hill in 1880, when he was sixty and she in her twenties. A vulnerable orphan, she was then recovering from a recent suicide attempt, the result of a love affair with a lawyer. Sharon was immediately attracted to her and offered her $500 to let him "love her." He would later testify that this was his usual offer to potential mistresses. Althea, however, declined his rather callous offer—even when he upped the ante to a cool $1,000. She insisted that she would not sleep with him unless he married her, a small obstacle that would become the root of all their trouble.

Always one to find an angle, Sharon ultimately agreed to "marry" her, although not in the traditional sense. Instead of exchanging vows, he explained, they could marry under Section 75 of a California civil code by simply agreeing to do so in writing. He also somehow convinced her to keep the marriage a secret. Any sort of surprise to the voters, he said, would interfere in his reelection campaign. In reality, he didn't want anything interfering with the affair he was having with a woman in Philadelphia.

Sharon was alleged to have drafted the following agreement:

In the city and county of San Francisco, state of California, on the twenty-fifth day of August, A.D. 1880, I, Sarah Althea Hill, of the city and county of San Francisco, state of California, aged 27 years, do here, in the presence of Almighty God, take Senator William Sharon, of the state of Nevada, to be my lawful and wedded husband, and do here acknowledge and declare myself to be the wife of Senator Sharon, of the state of Nevada.

SARAH ALTHEA HILL.

August 25, 1880. San Francisco, Cal. I agree not to make known the contents of this paper or its existence for two years unless Mr. Sharon himself sees fit to make it known.

S. A. HILL

In the city and county of San Francisco, state of California, on the twenty-fifth day of August, A.D. 1880, I, Senator William Sharon, of the state of Nevada, aged 60 years, do here, in the presence of Almighty God, take Sarah Hill, of the city of San Francisco, Cal., to be my lawful and wedded wife, and do here acknowledge myself to be the husband of Sarah Althea Hill.

WILLIAM SHARON, NEVADA, August 25, 1880.

Sharon "kept" Althea in the Grand Hotel, which was connected to The Palace by a covered bridge, known locally as "the bridge of sighs." When she first moved in, he wrote a short note of introduction to the hotel manager which read, "Miss Hill, a particular friend of mine, and a lady of unblemished character and of good family. Give her the best, and as cheap as you can." Obviously, the senator, while willing to indulge himself, desired to do so with a minimum of expense.

As it turned out, Senator Sharon was no more of a romantic than he was a sport. He furnished her room and gave her $500 a month spending money, the same amount he originally promised her if she became his mistress. The arrangement continued for about a year before Sharon tired of Miss Hill and, according to Althea, asked her to sign another piece of paper saying she was not Mrs. Sharon. He paid her $7,500 cash and had the hotel manager ask her to leave. When she delayed, he had the door taken off its hinges and the carpet removed to help her make up her mind.

With nowhere to go, she sought the help of Mammie Pleasants, a black woman said to have once been a slave for Althea's family in Missouri. Mammie's first plan was to teach Althea how to get the senator back—with a voodoo ceremony. Her instructions were to put a white powder around his chair, a black powder between the sheets, and his sock and shirt under a corpse in a fresh grave. While it is not known if Althea ever followed Mammie's initial "sartorial" plan, it is known that she agreed to adopt her second one—to sue the senator's pants off.

Mammie took Althea and her "marriage" document to a lawyer, who in turn called in an expert, David Terry. In September 1883, Althea, as advised by her new legal team, made a public disclosure of her marriage. She promptly had Senator Sharon arrested for adultery, and then sued him for divorce. Admitting to philandering with a long list of women, Sharon responded with his own suit in federal court for fraud, claiming the marriage document was forged. The two suits would bounce from one court to another for the next six years.

The divorce suit was the more titillating of the two. In sworn testimony, Althea shyly admitted to watching the senator and another woman go to bed together. When she spoke from the witness stand she actually conveyed an air of innocence. Sharon did not, and on Christmas Eve 1884, Judge J. F. Sullivan awarded Althea $2,500 a month alimony and granted the divorce.

Sharon, of course, had had merrier Christmases in his life. Down, but not out, he appealed and pressed for a decision in federal court regarding the authenticity of the document. He threatened to use every last dime to make sure Althea never got a single penny. The federal fraud case was even stormier than the divorce trial and through the long, hot summer of 1885, Althea's self-control began to disappear. Her shy demeanor was soon replaced by a raging temper and theatrical tirades. On more than one occasion she waved a pistol at her adversaries and the judge was assigned bodyguards for protection.

On November 15, 1885, the decision for the fraud case was set to be announced. Ironically, on that exact date, Senator William Sharon died, and the hearing was postponed until December 6. His death was said to be hastened by his aggravation from Althea and whatever other mistresses he was trying to juggle. Unfortunately for Sharon, he was not present when the court ruled in his favor, declaring the marriage contract a forgery. If Althea needed consolation, it can be presumed her attorney, David Terry, provided it. Twelve days later, they were married.

All was quiet in Althea's life until the divorce case was reopened two years later by Sharon's heirs. In this trial, the new Mrs. Terry displayed an even more violent temperament. At one point, she accused the judge of being on the take. Justice Stephen J. Field, who was actually a Supreme Court judge between high court obligations, ordered federal marshal J. C. Franks to remove Althea from the courtroom. When the marshal touched her arm, her husband took a swing at him and knocked a tooth out of the officer's mouth. Terry was restrained for a few moments, then released, after which he pulled out a knife. Only at gunpoint did he finally agree to relinquish the weapon. He later explained he went berserk to protect Althea, who was now expecting. The judge, however, was not very sympathetic and charged Terry with contempt of court. He received a six-month jail sentence and Althea thirty days. She subsequently suffered a miscarriage in prison.

Terry appealed the contempt case and the forgery case all the way to the Supreme Court. He also appealed the divorce suit to the California State Supreme Court. His efforts, however, were in vain, as he suffered three consecutive defeats. At this point, the story, which had begun nine long years before, should by all rights have ended. However, there yet remained one final—and fatal—chapter to be written.

On August 12, 1889, Justice Field was due back in California on an unrelated case. Because Althea and her husband were still in and out of court on a total of eight criminal charges, Attorney General William H. Miller convinced the judge to travel with a bodyguard. He agreed and hired Deputy David Neagle, the marshall who had disarmed Terry in court once before. By a strange twist of fate, the Terrys wound up on the very same train. That evening they spotted the judge and his bodyguard in the dining car. Althea saw Field first and bolted, giving all appearances that she went back to the train to get a gun. Terry, meanwhile, walked directly over to the judge's table and slapped Field across the face twice. With his gun poised, Deputy Neagle shouted for Terry to stop. As Terry raised his hand toward his chest, Neagle fired at point blank range, killing him instantly.

When Althea returned with her own gun tucked safely in her purse, she fell grief-stricken over her husband's body. She insisted the witnesses note that her husband was unarmed and murdered in cold blood. Field and Neagle were arrested for the murder of David Terry.

The arrest of a Supreme Court justice on a murder charge was so extraordinary that the California governor intervened and the charges were dropped. Neagle, on the other hand, was still in serious trouble. By the time the case reached the highest court, Neagle's entire defense rested on the issue of whether or not he had been working "in pursuance of a law of the United States." In other words, the murder was justifiable as long as it was legal for the judge to have hired him in the first place.

Interestingly, the Supreme Court ruled (with Justice Field abstaining) that the executive order appointing Neagle as a bodyguard for Justice Field was authorized under the presidential obligation to ensure that the laws are faithfully executed. Defining an executive order as the equivalent of a law of Congress, the Court ruled that Neagle had been acting "in pursuance of a law of the United States," even though there was no specific statute to provide the judge with a bodyguard. At the time, this was the broadest interpretation ever given to "implied powers" of the constitution. Also, this broad definition of "law" further asserted the supremacy of federal over state law. It is ironic that what began as an illicit love affair between a senator and his mistress became a turning point in constitutional law which had an impact for many decades. Most likely, the legal community found the trial results much more satisfying than Althea Hill Terry. In 1892, Mammie Pleasants had Althea committed to an asylum where she lived for the next forty-five years.

★ ★ ★

Regardless of the extent of Senator Sharon's womanizing throughout his career, at least it didn't interfere with the representation of his constituents, as was the case with a southern colleague, Florida Senator Charles W. Jones. Jones was so busy pursuing an affair with a wealthy spinster in Michigan that he forgot to show up in Congress—for almost two years!

Jones had been highly regarded during his first ten years in the Senate. As the first Florida Democrat elected to the Senate after the Civil War, he was a symbol of great changes in the South. But something went wrong. Although he attended Grover Cleveland's inauguration in March 1885, Jones did not show up when the forty-ninth Congress convened on December 7, 1885.

For more than two months, reporters searched for the missing senator. Finally, on February 9, 1886, the *Baltimore Sun* reported the shocking news—the senator was living in Detroit, where he was attempting to woo an unnamed spinster who was worth $2 million. Ten days later, a Jacksonville (Florida) newspaper published an article revealing a similar incident in Jones's past. Two summers before he had followed a woman around from Boston until he was threatened with force to leave her alone.

One paper christened him "the Love-Mad Man" while another commented that the senator had attracted more attention as an unsuccessful lover than he ever did as a statesman. Recognizing a good story, the press dug deeper into the affair. In April, The *Florida Times Union* finally reported a detailed description of Jones's antics. The object of the senator's fixation was Miss Clothilde Palms, "a plain looking woman of 35 years." After they first met in the fall of 1885, he visited her daily. "At first he was pleasantly received . . . [but kept] calling at all sorts of inopportune times, sent passionate notes and bo[u]quets until the violence of the courtship showed that he was not a fit person to be received." Her father, it was reported, put an end to it. As it turned out, Miss Palms was also the victim of a paralytic stroke.

Jones's colleagues in the Senate reacted with outrage at the reports, and on April 12, the Senate leadership ruled that Jones's place on various committees was "temporarily vacant." The most serious effect of this was the loss of his seat on the Commerce Committee which, overseeing all river and harbor legislation, was vital to Floridians.

While the constituents wanted to elect another senator, there was no process by which to replace a legislator who was not declared mentally or physically incompetent. Jones's seat remained vacant until his term expired in March 1887.

Once his job had been terminated, the former senator deteriorated. Within months, the "Love-Mad Man" was an unshaven beggar on the streets. In May 1890, a court judged Charles Jones insane and sent him to a St. Joseph's Retreat in Dearborn, Michigan, where he died seven years later. In reviewing the published accounts today, it is possible that he suffered from Alzheimer's disease during his last years in office.

★ ★ ★

One last volatile Capitol Hill love affair of the era became a turn-of-the-century "Fatal Attraction"—only in this sordid tale, Senator Arthur Brown was killed by the mistress. Brown, who was one of the first two U.S. senators elected after Utah gained statehood, died on December 13, 1906, in the Emergency Hospital in Washington, D.C. To many observers, his death was the logical conclusion to his turbulent eight-year affair with Anna Addison Bradley, the secretary of the fifth-ward Republican Committee.

The senator and Anna began an intimate affair in January 1899. Thirteen months later, she gave birth to a son she named Arthur Brown Bradley. At the time, however, she was still living, off and on, with her husband. Brown was then living with his second wife, Isabel.

Anna Bradley seemed to have a complete spell over Brown. He separated from his wife and promised to marry her. But Isabel decided to fight for her man. She had them followed by detectives and arrested for adultery, first in 1902 and again in 1903. At that time, Brown promised his wife to stop seeing Anna and hired a lawyer, Soren K. Christensen, to stay with him and make sure he behaved. Later, Christensen described the pitiful state to which the senator was reduced by his attraction to Bradley. At times, he recalled, the senator would "call . . . [Anna] vile names and abuse her, and at other times he would tell me he couldn't live without her."

That attraction once again got the better of Bradley when, a few months later, the senator gave his watchdog the slip and ran away to meet Anna in Pocatello, Idaho. Christensen and the senator's wife quickly followed to help Brown escape the influence of his mistress. The following is part of Christensen's deposition of the dramatic confrontation between the senator, his wife and his mistress:

> Mrs. Brown said to her, "How do you do, Mrs. Bradley? I have wanted to talk with you!" Mrs. Bradley sort of cowed over to the wall, and Mrs. Brown walked up towards her and grabbed her by the throat and threw her down, and intended to kill her . . . I separated them, they got up, and commenced talking in a very low tone of voice again, when Mrs. Brown grabbed her again. I separated them, and Mrs. Brown says, "Let me alone, I will kill her," and I says, "Not when I am here." . . . Finally Mrs. Brown rapped on the door of the room 11, and said, "Arthur, open the door or I will mash it in," and the door opened and the two women went in, when Arthur Brown came and called me, and said "come in, I don't want to be left alone here with them. . . ."

After the incident in Idaho, Brown gave Anna Bradley a revolver to carry as protection from his wife.

The real crisis in their relationship began when Isabel Brown died of cancer on August 22, 1905. That very night, the senator called Anna and told her to get a divorce, which she did. Brown, however, inexplicably developed cold feet. First he asked her to wait until the following June to marry—and even then he left her standing at the altar. In August, she pleaded with him to do the right thing. She was thirty-three, divorced, and had four children. Still, he put her off, saying he needed more time.

When the senator gave her a ticket for a rest in Los Angeles, she exchanged it for a ticket to Washington and broke into his hotel room. While he was out, she began snooping through his letters

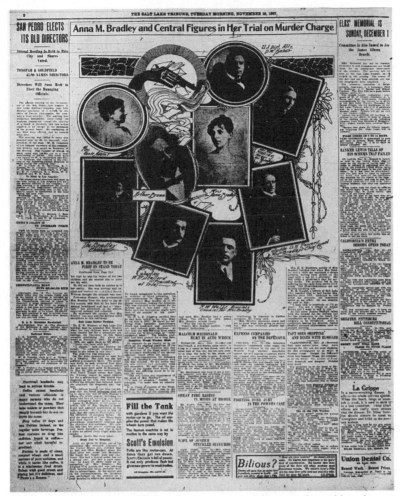

Anna Bradley was found ''not guilty'' in the murder of her lover, Senator Arthur Brown.

and discovered he was having an affair with Annie Adams Kiskadden, the mother of Maude Adams, the famous actress. This last blow was too much for her to bear. When Brown returned, she shot him. Ironically, she killed him with the same gun he had given her three years earlier as protection from his wife, Isabel.

Anna Bradley pleaded temporary insanity. In her murder trial, it was revealed that she had suffered several miscarriages and had undergone three abortions, one of which was allegedly performed by Senator Brown a few weeks before she killed him. The jury returned a verdict of not guilty.

"You Can't Cast the Man as Romeo"

Scandals in the Life and Times of Woodrow Wilson

THE SUCCESS OF GROVER Cleveland's two administrations confirmed, for the time being, that a candidate's public record was far more important than his personal one. But if the press was inspired to exercise a new restraint, it went untested. Until the administration of Woodrow Wilson, ten years later, there were few, if any, personal scandals to report. Presidents Benjamin Harrison, Theodore Roosevelt, and William Howard Taft were all moral family men. And President William McKinley's undying devotion to his wife, Ida, who suffered from epileptic seizures, was unparalleled. To best look after her, President McKinley broke from established protocol and insisted that he sit by her side at all official functions. Whenever she went into a seizure, he quietly placed a handkerchief or napkin over her face to conceal the contortions, and carried on with the business at hand. When the first lady was finished thrashing, he filled her in on what she missed. Mark Hanna, the political boss of Ohio, once said, ''President McKinley has made it pretty hard for the rest of us husbands in Washington.''

By the time Woodrow Wilson was elected president in 1912, the new crop of journalists chose to ignore the persistent rumors about his lifelong relationship with a woman named Mrs. Mary Hulbert Peck. Perhaps they had become too used to the total har-

147

mony in the White House. Or perhaps they were more concerned with the growing possibility of America's entry into World War I. Regardless of the reason, they missed an intriguing story.

★ ★ ★

Woodrow Wilson first met Mrs. Peck in 1907 in Bermuda while on his first vacation without Ellen, his wife of twenty-two years. In the early 1900s, Bermuda was an island paradise for high society. It was also where he became smitten with Mary Hulbert Peck, the wife of a manufacturer in Pittsfield, Massachusetts. Curiously, Wilson wrote his wife detailed letters about his new friend. He was careful, however, to diffuse any jealousy. "While she delights me," Wilson wrote, "you enslave me."

When she first met Wilson, Mary Peck was separated from her second husband, Thomas D. Peck. She had spent the winters in Bermuda ever since she was diagnosed with "melancholia," known today as manic depression. The colonial party life on the island seemed to act as an elixir for her troubled spirit. She golfed with the Governor, danced with admirals and lunched regularly with Mark Twain. An attractive, high-spirited and available woman, she yet had that unique quality of being nonthreatening to most of the wives, even Ellen Wilson.

When his three-week Bermuda vacation was over, Wilson returned to his post as president of Princeton University, but he could not stop his thoughts from returning to Bermuda and Mrs. Peck. He sent her two collections of essays, one volume of the English social scientist, Walter Bagehot's, and one volume of his own, and began a regular correspondence. A year later he returned to Bermuda, again without his wife, where he and Mrs. Peck resumed their relationship. At the same time, Wilson continued to reassure Ellen of the strength of their marriage. He wrote, "I brought two pictures of you with me . . . and Mrs. Peck is so charmed with them that she insists upon keeping one of them on the mantel-piece in her drawing room, so that it sometimes seems almost as if my darling were there."

Wilson discussed his most intimate thoughts with Mrs. Peck during that trip to Bermuda—including the idea that he might run

Woodrow Wilson (at right) in home of Mrs. Peck (to his left). Mark Twain is in the center of the group.

for president. While they sat under a tree overlooking the ocean, he told her:

"My friends tell me that if I will enter the contest and can be nominated and elected governor of New Jersey, I stand a very good chance of being the next President of the United States. Shall I, or shall I not, accept the opportunity they offer?"

"Why not?" she answered. "Statesmanship has been your natural bent, your real ambition all your life and God knows, our country needs men like you in her national life!"

"The life of the next Democratic President will be hell—and it would probably kill me."

"Oh, but you would rather die in harness, fighting for all the great things for which you stand than live up to a less than the best that is within you."

"Very well, so be it!"

As their relationship grew, their letters became more expressive and intimate enough to make Wilson vulnerable to potential blackmail. In one dated September 19, 1909, Wilson wrote:

It is easy on a day like this to think of you, and to realize what you would think and say, were I near enough to hear and share what was passing through your thoughts. You love nature so genuinely and so simply, respond to it so eagerly and entirely, grow so gay and excited, so like a delightful girl, when it is at its best, its most poignant phases of beauty, that a day like this, so sweet and yet so vivid, so still and yet so quick with life, seems as if it were meant to contain you and to draw out in you all that is sweetest and happiest. . . . There is an air about you like the air of the open, a directness, a simplicity, a free movement that link you with wild things that are yet meant to be taken into one's confidence and loved. And so you have seemed part of the day to me ever since morning.

Around the time Wilson announced his candidacy for the

1912 election, Mrs. Peck and her husband began their divorce proceedings, sparking a rumor that Wilson was about to be named in
the suit. A judge, so the rumor went, had been presented with one
of Wilson's letters as evidence. For a time, Wilson worried that
this rumor would ruin his candidacy, but in the final analysis, he
told his campaign intimates that he had never written a word to
Mrs. Peck that he would not feel comfortable reading to his wife.

Actually, the scandal might have become a serious campaign
liability had it also not been for Theodore Roosevelt, Wilson's
opponent on the Progressive Party ticket. Although the former
president was running hard for his third term, he refused to reduce
the campaign to scandalous attacks. He dismissed the adultery rumors as irrelevant, and added a little dig as well. "You can't cast a
man as a Romeo," he observed, "who looks and acts so much like
an apothecary's clerk."

Wilson won the presidential election and took his entire family to Bermuda ten days later, perhaps to stem the tide of gossip.
They even borrowed Mrs. Peck's house while she was away. In
1913, the Wilsons extended the invitation for her to visit them in
the White House and she did. During her week-long visit, Wilson
took her on long drives through Washington. When Ellen couldn't
join them, she sent Wilson's cousin, Helen Bones, to avoid any
appearance of impropriety. No longer did anyone seem particularly concerned about the risk of their letters. President Wilson wrote
Mrs. Peck at least thirty-four letters in 1912, thirty-two in 1913,
and twenty-nine in 1914.

Mrs. Peck's last White House visit was in 1915, after Ellen
Wilson had died from Bright's disease. Many speculated that Wilson would marry Mrs. Peck, but it wasn't in the stars. After Ellen's
death, Wilson was emotionally despondent. He confided to a
friend, "I never understood before what a broken heart meant."
He told another friend that he hoped he would be assassinated.

For Mrs. Peck, it was a trying time as well. Throughout 1914,
Wilson had been trying to help her financially. First, he wrote to
one friend in Boston to try to get her involved in interior decorating. Then, under a presidential cover letter, he submitted a cook-

ing article she wrote to *Ladies' Home Journal* and offered her the services of his secretaries so that she could work on a cookbook. He even loaned her $7,500 against her mortgages. Later, newspaper reports of the loan greatly embarrassed Wilson. The press probably would have made more of the president's relationship with Mrs. Peck at this time had it not been for the presence of another woman in Wilson's life, Mrs. Edith Bolling Galt, the woman President Wilson really wanted to marry.

Mrs. Galt was the widow of Norman Galt, a Washington, D.C. jeweler who died in 1908. She was introduced to the president in March 1915 by Wilson's cousin, Helen Bones, who had taken over as White House hostess after Ellen's death in 1914. The first meeting was actually unexpected. Helen had invited Mrs. Galt for tea, but she hesitated, saying that she wasn't dressed properly and besides, her shoes were muddy. It wasn't until Helen convinced her that the president was out playing golf that she agreed to stop by. As fate would have it, Wilson came home early and invited them for tea in the oval room.

The president must not have been too put off by her muddy shoes. He invited Mrs. Galt to dinner in the White House on March 23, and two months later, on the south portico of the White House, he proposed. Mrs. Galt was more shocked than flattered, answering, "Oh, you can't love me, for you don't really know me; and it is less than a year since your wife died." Unwilling to be hurried into marriage, she left without giving him an answer.

Wilson's top advisers were very concerned about the President's romance. During May and June of 1915, as war raged across Europe and the sinking of the *Lusitania* brought the United States to the brink of war, President Wilson wrote love letters to Mrs. Galt at least once a day. Some of the letters were twenty pages long. At the end of July, Colonel E. M. House, the president's top aide, recorded in his diary, "It seems the President is wholly absorbed in this love affair and is neglecting practically everything else." World War I was not the best time for the commander-in-chief to fall in love.

His advisers also feared that a courtship so soon after Ellen's death might mean political suicide. If the president remarried before November, it could even have a ripple effect on the whole Democratic party. In early September, the cabinet and top Democratic leaders had a secret meeting to decide how to nip the romance in the bud. First, Josephus Daniels, secretary of the navy, was nominated to tell the president about the general consensus of the meeting, but he declined. Many years later he wrote in his memoirs, "Neither my heart nor my head was enlisted and in the performance of which my official head might suffer decapitation."

Next, William G. McAdoo, Wilson's son-in-law and treasury secretary, planned a hoax to discourage a remarriage. He fabricated a story about an anonymous tip that Mrs. Peck was circulating her letters around town. The rationale of the lie was to remind the president of the dangers of the public's perception. But the McAdoo plan backfired. Instead of cooling off, Wilson rushed right over to Mrs. Galt's home and told her everything about Mrs. Peck. If his relationship with Mrs. Peck was going to explode into a scandal, she might as well hear it first from the president. As Colonel House later wrote, Wilson refused to live "having a sword continually hanging over his neck."

After baring his soul, Wilson told Mrs. Galt she was free to decide not to marry him. But a moment later he pleaded, "Stand by me—don't desert me!"

The next day, Mrs. Galt wrote to the president, "This is my pledge, Dearest One, I will stand by you—not for duty, not for pity, not for honour—but for love—trusting, comprehending love."

Finally, on October 6, President Wilson wrote an engagement announcement and gave it to the press:

The engagement was announced to-day of Mrs. Norman Galt and President Woodrow Wilson.

Mrs. Norman Galt is the widow of a well known business man of Washington who died some eight years ago. She has lived in Washington since her marriage in 1896. She was Miss Edith Bolling and was born in Wytheville, Virginia, where her girlhood was spent and where her father, the Hon. William H. Bolling, a man of remarkable character and charm, won distinction as one of the ablest, most interesting and most individual lawyers of a State famous for its lawyers. In the circle of cultivated and interesting people who have had the privilege of knowing her Mrs. Galt has enjoyed an enviable distinction, not only because of her unusual beauty and natural charm, but also because of her very unusual character and gifts. She has always been sought out as a delightful friend, and her thoughtfulness and quick capacity for anything she chose to undertake have made her friendship invaluable to those who were fortunate enough to win it.

It was Miss Margaret Wilson and her cousin Miss Bones who drew Mrs. Galt into the White House circle. They met her first in the early part of the present year, and were so much attracted by her that they sought her out more and more frequently and the friendship among them quickly ripened into an affectionate intimacy. It was through this association with his daughter and cousin that the President had the opportunity to meet Mrs. Galt, who spent a month at Cornish this summer as Miss Wilson's guest. It is, indeed, the most interesting circumstance connected with the engagement just announced that the President's daughters should have picked Mrs. Galt out for their special admiration and friendship before their father did.

Embarrassed on behalf of the love-struck president, *The New York Times* chose only to quote the first paragraph of his press release and paraphrase the rest.

At first, most newspapers were pretty upbeat about the news, running daily installments of the presidential courtship. If the details gave the nation a much-needed break from the war in Europe, the October 9th *Washington Post* must have provided the greatest relief of all with the most extraordinary typographic error in history. A front-page exclusive described the first couple's first day before the public. But instead of writing how the president spent the afternoon ''entertaining his fiancée,'' they accidentally printed that he spent the afternoon ''entering his fiancée.''

But while the courtship for the first couple was just beginning, the honeymoon with the press soon came to a grinding halt. The public just wasn't ready to forget Ellen Wilson so quickly. Almost immediately, vicious rumors circulated that Mrs. Edith Bolling Galt had been the brains behind a murder plot to kill the first lady. And Wilson was accused of callously neglecting Ellen's gravesite in Rome, Georgia. Just as women had held meetings to protest the Breckinridge affair, they began to organize against Mrs. Galt. When an old friend of Wilson's told him of all the activity, the president was brought to tears.

Two strategies were developed to halt the vicious gossip. First, Wilson decided to marry Mrs. Galt as quickly as possible. Second, he decided to come out in support of voting rights for women. While that decision did not help the suffragettes' cause much at the time, it did appease many of the women's groups as far as Wilson was concerned.

The president and Mrs. Galt were married on December 18, 1915, at her home in Washington. The new Mrs. Wilson wasn't nearly as understanding about Mrs. Peck as the first Mrs. Wilson had been; she quickly put an end to the relationship. Sadly, within four years, Mrs. Peck was reduced to selling books door-to-door. Still, when she was offered $300,000 for her Wilson letters, she refused.

Woodrow Wilson's difficulties in gaining acceptance of his remarriage raised some issues regarding press scrutiny of the first lady. Was it unfair for the public to want their president to remain a grieving widower forever? Was it any of their business who the president chose to marry in the first place? In hindsight, maybe it was. Woodrow Wilson became incapacitated by a series of debilitating strokes and First Lady Edith Wilson made key decisions for the president. She decided who Wilson would see and who would wait; which documents would be brought to his attention and when they would be signed. At times there was uncertainty as to who was actually running the country. This situation, much like the secret operation of Grover Cleveland, provided another argument for the twenty-fifth amendment, which called for a formal transfer of power in the event of presidential incapacity. Since it didn't yet exist, Edith Bolling Galt Wilson for a time was the acting chief executive, earning the nickname "Lady President."

"The Great Morality Panic of 1924"

Scandals in the Life and Times of Warren G. Harding

WARREN G. HARDING IS considered by many to be one of the rarest types of presidents of all—a total failure. Privately, this "happily" married man maintained two steady mistresses and even fathered a child by one. Publicly, he oversaw one of the most corrupt administrations ever. Key cabinet members, including three who were forced to resign, were involved in graft, fraud, conspiracy, bribery and cover-ups. Harding's interior secretary, Albert Fall, even gained the distinction of being the first cabinet member in history to go to jail for crimes committed in office. When the Harding Administration corruption was first exposed, Will Rogers called it the "great morality panic of 1924." But it would rattle the nation for a solid decade.

Warren G. Harding lived a lie from the moment he won the 1920 nomination at the Republican convention in Chicago. When no other candidate had emerged by one a.m. on the second day of balloting, Harding's hat was thrown into the ring. The politician from Marion, Ohio, seemed like a decent compromise candidate, but fifteen Republican power brokers first wanted to make sure Harding had no skeletons in the closet. In the wee hours, Harding was summoned to Suite 404-6 on the thirteenth floor of the Blackstone Hotel in Chicago, a meeting place that would go down in infamy as "the smoke-filled room." There George Harvey, editor of the *North American Review* and publisher of *Harvey's Weekly*, spoke first to the senator from Ohio: "But first, Senator Harding, I wish you to assure these gentlemen and myself, upon your sacred honor and before God, that you know of no reason, arising out of anything in your past life, why you should not stand with confidence before the American people as a candidate for the highest office within their gift." Harding excused himself from the room for ten minutes, and returned with his answer—"No, Gentlemen, there is no such reason."

It is presumed Harding telephoned Nan Britton, his young mistress who was in Chicago at that very moment with their illegitimate child. Of course, he also had to consider the situation with his more mature mistress, Mrs. Carrie Phillips, the wife of his old friend Jim. She would ultimately be paid off by the Republican National Committee who sent her, and her husband, on a slow cruise to the Orient so she wouldn't interfere with the election. Still, those in the smoke-filled room believed him when he said his life was scandal-free.

Most of the public scandals and all of the private ones, in fact, were revealed only after Harding died in his office on August 2, 1923, of a cerebral hemorrhage. Actually, it is remarkable that any information surfaced at all. On the eve of his funeral his wife, Florence, returned to the White House and began a systematic burning of Harding's papers, which continued for five evenings. When Calvin Coolidge and his wife moved into the White House, Mrs. Harding burned even more at Friendship, the sprawling estate of Edward B. McLean, owner of *The Washington Post* and *Cincinnati Enquirer*. Over the next six weeks, she destroyed some in a bonfire, others in a potbellied stove. In at least one instance, she burned some letters in the suitcase in which she carried them. This was just the beginning of the most calculated censorship in presidential history. But then again, Warren G. Harding had more to hide than most.

Many believe Harding meant well, but was basically in over his head as president. By his second year in office, he suffered severe depressions, and was once found crying on the White

House lawn. His history of mental disorders was later traced back
to the age of twenty-four, when he suffered a nervous breakdown
and was hospitalized in a sanitarium in Battle Creek, Michigan.
From time to time thereafter, he checked himself into various sani-
tariums to regain his emotional strength.

During his term, however, there was no retreating from the
stress and strain of his corrupt administration. Although he died
before the major scandals were exposed, he was around to see a
fair share. Charles R. Forbes, for instance, as head of the Veterans' Bureau, was caught skimming profits from war surplus
goods, bootlegging hospital drugs to narcotics dealers, and taking
kickbacks from purchasing agents. Forbes's assistant, Charles
Cramer, shot himself to death, leaving a suicide note addressed to
the president (which Harding never opened). Then Jess Smith, the
personal aide to Attorney General Harry M. Daughtery, also committed suicide. Harding had asked for his resignation after it was
disclosed that Smith had been the bagman for Thomas Miller, the
alien-property custodian who was also convicted of taking bribes.

But those scandals were insignificant compared to the ones
exposed six months after Harding's death. The worst was Teapot
Dome, the scandal that proved to be a major watershed in U.S.
political history. Teapot Dome was a naval oil reserve in Wyoming
that had once been set aside by the government for emergency use.
In 1920, however, Congress passed legislation to establish private
leasing of public mineral lands, and contracts for Teapot Dome
and other oil reserves were given to various bidders through the
secretary of the department of interior, Albert Fall.

Fall was an outspoken, rough-and-tumble senator from Montana who, with his thick moustache and black Stetson hat, looked
the part of a modern-day Buffalo Bill. Fall originally was under
consideration to be secretary of state, but Harding ultimately
appointed him to the interior post. The two men had met years
earlier while serving together on the Senate Foreign Relations
Committee, and soon thereafter became personal friends and
poker partners.

All was going smoothly for Fall until 1923, when a few peo-

ple began to notice that he was living way above the means afforded by a public servant's salary. He had bought an expensive
ranch in New Mexico that was certainly out of the range for someone who, after eleven years in the senate, had been nearly broke.
Only through the painstaking investigations of Montana Senator
Thomas J. Walsh was the source of Fall's outside income revealed. Fall had allowed Mammoth Oil Company to tap the Teapot
Dome reserve in exchange for $308,000 and a herd of cattle, which
he kept on the ranch paid for with a $100,000 bribe he got from Pan
American Petroleum and Transport Company, who were allowed
access to the Elk Hills reserve in California.

When news of the investigation first appeared in the press,
Fall acted incensed. He insisted when questioned by Walsh's investigating committee that the $100,000 loan to buy his ranch had
come from Edward B. McLean, the family friend with whom the
first lady stayed after President Harding's death. In a letter to the
committee, which he cleared with former Republican National
Chairman Will H. Hays and Harry F. Sinclair, the head of Mammoth Oil, Fall denied he had ever received "one red cent on account of any oil lease." Walsh, with his keen investigative skills,
didn't believe him and turned up in Palm Beach, Florida where
Fall and McLean were vacationing together. There, he got
McLean to admit he never loaned Fall any money at all. In January
1924, Walsh traced the loan to Edward Doheny, the oil magnate
who ran Pan American Oil and Transport Company. Doheny, under pressure from Walsh, ultimately testified that the money had
come from him. In 1929, Fall was found guilty of accepting the
bribe from Doheny. Fall, a broken man, had to be taken by ambu-
lance to prison where he served ten months of a one-year sentence.

★ ★ ★

While the Teapot Dome scandal stayed prominently in the
news throughout the decade, it was overshadowed for a time by a
scandal of a more personal and titillating nature. In June 1927,
three years after the death of Harding's wife, Nan Britton published *The President's Daughter*, a scandalous book that chronicled her illicit affair with the president. The first edition was

Miss Nan Britton says:

"The story of my life-long love for Warren Gamaliel Harding and his love for me and our love for our child is told in these pages, together with the family, community, and political circumstances under which this relationship continued for the six and one-half years preceding the sudden passing of the President on August 2, 1923.

The author has had but one motive in writing for publication the story of her love-life with Mr. Harding. This motive is grounded in what seems to her to be the need for legal and social recognition and protection of all children in these United States born of wedlock."

The Elizabeth Ann Guild~Inc.

announces the publication of THE PRESIDENT'S DAUGHTER, a fact-story revealing the love-tragedy of Warren Gamaliel Harding, twenty-ninth President of the United States.

Fathers, mothers, lovers, students of human na-

This is an actual portrait of Elizabeth Ann, only daughter of President Harding. The moving, tragic story of her coming into the world is now told for the first time.

ture, the American public, and voters of all political parties, are eager to read this mother's true narrative of the circumstances surrounding Mr. Harding's only child, a little, daughter now seven and one-half years old, and hitherto unknown to the world.

This book is being talked about everywhere~ For a copy ~ Mail this form at once!

ELIZABETH ANN GUILD, Inc.
20 WEST 46th STREET, NEW YORK

Please send postpaid "The President's Daughter" (455 pages and 48 illustrations). Enclosed is my check for $5 (If you prefer to pay postman on delivery omit remittance with this coupon). If not entirely satisfied, I have the right to return the book within a week and you will refund my payment.

Name _____

Address _____

City_____ State _____

This coupon brings you this astonishingly beautiful book by return mail!

Nan Britton self-published her book, The President's Daughter.

almost censured when the Society for the Suppression of Vice entered the printing plant and confiscated the plates and printed pages. But a magistrate's court dismissed the case and returned the material.

The book's intimate details were shocking. Nan Britton had been in love with Warren Harding ever since she was fourteen. At the time, Harding, who was thirty years older than she and a friend of her father's, had just lost his bid for governor in Ohio. To Nan, who hung his posters in her bedroom, Harding was a misunderstood hero.

Seven years later, Nan wrote a letter to Harding, who had become a U.S. senator, to see if he could help her get a job. He did a lot more than that. He met her at the Manhattan Hotel and registered in the bridal chamber. Between kisses he tucked $30 in her silk stockings and suggested she not take a job in Washington but stay in New York, where it would be easier to rendezvous.

In the following weeks, they met in various hotel rooms and train compartments, but never got past heavy petting. She wrote, "I experienced sweet thrills from just having Mr. Harding's hands upon the outside of my nightdress." But on July 30, 1917, having arrived in a pink linen dress, she lost her virginity to him in a hotel overlooking Broadway. Their room was a perfect love nest—until it was raided by two men who appeared to be vice squad. Amazingly, Harding was able to bribe them with a mere $20. The unabashed philanderer later expressed delight that it hadn't cost him $1,000.

By January 1919, they had begun having sex in his senate office, as he said he wanted Nan's memory to last through his work day. That is also where, Nan speculated, they conceived their child, who was born October 22, 1919. Throughout the relationship, Harding supported Nan and Elizabeth, providing up to $1,000 a payment. Although the money was paid on an "as-needed" basis, the installments must not have come too easy for the president, as when he died, he owed $180,000 to his brokerage firm.

Although Nan Britton intended her published version of the affair with Harding to be intimate and wonderful, it was, instead, a sad tale of a young girl who was delighted with every little morsel of love thrown her way by a manipulative lover. While Harding never met his daughter, Nan was grateful that he even looked at pictures of her. She was happy having sex with the president in an office closet at the White House, and his forty-page love letters

Nan Britton and her daughter, Elizabeth Ann, who resembled Warren G. Harding.

written on scratch paper in pencil were enough to carry her from visit to visit. She believed they would be married after Florence died.

No one thought of the possibility that Harding would die first. When he did, Nan unexpectedly found her funding cut off and no one to help. At Harding's request, she had destroyed all letters and evidence of their affair. In dire straits, Nan went to Harding's sister, Daisy, and brother, George. They gave her a $40 check, but refused to accept her story. Harding and his wife had no children of their own, and they refused to believe he had one with Nan. It was finally out of desperation that Nan went public with the book.

Perhaps because some people who knew the truth were still alive, or perhaps because it seemed to be well-documented with dates and places, Nan Britton's book was quickly accepted as truth. And on November 13, 1927, she held a press conference to introduce six-year-old Elizabeth Ann to the public.

There was no hard evidence to corroborate Nan's story until October 1963, when a box of love letters written by Harding were discovered in a shoebox in Marion, Ohio. These letters matched precisely the type of letters described by Nan Britton. Most were written in pencil on scratch paper. Some stretched forty pages and they were relentlessly, explicitly sexual. One letter was written on stationery from the Witherill Hotel at Plattsburgh and dated August 17, 1918. In *The President's Daughter*, Nan had written that she and Harding had spent that very weekend at the Witherill together. But while the discovery of the letters may have vindicated Nan, they did not put her affair in a better light. The August 17 letter, along with all the rest, was written by Harding not to Nan but to his other mistress, Mrs. Carrie Phillips.

The Hardings and the Phillipses had long been close friends. Carrie had been a schoolteacher when she married Jim, a successful dry goods merchant and partner in Uhler-Phillips of Marion. In 1904, the Phillips's two-year-old son died, which threw them both into serious depression. The following year, Harding arranged for Jim to go to the sanitarium in Battle Creek, Michigan, where he had recovered from his own nervous breakdown. He had a much more personal remedy, however, to lift Carrie's spirits.

Conveniently, Florence was recovering from a kidney operation when Harding slipped away to visit Carrie. He found her alone in the bedroom. The seduction began the very first night, as did the deception of their spouses. In 1909, it went on right under their noses, as when the Hardings and the Phillipses took a cruise

Warren G. Harding and his wife, Florence.

to Europe together. According to the letters, when Jim and Florence were asleep, Harding headed for the lifeboats with Carrie to grab a quick embrace.

Florence eventually caught on to the affair and dragged her husband to a divorce lawyer. Somehow, while at the lawyer's office, Harding was able to convince her to give him a second chance. This forced him to observe a brief cooling-off period with Carrie. But just a few weeks later, he resumed their affair with more abandon than ever.

In a letter he sent to Carrie sometime in 1911, Harding wrote, "I love you garbed, but naked more," underlining "naked" twice. He wrote a poem which began "Carrie, take me panting to your heaving breast," and more. At one point, Harding took all the letters back but, strangely enough, he returned them to her. By the

Warren Harding's mistress, Mrs. Carrie Phillips.

time he ran for president, it cost him dearly. In his last letter, he promised her $5,000 a year "to avoid disgrace in the public eye, to escape ruin in the eyes of those who have trusted me in public life. . . ."

That wasn't enough for Carrie, who had already received a Cadillac from Harding. Through Albert Lasker, an advertising expert who served as Harding's campaign manager in 1920, she received $25,000 down, $2,000 a month thereafter, plus an extended trip to the Orient, all compliments of the Republican National Committee.

★ ★ ★

Today, there are still many questions that remain unanswered about Harding's life. After his death, most of the documents that Florence Harding didn't burn were then suppressed by the Harding Memorial Association, an organization established by the first lady and run by Dr. Carl Sawyer, the son of Harding's White House physician and close friend. Ironically, it was the eventual release of some material from the Association to the Ohio Historical Society in 1963 that led to the discovery of the Phillips letters. Among the handful of biographers to descend on Marion, Ohio, to review the newly available papers was Francis Russell. While in the process of soaking up the local color of the former President's hometown, Russell met Don Williamson, the attorney who had been the legal guardian of Mrs. Carrie Phillips, who had died only four years before. Incredibly, Williamson had a shoe box containing one hundred letters from Harding written over a period of ten steamy years.

Although considered quite a find, the discovery of the letters unfortunately triggered a new wave of censorship. Through a series of legal maneuvers, the letters wound up under the control of the Harding family. By law, letters belong to the recipient, although the contents belong to the writer. Since Carrie Phillips had a daughter, Isabell, the letters rightfully belonged to her. But since Carrie Phillips died owing over $11,000 for nursing home and legal costs, a judge ruled that Isabell could only have the valuable letters, estimated to be worth $25,000, after the debts were paid. Not surprising, Dr. George T. Harding III bought the letters from Isabell. And only after eight years of pressure from historians did he finally agree to give the Phillips letters to the Library of Congress. Unfortunately, he negotiated the condition that they remain sealed until July 29, 2014. From time to time, however, passages from the letters have leaked out. In 1976 the *Washington Post* ran one of Harding's more erotic efforts: "There is one engulfing, enthralling rule of love, the song of your whole being which is a bit sweeter—Oh Warren! Oh Warren—when your body quivers with divine paroxysms and your soul hovers for flight with mine."

When the rest of the material is released, it will no doubt generate even more news coverage and analysis of Warren Harding. And while other political scandals through history may have had more dramatic aftereffects, those of the Harding Administration managed to have an ironic one—they inspired a future president. As a boy of eleven, Richard Milhous Nixon became so outraged by daily news reports of the Teapot Dome and other scandals that he decided to become a public servant. According to his mother, he said, "When I get big, I'll be a lawyer who can't be bribed."

An Unwritten Code of Privacy

Scandals in the Life and Times of
Franklin D. Roosevelt

T HE PRESIDENCY OF WAR-
ren Harding leads to one natural question: Is there any connection
between a politician's sexual or marital profile and his leadership
ability? In Harding's case it did appear that personal deceit and
infidelity were correlative with public corruption. But if ever there
was an argument that an unorthodox sex and family life has nothing to do with the ability to serve, and lead, a country, it is in the
record of Franklin D. Roosevelt, the thirty-second president of the
United States. While he is considered one of the most popular and
successful presidents, his private life was nothing less than bizarre. He loved two women other than his wife—and one lived
with him in the White House. First lady Eleanor Roosevelt also
had a friend living in the White House—a former AP reporter
who, according to evidence available today, was a lesbian.

President Roosevelt's accomplishments were many. He led
the country out of the Depression with the New Deal, a federal
relief and economic regulation plan which solved the banking crisis, established the Securities and Exchange Commission, fed and
housed the poor, created jobs and more. His Tennessee Valley
Authority (TVA) harnessed the power from the Tennessee River to
provide for low-cost electricity to severely depressed areas. Under
FDR's administration, prohibition was repealed, ending much of
the crime related to bootlegging. FDR was the first president since

169

the Russian revolution to renew diplomatic relations with the Soviet Union and, most critical, he led the United States through World War II.

Throughout Roosevelt's administration, there wasn't one scandal that produced an indictment, or even forced a resignation of any White House staff member or major New Deal administrator. His secretary of the interior, Harold Ickes, was known to have blown his stack when learning that forty-seven dollars-worth of cement was misused by the Public Works Administration, which provided grants-in-aid to cities and states to fund large-scale construction projects. His record of integrity and commitment endeared him to the entire nation.

Eleanor Roosevelt was a strong leader in her own right. She was the first first lady to endorse causes of any substance. She was an early and strong supporter of the black civil rights movement. When the Daughters of the American Revolution (DAR) refused to allow black singer Marian Anderson to perform in Constitution Hall, she resigned her membership in protest. She served as co-chairman of the office of Civilian Defense, and she walked through the coal mines to bring attention to poor working conditions. After the death of her husband, she continued in public service, chairing the United Nations Commission on Human Rights, supporting the establishment of Israel, and more.

Despite their extraordinary accomplishments, it is doubtful the first family could have stood up under the examination public servants get today. Fortunately, for a number of reasons—Roosevelt's illness, his popularity and his wife's, and the dire nature of the time, first, during the Depression and then, World War II—they enjoyed a certain immunity from the type of scrutiny to which the press had subjected many previous presidents.

★ ★ ★

Franklin Delano Roosevelt and (Anna) Eleanor Roosevelt were married on March 17, 1905. They were fifth cousins once removed, and both were related to former President Theodore Roosevelt. During the early years of their marriage, Eleanor was a shy, homely girl, dominated by her mother-in-law, and a very dif-

Lucy Page Mercer, as she looked when working as Eleanor Roose-velt's social secretary.

ferent person from the strong-willed woman who would later be called "The First Lady of the World." Sadly, her growth and movement toward independence began in 1918, when she discovered her husband was having an affair with her social secretary, Lucy Page Mercer. Eleanor found out about them when Roosevelt, who was then serving as assistant secretary of the Navy, returned from a trip to Europe with double pneumonia. While sorting out his mail, Eleanor found a stack of love letters from Lucy. According to biographer Joseph P. Lash, one of the few people with whom she ever discussed the incident, Eleanor was devastated. Twenty-five years after discovering the affair she wrote to Lash, "The bottom dropped out of my own particular world and I faced myself, my surroundings, my world, honestly for the first time. I really grew up that year."

In 1973 their son, Elliot Roosevelt, broke the family silence about that fateful day. "Mother came up to kiss me good night and dissolved into tears on my pillow. I had not heard her cry before in this uncontrolled, hopeless way. . . . Later, I came to realize it . . . those were the early days of Father's involvement with Lucy. Mother was facing the breakup of the marriage and she felt at the moment that she was powerless to do anything to prevent it from happening."

According to various accounts, Eleanor offered to give Franklin a divorce, but he declined. Besides the effect of divorce on the children, there were other considerations. First, there was his domineering mother, Sara, who controlled the family purse strings. She threatened to cut him off if he didn't stop seeing Lucy. Next, there was the inevitable fact that Lucy, a Catholic, would never marry a man who was divorced. Finally, and perhaps most importantly, FDR knew a divorce meant political suicide. With that in mind, he agreed to stop seeing Lucy and try to repair the damage.

The Lucy Mercer affair did not end their marriage but it changed it in a very pronounced and irrevocable manner. Elliot Roosevelt later recalled: "Through the entire rest of their lives, they never did have a husband-and-wife relationship, but . . . they

Missy Lehand, FDR's personal secretary, lived in the White House.

struck up a partnership arrangement. This partnership was to last all the way through their life; it became a very close and very intimate partnership of great affection—never in the physical sense, but in a tremendously mental sense.''

Although FDR stopped seeing Lucy, he soon began a second affair with yet another woman, Marguerite Alice LeHand, better known as Missy. They first met in 1920, during FDR's campaign for vice president on the Democratic ticket with James M. Cox against Warren Harding. Missy was a campaign worker in the Washington, D.C., headquarters. Although Roosevelt lost his bid for vice president, he gained a loyal secretary and intimate companion in Missy. She would remain close by him for the next twenty years.

No one knows what arrangement they actually struck, but FDR never hid his relationship with Missy from Eleanor, who accepted the young woman as her husband's mistress. Elliot wrote:

"It was no great shock to discover that Missy shared a familial life in all its aspects with Father. What did surprise us was the later knowledge that Mother knew, too, and accepted the situation as a fact of life like the rest of us.''

Their intimacy began sometime after 1921, when FDR's political life was interrupted by polio. Through the endless months of rigorous rehabilitation, Missy remained constantly by his side. She swam with him, she worked with him, she kept his spirits high. It is difficult to say exactly when they first became romantically involved, but it was well known among those close to the president that Warm Springs, Georgia, where he frequently went for hydrotherapy, was his private retreat with Missy.

While FDR focused his personal attention upon Missy, Eleanor began to build a life for herself. Although his mother disapproved, FDR gave Eleanor a tract of land a mile and a half east of the family home, where she built a home called "ValKill," meaning "valley stream" in Dutch. As time went on, Eleanor socialized more with women than men. Franklin described many of these women as "she-males." Two friends moved in with her—Nancy Cook, the cigar-smoking head of the women's division of the New York Democratic party, who wore her hair cropped short like a man's and made cabinets as a hobby; and Marion Dickerman, who ran the private school where Eleanor was a part-time teacher. But neither of those friendships matched the one she developed with Lorena Hickok, better known as "Hick."

Most of what is known about Eleanor Roosevelt's relationship with Lorena Hickok comes from the contents of 3,000 letters they wrote to each other. In the last years of her life, Hick donated them to the Franklin D. Roosevelt Library in Hyde Park under the condition that they would not be opened until ten years after her death. She died in 1968, and ten years later, on May 1, 1978, eighteen cardboard boxes of letters were unlocked, as were many secrets of the Roosevelt era.

Eleanor had first met Hick in 1932, during FDR's presidential campaign. Hick was a cigar-smoking, Associated Press reporter assigned to the Democratic candidate's wife. According to at least one female coworker, Lorena Hickok was an acknowledged lesbian. One night, while the two women shared a room on assignment, Hick made a lesbian overture. Rebuked, Hick apologized, adding that she tried to keep her "tendency" in check, but sometimes "went off the deep end" over women.

She must have gone off the deep end over Eleanor Roosevelt. The first lady wore Hick's sapphire ring to FDR's Presidential inauguration on March 4, 1933. The inauguration was strange all around. The night before, Eleanor and Hick shared a room at the Mayflower Hotel. The following day, Franklin sent a private limousine for his old flame Lucy, who was now married and known as Lucy Mercer Rutherfurd. Neither Eleanor nor Missy were aware of her presence. But neither Missy nor Franklin were aware that Eleanor was wearing Hick's ring, either.

Three days after the inauguration, on Hick's fortieth birthday, Eleanor Roosevelt wrote to her about the ring and what it meant to her.

> Hick darling, All day I've thought of you & another birthday I will be with you. . . . Oh! I want to put my arms around you, I ache to hold you close. Your ring is a great comfort. I look at it & think she does love me or I wouldn't be wearing it!

Eleanor wrote in another letter, which totalled fourteen pages in length: "Most clearly I remember your eyes, with a kind of teasing smile in them, and the feeling of that soft spot just northeast of the corner of your mouth against my lips." It ended, "Goodnight, dear one. I want to put my arms around you and kiss you at the corner of your mouth. And in a little more than a week now— I shall!"

Some of the emotional aspects of the relationship between Eleanor Roosevelt and Lorena Hickok, which began with a series of AP interviews, were not that difficult to understand. Hick's highly personal interview style had almost been cathartic for Eleanor, who had repressed much hurt and anger over the years. The women had exchanged stories about their childhoods, their hopes,

*Eleanor Roosevelt and Lorena Hickok penned 3,000 letters to
each other.*

their fears, their pains. Eleanor had had an awkward adolescence and had emotional scars from her aunts who called her an "ugly duckling." Hick had been raped by her father. Their bonding was so intense that Hick eventually resigned from her newspaper job to lend the much needed emotional support to the woman who would become the most beloved first lady ever. Outwardly Eleanor was in command, but inwardly, she feared losing the independence she had worked so hard to gain. She was hanging on for her very survival—with Lorena Hickok by her side.

Hick, who had been a frequent guest at the White House, often staying months at a time, officially moved in on January 2, 1941, and maintained a permanent residence there for the following four years. According to Lillian Rogers Parks, a White House maid during the Roosevelt administration who described her life in the Roosevelt White House in her book, *The Roosevelts: A Family in Turmoil*, the living arrangements were strange. Although Hick had her own room, she often slept on the daybed in Eleanor's room. When Hick stayed in her own room, which was across the west hall on the north side of the house, the first lady could be seen running back and forth between the rooms. Complicating matters for the household staff even more was Missy LeHand, who had her own suite in the White House consisting of a living room, a bedroom and bath. It was not uncommon to see Missy in the president's suite at night in a nightgown, or in the Oval Office on his lap. The extent of Missy's discretion, according to Parks, was in not remaining in the president's bedroom when his breakfast tray was served.

The setup had been the same, years before, in the executive mansion in Albany while Franklin was governor. There, Franklin took the master bedroom which adjoined Missy's by a curtained French door. Eleanor took a back bedroom down the hall on the second floor. Everyone, including the children, had accepted the arrangement, and it wasn't unusual for them to catch Missy in their father's room, wearing a nightgown.

While Eleanor didn't seem to mind Missy, the president wasn't a big fan of Hick's. One day he was heard yelling, "I want that woman kept out of this house!'' From that moment on, the White House maids quietly worked to make sure the two didn't cross paths. In the mornings, Hick would try to leave the White House after breakfast with Eleanor. In the evenings, she'd return to her room before the President left his office in the West Wing.

Matters were not helped any when Hick, while still living in the White House, found a new love interest—a female tax court judge named Marion Janet Harron. Judging by the contents of their letters, they were deeply in love. Then, FDR's personal life was thrown into as much turmoil as Eleanor's when, in the summer of 1940, Missy LeHand had a cerebral hemorrhage and was moved permanently out of the White House. She died three years later.

Lucy and FDR had been seeing each other again since 1941, during the period her husband Winthrop was dying from a stroke. Secret service agents used to drive the president to a rendezvous point on Canal Street outside of Georgetown and from there, FDR and Lucy drove around in her car for a couple of hours before he returned to the White House. After her husband's death, Lucy began visiting the White House when Eleanor was away. FDR suffered his fatal stroke on April 12, 1945, while in Warm Springs with Lucy Mercer Rutherfurd. Lucy was rushed from the house in an effort to conceal her presence from Eleanor. Later, Eleanor was sad to discover that her daughter, Anna, had known about the clandestine visits.

Although FDR died in the company of Lucy, his will was the clearest reflection of his heart. He left half of his $1.9 million estate to pay for Missy's medical bills, and the other half to Eleanor.

While few questions remain about FDR's romantic feelings, many remain about Eleanor's. The most striking: Was Eleanor Roosevelt a lesbian? For certain, Lorena Hickok was. But historians will probably forever debate whether or not Eleanor Roosevelt was, too. Elliot Roosevelt, for one, doesn't believe so. He explained, ''Her sensibilities were not tuned to sexual attraction of any kind, whether it existed between a man and a woman or between members of the same sex. On the strength of their appearance and knowledge of their living patterns, I suspected that some of the women, all dead now, who flattered my unwitting mother with their attentions were active Lesbians.''

In the final analysis, Franklin and Eleanor Roosevelt were fortunate to be left alone by the press. They occupied the White House at a time when press photographers honored Roosevelt's privacy code to the point of never showing him in his wheelchair. With such little concern about disclosure, the president and first lady could be as indiscreet as they desired. But, with the benefit of hindsight, the handful of personal scandals the American public was unaware of at the time is not all that significant. It remains a far more sobering exercise to wonder what contributions might have been sacrificed had the Roosevelts lived in the press climate of today.

"A Gift Is Not Necessarily a Bribe"

Scandals in the Life and Times of Harry S Truman and Dwight D. Eisenhower

W**ITH ROOSEVELT DEAD** and World War II over, the press took their kid gloves off and put their boxing gloves on, and a new era in scandal coverage began. Throughout the administrations of Harry S Truman and Dwight D. Eisenhower, the media began to probe more personal questions about public officials, most notably their acceptance of expensive gifts. And with the rapid growth of the White House staff, there were that many more politicians to scrutinize.

Franklin D. Roosevelt was the first president to greatly expand the number of political appointees to his personal staff. Jefferson had eked by with only one secretary and a messenger. Wilson plowed through World War I with only seven aides. Following the advice of a report by a presidential commission, Roosevelt increased the staff to 170. While FDR's staff adhered to the high political standards of its leader, the same couldn't be said for its successors.

Like too many presidents, Truman had appointed his White House staff on the basis of friendship and loyalty rather than experience or talent. As two early biographers said of his "Missouri Gang," "Never was there such a large, weirdly assorted, and variegated crew, and never one which ran so instinctively and unerringly to the banal and second-rate."

The list of scandals in the Truman Administration grew so

long, the press found it difficult to give each case the coverage it deserved. When all was said and done, a White House secretary went to jail, two White House aides were censured, and many more hung on to their jobs only by the grace of Truman's loyalty. It wasn't surprising that after the endless scandal exposures in the press, "Give 'em Hell Harry" suffered the lowest popularity rating in the polls of his entire career and chose not to run for reelection. It was a sad way to end a career that had been built on a reputation for honesty. As a senator, Truman had gained high marks as chairman of a committee that investigated mismanagement, fraud, and conflict of interest in connection with military contracts distributed during World War II. Ironically, because of his poor judgment in appointments, he became the target for similar probes.

One of the most notorious stories of wrongdoing was the "deep-freeze" scandal. It began when Brigadier General Harry Vaughan, Truman's top military aide, had hinted to a manufacturer named Harry Hoffman that he and Truman needed new deep freezer units in their homes. The Milwaukee manufacturer obliged, and not only sent one each to Vaughan and Truman (for his residence in Missouri), but he also sent freezers to four other Truman "cronies," including John Snyder, the federal loan administrator; Fred Vinson, the secretary of the treasury; and James K. Vardaman and Matthew Connelly of the White House staff. Only Vinson sent his back.

While the Constitution forbids the president to accept personal gifts from a foreign government, there is no law that prohibits gifts from fellow Americans. Still, earlier presidents had abided by an unwritten code of ethics regarding the practice. John Quincy Adams didn't want his wife to keep soap given to her by a manufacturer. Andrew Jackson went to Congress to find out what to do about two horses and a lion given to him. Polk wouldn't accept anything more valuable than a book, and Buchanan even refused gifts from his personal friends. Truman's soft standards opened the door for abuse.

Donald Dawson, the White House personnel director, admitted to accepting free accommodations from the Saxony Hotel in Florida, an apparent breach of ethics. The hotel had received a $1.5 million loan from the Reconstruction Finance Corporation (RFC), a government agency which wound up under Senate investigation for influence peddling. Dawson, a former personnel director for the RFC, was charged with accepting a payoff. He denied that he ever used influence to help secure loans for the Saxony and was permitted to remain on the White House staff, another example of Truman loyalty that drew great criticism.

Matthew Connelly, the president's appointments secretary, accepted a top coat, two suits and a $7,000 oil royalty from a lawyer whose client was under investigation by the Bureau of Internal Revenue. He was charged with bribery, perjury, and conspiracy. His presidential connection, however, could not rescue him as he was tried, convicted, and sent to jail.

E. Merl Young, a former RFC examiner, created a scandal when it was discovered that he accepted a royal-pastel mink coat for his wife, who was a White House secretary. The gift was from a lawyer who had represented a furrier who had applied for a loan from the RFC. The ethics of accepting mink would be argued throughout the entire 1952 political campaign—especially by vice-presidential candidate Richard M. Nixon, who noted his wife's "Republican cloth coat" was just fine.

Even Truman's White House physician, Brigadier General Wallace H. Graham, was investigated by a Senate subcommittee for fraud and corruption. Graham admitted to insider trading on the commodities exchange and added to Truman's disgrace.

Besides the White House staff, entire governmental departments were investigated for corruption and influence peddling. The investigation of the Bureau of Internal Revenue resulted in the resignation or firing of 166 tax officials, many of whom went to prison. The Department of Agriculture began to fall apart when it was discovered that $10 million was missing and presumed stolen. Finally, even the Justice Department, which was supposed to investigate everyone else, was found to be corrupt. An assistant attorney general took a $5,000 commission on the sale of a friend's airplane to a relative of a man involved in a tax case. He was fired, tried, and jailed.

Of all the scandals in the Truman era, the most infamous and far-reaching had little to do with the president but involved the anti-communist crusade of Senator Joseph R. McCarthy. With postwar anti-communism at its peak, Joseph R. McCarthy adopted the "red scare" as his personal crusade. His attacks took a heavy toll: scores of private citizens lost their jobs, many being forced to change their names and move to other cities; ten Hollywood screenwriters went to jail; political opponents lost bids for reelection; Secretary of State George Marshall (who later won the Nobel Peace Prize) was accused of being a "traitor"; and Senator Lester Hunt of Wyoming committed suicide. Yet not one communist was ever found nor was one spy convicted.

All this damage was caused by McCarthy who, years before, had been voted the "worst" U.S. senator by the Washington press corps. Facing a sure defeat in his bid for reelection, the communist scare seemed to be the perfect issue to help his constituents forget his dismal record.

The McCarthy era unofficially began on February 20, 1950, when McCarthy took his case to the Senate floor and detailed fifty-seven cases of "known" communists in the State Department. This forced an investigation by a subcommittee of the Senate Foreign Relations Committee which was chaired by Millard Tydings of Maryland. After Tydings found McCarthy's charges to be unsubstantiated, McCarthy quickly turned on him as well. Before the November election, McCarthy circulated a doctored photograph that showed Tydings listening attentively to the leader of the United States Communist Party. Sadly, it cost Tydings reelection.

McCarthyism took an even greater toll on Senator Lester Hunt, who attempted to stem McCarthy's abuses by introducing a congressional bill (S.782) which provided "for civil suits against the United States by persons suffering damages as a result of defamations committed by Members of Congress in the course of their official activities." The bill failed, as did his warning: " . . . [T]here have been many suicides due to the smearing received either in Committee hearings or from remarks made in the United States Congress.''

McCarthy vowed revenge, and not long after found a perfect opportunity. Lester Hunt, Jr., the president of the student body at the Episcopal Theological School of Cambridge, Massachusetts, had been arrested in a Washington, D.C., park after agreeing to engage in a homosexual act. Since the charge was only a misdemeanor and it was his first offense, police agreed not to prosecute. But McCarthy threatened to expose the incident if Hunt sought reelection.

When Hunt refused to be bullied, two senators, at McCarthy's behest, pressured the police department into bringing his son's case to trial in October 1953. Hunt, Jr. was found guilty and admonished by the judge that the charge was one of the most degrading that could be made against a man.

Although thirty-six Wyoming newspapers had refused to carry the story, a handful did publish the item and Hunt was pressured to resign immediately. On Saturday, June 19, 1954, Hunt drove to his office and shot himself in the head with a .22 caliber rifle. He left three notes. One was to the president of an oil company whom he asked to help his son find a job. The second was to his wife. The third was to his son, saying his suicide had nothing to do with him.

In the end Joseph McCarthy self-destructed, as did Roy M. Cohn, the attorney who had served as his top aide and hatchet man. On April 22, 1954, after enduring many false charges of subversion, the U.S. Army fought back. They charged that Cohn had promised to ''wreck the army'' when they refused special treatment for a friend of his. Over thirty-six days of televised hearings, the army revealed for all to see the illegal and unethical methods McCarthy and Cohn had used to destroy hundreds of innocent people, exposing their doctored photos and other assorted lies. The following December, McCarthy was condemned by the Senate and died a broken man three years later. Cohn died in August 1986, of AIDS.

★ ★ ★

In his bid for the Presidency in 1952, General Dwight David

Eisenhower founded his campaign on the promise to "clean up the mess in Washington" created by Harry S Truman. Before the election, however, a scandal arose in his own camp involving his vice-presidential running mate, Richard M. Nixon. On September 18, the *New York Post* disclosed details of a "slush fund" of $18,000, which Nixon had received from a group of California businessmen. It was especially embarrassing in light of the Republican attacks on Truman's "mink dynasty." Such an untimely exposé might have proved fatal to many other candidates, but Nixon's masterful handling of the crisis would serve as the ultimate guide to surviving a political scandal in the second half of the twentieth century.

When the news first broke, Eisenhower initially resisted pressure to dump Nixon, choosing to play for time and see if the crisis would fade. But rather than subside, the crisis only intensified as political demonstrations and newspaper editorials called for Nixon to step down. Finally, just as Eisenhower appeared ready to drop him, Nixon sprang into action and the "new politician" emerged.

On September 23, Nixon delivered a thirty-minute televised address to the nation, one of the most brilliant public-relations speeches ever. While he admitted the slush fund existed, he denied any of it went for his personal use. He went on to list the details of his personal assets, which included a 1950 Oldsmobile, $3,000 equity in his California home, $20,000 equity in his Washington home, and $4,000 in life insurance. He also listed his liabilities— $10,000 mortgage on the California home, $20,000 mortgage on the Washington home, $4,500 bank note, and a $3,500 debt to his parents. After completing his unprecedented accounting, Nixon did admit accepting one gift from a supporter in Texas—a cocker spaniel his six-year-old daughter Tricia had named "Checkers." In closing, the candidate warned, "I just want to say this, right now, that regardless of what they say about it, we are going to keep it."

Known today as the "Checkers speech," it was direct, to the point, and highly emotional. You didn't have to love dogs to forget about the slush fund. In one tear-jerking moment, Nixon had delivered one of the greatest responses to charges of corruption ever, one that saved his political career (for the time being) and cemented his place on the 1952 Republican ticket. Eisenhower happily met Nixon at the airport the following night, put his arm around him, and proclaimed, "You're my boy!" They both went on to an election victory.

While Nixon survived his scandal, other Eisenhower staff members involved in their own scandals did not. In 1958, Sherman Adams, the House chief of staff, was accused by the House of Representatives of manipulating the Securities and Exchange Commission (SEC) and the Civil Aeronautics Board (CAB) in exchange for a $700 vicuña coat and a $2,400 oriental rug, both from a New England industrialist named Bernard Goldfine. It was also discovered that Goldfine had paid hotel bills for Adams at the Waldorf Hotel in New York in 1954 and the Boston Sheraton Plaza between November 1955 and May 1958.

In testifying to a June 1958 House Special Subcommittee on Legislative Oversight, Adams said, "If there were any errors here . . . there were errors perhaps of inexperience." President Eisenhower stuck by his chief White House aide, issuing a statement that noted, "A gift is not necessarily a bribe. One is evil, the other is a tangible expression of friendship." But through the following months, the vicuña coat issue returned again and again to haunt Eisenhower at his press conferences. Finally, on September 18, either of his own volition or at the behest of the president, Sherman Adams resigned.

One reason Eisenhower might have been so supportive of Adams was that he, too, had accepted expensive gifts from political supporters, many of them for his Gettysburg farm. He had accepted a $4,000 tractor with a cigarette lighter attached, a $1,000 bull, and an estimated $40,000-worth of other farm equipment and livestock. And, like his former chief of staff, Eisenhower was under attack by the press. (Syndicated columnist Drew Pearson would later estimate the total worth of gifts, which included yet another vicuña coat, at a shocking $300,000.) When questioned about the various revelations, which had also appeared in *Newsweek*, *U.S.*

News and World Report, and the Cowles newspapers, Eisenhower replied, "The conflict-of-interest law does not apply to me."

Public opinion didn't reflect the views of the president. Neither did the Association of the Bar of the City of New York who, in 1958, established a Committee on the Federal Conflict of Interest Laws, which insisted that the president must set "the standard of sensitivity to ethical problems which will govern the conduct of millions of subordinates." While they acknowledged it would be impossible to stop the flow of gifts to the White House, they suggested donating the gifts to charities or museums, a practice more or less followed today.

While the press had become much more interested in the personal lives of politicians, extramarital matters were still clearly off limits. Such was the case regarding the wartime "romance" Eisenhower had with his personal driver. Eisenhower, then a general, had met Kay Summersby in May 1942, when the former model and movie actress was assigned to him on his ten-day visit to London. When he took over command of the European Theater of Operation the following month, he requested her full-time. She was beautiful, he was far from home, and a special relationship developed, the extent of which was kept secret for thirty years.

The first published hint of any romance appeared in Merle Miller's *Plain Speaking: An Oral Biography of Harry S Truman* (1973). Miller quoted Truman as saying "Why, right after the war was over, he [Eisenhower] wrote a letter to General Marshall saying that he wanted to be relieved of duty, saying that he wanted to come back to the United States and divorce Mrs. Eisenhower so that he could marry this Englishwoman." Truman claimed to have seen the letter, along with Marshall's blistering reply, in Eisenhower's Pentagon file. Truman also claimed that one of the last things he did as president was destroy the letters.

Truman's comments may have inspired Kay Summersby to write her own book. Two years after *Plain Speaking* hit the stands, she published *Past Forgetting: My Love Affair with Dwight D.*

Kay Summersby holding the puppy given to her by Dwight D. Eisenhower.

Eisenhower. While her earlier memoir, *Eisenhower Was My Boss* (1948), failed to mention any romance at all, this was a full confession. But even her own version of the most romantic moments left much to be desired. The Eisenhower-Summersby romance didn't even fall into the category of one of those things that happens in a war. It was more like one of those things that didn't happen in the war.

According to Summersby, Eisenhower was impotent—in London, in North Africa, and in Germany. She described one occasion:

> Ike refilled our glasses several times and then, I suppose inevitably, we found ourselves in each other's arms in an unrestrained embrace. Our ties came off. Our jackets came off. Buttons were unbuttoned. It was as if we were frantic. And we were.
>
> But this was not what I expected. Wearily, we slowly calmed down. He snuggled his face into the hollow between my neck and shoulder and said, "Oh, God, Kay. I'm sorry. I'm not going to be any good for you."

That was the general level of their futile attempts at lovemaking. The last try was in Germany on October 14, 1945, Eisenhower's birthday. Summersby recalled:

> I remember thinking, the way one thinks odd thoughts at significant moments, Wouldn't it be wonderful if this were the day we conceived a baby—our very first time. Ike was tender, careful, loving. But it didn't work.
>
> "Wait," I said, "you're too excited. It will be alright."
>
> "No," he said flatly. "It won't. It's too late. I can't." He was bitter. We dressed slowly. Kissing occasionally. Smiling a bit sadly.

Kay wrote Eisenhower's impotency off to the pressures of the war. Perhaps it was really out of faithfulness to his wife, or perhaps guilt, or both. But while they had never become lovers in the physical sense, Eisenhower and Kay did develop a strong emotional bond during the war where they braved life-threatening missions together. At first, their relationship was strictly business. She was engaged to an American soldier and Eisenhower was loyal to Mamie. But the death of her fiancé in North Africa seemed to strengthen their bonds. Eisenhower bought Kay a puppy to help console her and found himself accidentally calling his wife ''Kay'' on his visits back home.

Whatever the relationship was during the war, it was over the day Eisenhower left Europe for home. When Kay dropped in on him at the Pentagon a few times, she received an icy reception. When she dropped in unannounced to his office at Columbia University in New York, where he had been appointed president, he was annoyed.

Kay later married and worked as a fashion consultant in the film industry. Her last job was for *The Stepford Wives*. In 1973, after her doctors gave her six months to live, she said, ''I would like the world to know the truth of the Eisenhower affair.'' Unfortunately for those seeking to read of a torrid romance, the truth, while revealing in many other ways, left much to the imagination.

A Tarnished Camelot

Scandals in the Life and Times of John F. Kennedy

WHEN JOHN F. KENNEDY was sworn in as the United States' thirty-fifth president, he ushered in a new era, one which marked the coming of age of an America with style, progressive ideas, and sex appeal. His presidency would come to be known as the "Camelot" years, when for "one brief, shining moment" the United States realized the promise of its youth and took its place as the world's leader.

It was a charmed time in which a president could be a known womanizer and his supporters would love him for it. Presidential speechwriter Theodore Sorensen got laughs when he promised that this administration would do for sex what Eisenhower's did for golf. And when Marilyn Monroe sang a breathy "Happy Birthday" to the president in Madison Square Garden, the nation cheered and thought JFK was that much more dynamic, that much more in charge. Everyone loved the sex appeal of Camelot, especially the media who, in those days, still had a policy of keeping the well-known stories of the president's indiscretions among themselves.

In overlooking JFK's womanizing, however, the media became a willing co-conspirator in the "Camelot myth." And following John Kennedy's assassination, unwilling to accept that Camelot was over, the media tried to recapture it with all the other Kennedys for many years to come, first with Bobby and then again

The Kennedy family aboard the Normandie in 1935.

with Ted. All this helped make the Kennedys, through thick and thin, the greatest media darlings in American history—until Chappaquiddick, the most critical turning point in twentieth-century coverage of private lives of politicians. From that fateful moment on, the rules changed—forever.

Eventually, this unofficial conspiracy of silence had to end, if only because of the Kennedys' own lack of discretion and their tragic tendency to push their luck to the limit. Of all the Kennedys, Ted, in particular, exhibited a tremendous recklessness in his personal life, which only escalated after the violent deaths of his brothers. On one occasion in the spring of 1969, he boarded a plane in Anchorage, Alaska, visibly drunk, and continued to guzzle even more liquor from a silver flask that had once been Bobby's. He threw a pillow at a stewardess and a dinner roll at network correspondent Cassie Mackin. When he went weaving down the aisle with a cup of scalding coffee, he terrified a passenger who cradled a newborn in her arms. A *Newsweek* reporter on the plane filed a memo to his editor describing the incident and noting that Kennedy was "under terrible stress, an accident waiting to happen." Not one word on Ted's behavior, however, found its way into the press.

Finally, on July 18, 1969, the media's hands-off policy changed, suddenly and irrevocably, when Ted Kennedy drove his 1967 Oldsmobile off the Dike Bridge at Chappaquiddick. Although Ted swam free to safety, his companion, Mary Jo Kopechne, a young woman he was taking to a campaign party, drowned. From that point on, the media abandoned its unspoken policy of looking the other way. Never again would the memos stop at the editor's desk. In fact, the personal lives of all the Kennedys—including the martyred president—were now considered fair game.

While it is often argued that no one wrote about JFK's philandering until after his death, it is more the case that no one wrote about it until after Chappaquiddick. Almost overnight, revisionists went to work analyzing and reanalyzing the entire Kennedy family. And just as with the John Adams dynasty, recurring family patterns, reflecting both accomplishments and recklessness, were revealed in the new histories.

The Kennedy story begins with Joseph Patrick Kennedy, Sr. Joe Kennedy was a figure right out of the Great Gatsby. A third-generation Irish-American who graduated from Harvard, he became a bank president by the age of twenty-five and a millionaire at thirty-five. In the twenties, he amassed one of the greatest fortunes on Wall Street. And by selling short during the stock market crash of '29, he made millions more. Soon after, he branched into the movie industry, earning yet another fortune in Hollywood and engaging in a steamy love affair with box-office superstar Gloria Swanson. The romance not only added greatly to his playboy mystique, it also seemed to later influence, or at least presage, similar traits in his sons.

Having become disillusioned with the movie business, Kennedy accepted a post as Chairman of the Securities and Exchange Commission under Franklin D. Roosevelt. Ironically, as SEC

Joseph and Rose Kennedy.

Chairman, he ended many of the speculative stock market practices he used to build his own fortune. From 1937 to 1940, Kennedy served as ambassador to England where he began to get the itch
to run for president. Actually, had FDR not run for a third term,
Joseph P. Kennedy might have been the Democratic nominee. But
as FDR's popularity was unfailing, Kennedy missed his chance.
It was this failure to realize his own political ambitions that created the Kennedy legacy. If Joe, Sr. couldn't be president, his
sons would.

Just as John Adams placed his political hopes in his children,
Joe Kennedy, Sr. exerted intense pressure on his children to fulfill
the political aspirations he had never realized. From the oldest,
Joseph P. Kennedy, Jr., to the youngest, Ted, all nine children
were groomed for their political roles. When his young sons went
sailing in Nantucket Sound, Joe, Sr. would follow behind, taking
notes on every mistake. If he thought one of his sons was slacking
off, he would send him to have dinner in the kitchen in disgrace. So
ever-present was the spirit of competition and the need to win—
despite the risks—that the children would try anything, no matter
what the danger. "Second best," they were taught, "is a loser." It
wasn't how you played the game; the only thing that mattered was
winning. The logic was simple: winning was the only way to the
oval office.

Rose Kennedy's influence on her children was just as powerful as her husband's, if less apparent. When Kathleen, the second
oldest daughter, announced her plans to marry Peter Fitzwilliam,
the wealthiest man in Ireland, Rose threatened to disown her. Fitzwilliam had been married, and by marrying a divorced man, Kathleen would be denied the sacraments forever. While Joe Kennedy
hoped to get a special dispensation from the Pope, Rose stood her
ground. Reducing Kathleen to tears, she demanded the wedding
plans be called off. In protest, Kathleen and Fitzwilliam took off
for the south of France to get away from the pressure.

On May 13, 1948, Kathleen and Fitzwilliam were killed
when their private eight-seater airplane crashed into a mountain.
They had stopped off near Paris to visit friends and service the

plane. When they returned to the airport, a storm blew in and the pilot urged them to delay the trip. But overly anxious to reach Cannes, they took off into the treacherous weather. Rose refused to attend her daughter's funeral.

★ ★ ★

The first real presidential plans were laid for Joseph, Jr., the oldest of the Kennedy children. From the time he was a teenager, he embraced unquestioningly his father's wishes for him to become the first Catholic president of the United States. In 1941, at the age of twenty-five, he volunteered for military service, where he received his commission as a Navy pilot. In June of '44, after two tours of combat duty and fifty missions against Germany, he was ordered home. But instead of packing his duffel bag and heading back to Boston, he volunteered for one last, dangerous mission. It shouldn't go unnoticed that a year before, his younger brother John had been awarded a purple heart for his bravery during the sinking of his PT boat. It is quite possible that his decision to accept the mission was as much due to the Kennedy competitive drive as to his sense of duty.

On August 12, 1944, Joe, Jr. took off on a mission in a Liberator Bomber, an experimental plane carrying eleven tons of an explosive more unstable than TNT. Once it reached its designated altitude, it blew up. Joe's body was never found. It has never been suggested that Joe, Jr. had any kind of a death wish. It is perhaps more the case that he, like the rest of the Kennedys, never thought he was at risk. It was this sense of destiny that gave the Kennedys an aura of invulnerability, an aura that would be tragically shattered time and time again.

★ ★ ★

Although Joe, Jr.'s presidential ambitions were dashed prematurely, Joe, Sr. was not without recourse. He soon passed the torch to the second-born son, John Fitzgerald. John had always adopted his father's expectations as his own, and running for president was no different. He once said, ''Just as I went into politics because Joe died, if anything happened to me tomorrow, my brother Bobby would run for my seat in the Senate. And if Bobby died,

Marilyn Monroe sang for President Kennedy on his nationally televised birthday party in 1962.

Teddy would take over for him.'' Joseph Kennedy, Sr. would live long enough to witness that very chain of events.

If anything, JFK's fearless, and at times reckless, behavior grew even more so after his election to the presidency. On one occasion, he tried (although unsuccessfully) to convince a helicopter pilot to land on a 1400-foot crater at a Nevada atomic test site.

Traveling to the same area in Caracas, Venezuela, where Nixon had been threatened by rioters, he refused routine security measures, and plunged headlong into the uncontrollable mobs. And he was the most notorious womanizer of all the presidents—a distinction that some have speculated might even be linked to his assassination.

JFK has been romantically linked with hundreds of women, from two blonde secretaries nicknamed Fiddle and Faddle to more exotic types such as Jayne Mansfield, Angie Dickinson, Stripper Blaze Starr, and painter Mary Pinchot Meyer, with whom he smoked pot in the White House. JFK's love affair with Marilyn Monroe became perhaps the most widely reported after a private detective and a B-movie producer claimed the blonde bombshell's death in 1962 was somehow connected to her romantic involvement with both the president and his brother Bobby.

Although many mysterious circumstances still surround her "apparent suicide," as her death certificate reads, Marilyn was said to have been despondent over the cold shoulder she had been getting from both brothers. In twenty years, no one has been able to prove whether her death was suicide or murder. The arguments presented in books, magazines, and documentaries have been convincing on both sides. But regardless of the way in which she died, it is known that her last desperate phone call was made to actor Peter Lawford, the Kennedys' brother-in-law.

While womanizing with Marilyn proved to be risky, it wasn't nearly as reckless as JFK's romance with Judith Campbell—the mistress of Sam Giancana, a notorious underworld figure. Sam Giancana was the top banana of the Chicago Crime Syndicate, a position he held longer than his predecessor, Al Capone. Overseeing a criminal empire that included an estimated fifty thousand bookies, loansharks, drug dealers, counterfeiters, fences, assassins and other assorted gangsters, he controlled an annual illegal revenue of $2 billion. Incredibly enough, Kennedy's affair with Campbell was finally uncovered during an investigation by the Senate Committee on Intelligence Operations in 1975, which revealed that Giancana had been hired by the CIA in an assassination plot against Fidel Castro.

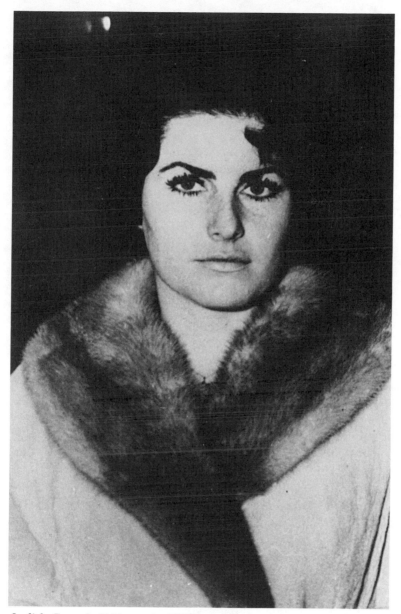

Judith Campbell Exner in 1960, the year she met JFK.

Committee chairman Senator Frank Church, a Democrat from Idaho, had made great efforts to keep the story in a low profile, deleting references to Judith Campbell by name or even gender in his final report. She was only called ''the president's friend'' in such contexts as the White House telephone log, which showed seventy calls between the White House and ''the president's friend'' who ''was also a close friend of John Roselli and Sam Giancana and saw them often during this same period.'' When Giancana and Roselli were both murdered following the Church committee disclosures, the media smelled a story, and eventually the details regarding Judith Campbell were revealed.

JFK, as it turned out, had been introduced to Judith Campbell by his good friend Frank Sinatra on February 7, 1960, in the lounge of the Sands Hotel in Las Vegas. Judith had been Sinatra's ''squeeze'' for a while, which made her more appealing to Kennedy. The fact that she rejected a pass made by Ted later that evening made the pursuit even better.

Despite a lot of phone calls and roses, JFK didn't get together with Judith until she flew to see him at the Plaza Hotel in New York on March 7—the eve of the New Hampshire primary. In her own published account of the relationship, called *My Story*, Judith described the ''big event'' as unspectacular. ''I was to learn in my relationship with Jack,'' she recalled, that ''his attitude was that he was there to be serviced. Partly this was due to his back problem, and partly I think he had been spoiled by women.''

According to Judith, she rendezvoused with JFK at his family home in Georgetown, a private home in Palm Beach, and the Hilton Hotel in Los Angeles on the eve of the Democratic Convention. The Hilton was where they had their first lover's spat—after Kennedy invited another woman to his room to interest Judith in a ménage à trois. When JFK's recklessness was at its peak, she visited him in the White House and swam in the pool. JFK even invited her on to Air Force One.

The affair made JFK more vulnerable to blackmail than anyone could have ever imagined. On February 27, 1962, FBI Director J. Edgar Hoover sent Kennedy a memo stating that Judith

Campbell, whom he knew was the president's mistress, was also Giancana's mistress. The memo was certain to put him in a difficult position with Hoover, one of Kennedy's most powerful adversaries in Washington. The president had been actively trying to limit Hoover's considerable power. An early warning sign of the changing tide for the FBI director was when JFK insisted that Hoover report only to his brother, Bobby, who served as attorney general. While the attorney general's office had jurisdiction over the FBI, Hoover, in the past, had only reported directly to the presidents he served. And now, Hoover could regain the political leverage he badly needed.

Hoover's memo was equally embarrassing to Bobby Kennedy, who had recently embarked on the most ambitious crackdown on mob activities ever. While his Justice Department was hoping to prosecute leading gangsters, the president was dating one of their girlfriends. Fearful of the repercussions of the potential exposure of the memo, Bobby ordered round-the-clock harassment of Giancana. JFK, meanwhile, stopped seeing Judith Campbell and Frank Sinatra. And only recently has Judith admitted that she, indeed, was the conduit between Kennedy and Giancana.

JFK was assassinated on November 22, 1963, bringing a sudden halt to Camelot. With his death, the presidential torch was passed to Bobby, an equally dynamic Kennedy, who seemed to rekindle the national spirit that had died with his brother. Bobby seemed fully prepared for the task, having been groomed by Joe, Sr. in the same way as his older brothers. One of the favorite family stories was how Bobby, at age four, threw himself off the family sailboat to teach himself how to swim. When Joe, Jr. pulled him out to safety, he jumped in again. JFK later recalled, "It showed either a lot of guts or no sense at all depending on how you looked at it."

In sports, Bobby had competed so intensely that he once completed three plays in a practice scrimmage after having broken his leg. No one knew until he collapsed and was carried from the field.

And although he was considered the "runt of the litter," Bobby, through sheer determination, became the only Kennedy to win a football letter at Harvard.

Bobby's fearless approach to life was yet another manifestation of the Kennedy legacy of reckless behavior. When the Canadian government named their highest unscaled mountain after JFK, Robert decided to be the first to ever climb the 13,000-foot peak. In March 1965, soon after his election to the Senate, he scaled it despite his crippling fear of heights. In November 1965, he took a canoe trip in the Amazon Valley in the middle of a tropical storm. With visibility less than six inches, the native guides refused to go. When he returned forty-five minutes later with four fish, the native guides admitted they were surprised to see him alive. The following day, feeling even more invulnerable, he took a 1937 plane to a remote part of the jungle, telling his wife, "I must be crazy to be on this light thing."

During his 1968 campaign for president, Bobby ignored all security warnings. His staff was frightened by the emotional frenzies he could whip up in a crowd. One *Life* magazine reporter wrote that Kennedy "deliberately and repeatedly [exposed] himself to the bad possibility. . . . He definitely did not want to be protected." On June 5, 1968, that "bad possibility" became a reality as Bobby Kennedy was assassinated in the Ambassador Hotel moments after delivering his California primary victory address.

★ ★ ★

The pressure for Ted to run for president started all too soon. Even as he rode in the elevator accompanying Bobby's corpse to the Good Samaritan Hospital autopsy room, anti-war strategist Allard Lowenstein turned to him and said, "Now that Bobby's gone, you're all we've got. You've got to take the leadership." Without a second thought, he assured Lowenstein he would "carry on."

As the 1968 Democratic convention neared, Ted gave his first political speech since Bobby's death. He told eager reporters, "Like my brothers before me I pick up a fallen standard." There was little doubt the 1972 presidential nomination could be his. But ultimately, the same sense of invulnerability and reckless behavior patterns—especially behind the wheel—would prove to be his undoing.

Ted had always been a ferocious driver. As a University of Virginia law student in the '50s, he was convicted of numerous traffic violations ranging from speeding, to reckless driving, to failure to stop for a red light. During his first Senate term, he once pressured a driver to speed things up on the way to the airport. The driver was already going one hundred miles per hour. As a future presidential candidate, his recklessness got even worse.

By his own admission, the events that surrounded the Chappaquiddick accident came close to criminal irresponsibility. After his 1967 Oldsmobile swerved off the bridge and into the water, Ted swam to safety and went to the party to get help. He did not call the police. Instead, he returned to the scene of the accident with his cousin and together they took several dives into the icy waters. At 2:30 a.m., he made an appearance in the lobby of his motel, after which he returned to his room and made seventeen phone calls. None were to the police. In fact, he didn't call the police until the next day—after Mary Jo Kopechne's body was found.

Interestingly, the Chappaquiddick scandal did not ruin Ted's political career entirely, a point many credit to his effective use of television. On July 25, Kennedy pleaded guilty to charges of leaving the scene of a fatal automobile accident and was given a two-month suspended sentence. That evening, he delivered a ten-minute statement from his father's home in Hyannis Port where he denied driving under the influence of liquor and appealed to the citizens of Massachusetts for advice as to whether or not he should resign from the Senate.

The appeal was written by Ted Sorenson, best known for JFK's "Ask not what your country can do for you" address. Although Chappaquiddick was a tougher assignment, he prepared a statement that seemed to work. Kennedy began, "It has been seven years since my first election . . . and so I ask you tonight, people of Massachusetts . . . in facing this decision I seek your advice

1962 photo of Mary Jo Kopechne.

Car approaching Dike Bridge (site of Chappaquiddick accident), traveling in the same direction as Ted Kennedy's car had on that fateful night.

and opinion." He continued, "The ultimate decision will be where it should be, and that is with the public and with the people of Massachusetts." Later in the telecast, he recounted his actions in a way that sounded more heroic than negligent as he recalled diving back into "dark and murky waters." Some said it was slightly reminiscent of JFK's heroic rescue efforts as commander of the PT 109, during World War II.

According to a 1970 study published in *Television Quarterly* by M. J. Robinson and P. M. Burgess, of every four persons who supported Kennedy before Chappaquiddick, one had left the fold by the time of the address. As a result of the telecast, however, half of the defectors returned to his support. The authors concluded, "When any man with some public notoriety . . . puts his case humbly before the television audience, and puts it there knowing that nobody is going to pan him after the performance, he can only come out ahead regardless of what he has to say."

The most painful defection after Chappaquiddick turned out

Ted Kennedy and wife Joan en route to Mary Jo Kopechne's funeral.

to be the senator's wife, Joan. While she stood by her husband's side through the scandal, and bravely accompanied him to Mary Jo Kopechne's funeral, the years of being a Kennedy wife had taken its toll. A month after Chappaquiddick, Joan miscarried what would be their last attempt to have another child. The marriage had eroded and it was increasingly apparent that Joan had become an alcoholic. She eventually left the Kennedy clan behind and moved into an apartment of her own in Boston. She sought treatment for her alcoholism and was successfully rehabilitated, after which she left Ted for good.

★ ★ ★

As with the Adamses, the greatest toll of the family expectations was taken on the third generation, who was made well aware of its Kennedy responsibilities. The day of JFK's funeral, Robert Kennedy had written to his son Joe II, "You are the oldest of all the male grandchildren. You have a special and particular responsibility now which I know you will fulfill. Remember all the things Jack started—be kind to others that are less fortunate than we—and love our country." Perhaps the weight was too much for a younger person to bear. In 1973, Joseph II wrecked a jeep after driving it wildly through the woods, spinning in circles. Pam Kelly, a passenger, was left paralyzed from the waist down. His younger brother, David, suffered a fractured vertebrae.

The following summer, Bobby Jr. took a death-defying raft trip down the Apurimac River at the headwaters of the Amazon where an estimated 300 Indians a year were smashed to death in its rapids. Before the group began their journey, Bobby insisted on jumping in for a swim, daring the others to follow. Twice he was sucked down in the treacherous undertow, swept out of their view. The others thought he had actually drowned until he finally surfaced downstream where he dragged himself to safety.

Bobby and his entourage survived the Apurimac—ragged, battered, but with their invulnerability level boosted. On the eleven-hour trip back to Lima through the mountains, Bobby climbed out the window to the roof of the moving bus to get a sweater out of his duffel bag. Bobby, Jr. had expressed such reckless arrogance as early as 1971, when at the age of seventeen he was arrested after spitting an ice cream cone in a cop's face. That same year he helped get his brother David, sixteen, suspended from Middlesex High School after selling him a pound of marijuana. David kept the pot at school in a suitcase, which mysteriously disappeared. When he heard what happened, Bobby came to school, disguised as a tough drug dealer, and threatened the other students. The intimidation, however, backfired. One frightened student went to the school authorities who threw David out of school.

Drugs remained a serious threat to many of the Kennedy grandchildren. In 1973, Ted and Joan's fourteen-year-old daughter, Kara, began to experiment with drugs. On several occasions, she ran away from home, only to wind up in halfway houses. In 1976, David was hospitalized for six weeks in Massachusetts General Hospital after a forty-day heroin shooting binge. Over the next few years he was in and out of detoxification programs, and in and out of trouble. One drug dealer stabbed him in the stomach during a heroin transaction. In Harlem, where he was nicknamed ''White James,'' he was mugged during another drug buy and then arrested by the police who found his behavior suspicious. In 1983, Bobby, Jr., who had become an assistant district attorney, was arrested for possessing a gram of heroin after having been carried off a Republic Airline plane. On April 25, 1984, David finally lost his running battle with drugs and was found dead from an overdose.

Behind the Kennedy legacy is what many have called ''the shadow legacy,'' a force that represented a contempt for all rules and ''an arrogance toward the laws that bound everyone else.'' As Chris Lawford, another Kennedy grandchild, said, ''The Kennedy story is really about karma, about people who broke the rules and were ultimately broken by them.'' Still, the legacy marches forward. In 1986, Joseph Kennedy II was elected to the House of Representatives from Massachusetts, becoming the first of his generation to enter politics. His older sister Kathleen tried, but lost her bid for a congressional seat in Maryland.

"Move Over, This Is Your President"

Scandals in the Life and Times of Lyndon Baines Johnson

ALTHOUGH PRESIDENT Lyndon Johnson's crude Southern charm was a far cry from the Kennedy Camelot style, the crass Texas Democrat was involved in almost as many romantic scandals as his predecessor. One of the more amusing tales involved the seduction attempt of a woman on his staff. While visiting the Johnsons' ranch in Texas, the female aide was startled in the middle of the night when a man in a nightshirt appeared at the foot of her bed. There was little she could see except for the light of his flashlight. There was little she heard other than the familiar voice who uttered what just might be the greatest seduction line in history: "Move over, this is your president."

While LBJ openly boasted of his sexual prowess throughout his administration, the media kept this tale, and many more, under wraps. But since his death in 1973, the truth about Johnson's womanizing has been slowly revealed to the public. Even today, LBJ sex scandals continue to surface, the most recent coming to light in June 1987, after thirty-six-year-old Steven Brown filed a $10.5 million patrimony suit claiming he is the illegitimate child, and only male heir, of the former president. His mother, sixty-two-year-old Madeline Brown, claims she was Johnson's mistress for twenty-one years.

Details of the suit were widely reported, although the public, fairly desensitized to such matters, has apparently taken them in stride. According to Madeline, her "purely physical" love affair with Johnson was well-hidden from his wife, Lady Bird, and their two daughters, Luci and Lynda. In return for her discretion, Madeline claims she was set up in a two-bedroom home with a maid, unlimited charge cards, and a new car every two years. Although no love letters or official confirmation exist, Madeline claims a letter from a now-deceased Dallas attorney, Jerome T. Ragsdale, is proof of her affair with the president. Written soon after Johnson's death in 1973, the letter gave Madeline Ragsdale's "personal assurance" that he would "continue with the financial arrangements that Lyndon provided for you and Steve through the past." He added, "I will continue to make weekly home visits to verify you [sic] and Steve's welfare."

While Madeline Brown may have been a purely sexual playmate, another mistress was an emotional touchstone for LBJ. In 1982, award-winning biographer Robert A. Caro revealed the poignant story of the thirty-year affair LBJ had with Alice Glass, a six-foot-tall Texas beauty with sparkling blue eyes and hip-length strawberry blonde hair.

LBJ first met Alice Glass in 1937 at "Longlea," an eighteenth-century-styled manor in northern Virginia where she lived with her common-law husband, Charles E. Marsh, and their two children. Despite her southern upbringing, Alice didn't believe in marriage, not even to Marsh, the affluent newspaper mogul who left his wife and children for her when she was still in her teens. In the 1930s, her lifestyle was considered scandalous. Alice's sister, Mary Louise, described her as "A free spirit—very independent—in an era when women weren't that way."

Longlea, where LBJ soon became a regular visitor, was an elegant meeting place for leading journalists, politicians, and academicians who would come to sit on the elegant terrace, sip champagne and exchange ideas. In many ways, LBJ's courtship of Alice at Longlea was reminiscent of George Washington and Sally Fairfax at Belvoir.

LBJ and Alice Glass shared a common bond of idealism. At

the time they met, Alice raised money and organized efforts to help persecuted Jews flee Hitler. Johnson was a young congressman ready and willing to help her. Many of the refugees came directly from Europe to Longlea, including a twenty-five-year-old conductor from Vienna who arrived on a temporary visa. When it appeared that his visa would not be extended, Alice turned to LBJ, who arranged for the conductor to travel to Cuba and return with a "permanent resident" status. Alice was dazzled. Here was a man who was not only ready to change the world, but could also back his ideals with actions. And not only did he oppose religious persecution, she learned, he also crusaded against poverty, racial prejudice, and other such wrongs of society.

By late 1938 or early 1939, Alice told her sister and her cousin that she and LBJ had become lovers. Johnson, however, told no one. Ironically, the fact that Johnson never spoke of the sexual aspect of their relationship was proof to many of his profound love for her. As LBJ was often boastful, even exhibitionistic about his other affairs, his silence about Alice was notable.

While Johnson had fallen deeply in love, he never let his feelings get in the way of a good political opportunity. Even with the love affair in full bloom, Johnson became a political protegé of Alice's common-law husband. Marsh, who was apparently unaware of the affair, helped Johnson both politically and financially. In 1938, his newspaper, the *Austin American-Statesman*, ran only pro-Johnson articles—and a lot of them. The following year, when Marsh noticed that Johnson couldn't get by on his $10,000 congressman's salary, he sold him a nineteen-acre tract of land for the below-market price of only $12,000. That one purchase, actually paid for by Lady Bird, permanently secured the Johnsons' financial future.

Perhaps Lady Bird felt it was an opportunity owed to her, as it is almost certain she knew of LBJ's affair with Alice. When Johnson went off to Longlea for the many weekends he spent there with Alice, Lady Bird was shuttled off to Texas or Washington for one domestic chore or another. But in the end, Lady Bird won her man. The relationship between LBJ and Alice Glass ended just as it began—over issues of social conscience—only now the focus was Vietnam. By 1967, even the possibility of a friendship was off. In protest, Alice had burned LBJ's love letters to her. Apparently, she didn't want her granddaughter to know she had ever been associated with the man she considered responsible for the war in Vietnam.

★ ★ ★

In light of the variety of LJB's extramarital affairs, it is ironic that a sex scandal that had nothing to do with him almost cost him the presidency. On October 14, 1964, just weeks before the election, the news media discovered that Walter Jenkins, Johnson's White House chief of staff, had been arrested in the men's room of the YMCA, where he was found engaging in homosexual activities with a sixty-year-old resident. What's more, the media discovered that Jenkins had been arrested on the same charge in the same men's room five years before.

At the time, homosexuality was considered one of the more serious political liabilities. Little had changed since a 1950 congressional report titled "Employment of Homosexuals and Other Sex Perverts in Government," Document No. 241, noted that homosexuals were prime targets for foreign governments recruiting spies. It defined homosexuals as perverts lacking in "moral fiber," who "violate moral codes and laws and the accepted standards of conduct." It was in such a moral climate that the Jenkins scandal erupted.

When the press first learned of the Walter Jenkins incident, a week after the actual arrest, Johnson was campaigning in New York. When Jenkins could not make telephone contact with the president, he turned to Abe Fortas, LBJ's top legal adviser. Fortas quickly had Jenkins admitted to a hospital. Then, while Jenkins was checking in, Fortas visited the editors of the three major newspapers to ask them to hold the story until the chief of staff could inform his family and resign from office. Although all three agreed to Fortas's request, United Press International broke the story later that afternoon. But by that time, Jenkins was in the hospital under medical observation, and Johnson was prepared to accept his resignation.

As part of his damage-control efforts, Johnson then called upon his old friend, J. Edgar Hoover. Hoover, who enjoyed a stronger relationship with LBJ than he had with the Kennedys, responded immediately, issuing a report within one week that assured the country Jenkins had not compromised national security in any way. While Hoover's report helped Johnson, the furor over the scandal did not die down until a more serious news story took over front-page headlines—China had exploded its first nuclear bomb.

From time to time during the campaign, Republican challenger Barry Goldwater tried to revive the Jenkins scandal with derisive references to Johnson and his "curious crew." And among the president's detractors, the campaign slogan "All the Way with LBJ" was changed to "Either Way with LBJ." But due to his keen political manuevering the damage to the president was minimized. In fact, while the Jenkins incident had caused Johnson considerable embarrassment, it also had one indirect benefit for the president. When Jenkins was called as a witness in a Senate investigation of Senate Secretary Bobby Baker, his physicians said he was too weak to testify. It must have provided at least some degree of relief for LBJ, as Jenkins was the key in linking Johnson with Baker in what some called "the most bizarre Washington scandal of the sixties."

In 1955, Johnson, then senate majority leader, selected Robert G. Baker as the majority secretary. For the following six years, Baker was Johnson's protegé. At one time Johnson said, "If I had a son, this would be the boy." But by the time Johnson reached the White House, this "boy" was an embarrassment. In 1963, Baker was sued for using his influence to secure contracts with the Defense Department for his vending machine firm. As the Rules Committee probed the allegations, they found even more improprieties, some of which led to the president.

Johnson had purchased a $100,000 life insurance policy from Don B. Reynolds, owner of an insurance firm that employed Bobby Baker as a vice president. Reynolds claimed that shortly after he sold Johnson the policy, Walter Jenkins suggested that Reynolds buy one thousand dollars in advertising time on an Austin, Texas, television station owned by Lady Bird. After that, Baker also urged him to buy Mrs. Johnson a stereo system that she had her eye on. Although he had no need for it, Reynolds bought the advertising time and sent the Johnsons the $600 stereo, invoice and all. When a Washington newspaper uncovered the story, which had all the appearances of a kickback scheme, it sent the White House an advance copy. Abe Fortas again tried to suppress the story, but this time he couldn't.

The extensive Senate investigation of Baker's activities ultimately led to nine counts of fraud, conspiracy to defraud the government, and income tax evasion, but it failed to implicate the president. Although his opponents cried ''Whitewash'' in true election-year fashion, Johnson and Jenkins were cleared of all allegations of wrongdoing in the life-insurance deal. Baker wasn't as lucky. He was convicted of seven of the nine counts.

As a result of the Baker scandal, the Senate, in 1964, set up a permanent ethics committee. The House of Representatives followed suit in 1967 following an investigation of Adam Clayton Powell, which found that the flamboyant Democrat from Harlem had used government funds for personal airline travel; that his wife had received a $20,000 annual salary which he banked in his own account; and that he was rarely attending Congress. The power of both ethics committees was strengthened in the late 70s, as a result of the widespread misconduct in the Nixon administration.

"Obscene Matters"

Scandals in the Life and Times of
J. Edgar Hoover

IN HIS FORTY-EIGHT YEARS as director of the Federal Bureau of Investigation, J. Edgar Hoover perhaps wielded more power than any one person in American history. In the '30s, he rose to national prominence after his G-men all but eliminated bank robberies and kidnapping in the United States. In the '40s, his power grew as he waged—and won—his war against Nazis and spies. In the '50s, he made himself indispensable after claiming a victory over internal communism, although some later questioned whether he created the very threat in the first place. But by the '60s, Hoover seemed to run out of the high-profile crime crusades on which he had built his reputation. He was hesitant to tackle organized crime out of fear he could never truly win that war. So instead, Hoover drew on the ultimate weapon to ensure his power for life—his files.

Hoover kept detailed files on the personal lives of the eight presidents he served. He made sure each new member of Congress had a secret FBI dossier. In the '60s, he expanded surveillance operations, bugging the bedroom of Martin Luther King and the telephones of a secretary who had been at the Chappaquiddick party the night Mary Jo Kopechne died. But he wasn't only interested in public figures and their employees. His 6.8 million files and 55 million index cards carried information on thousands of private citizens as well.

Not all his investigations had a direct link to national security. When Hoover died in 1972, files containing information about the philandering and drinking habits of a handful of presidents and at least seventeen senators and congressmen were found in his office. It is speculated that many more were shredded or spirited away to a secret location. But perhaps far more important than their contents was their mere existence, which stands today as a testimony of his enormous abuse of power. His files made him one of the most feared figures in twentieth-century American politics, a fact especially disturbing since he never held elective office.

In many ways, his political sex files seem to indicate that Hoover lived vicariously through the sex lives of others. While his supporters believed Hoover was a puritan at heart, trying to uphold his vision of the "American Way," his critics were convinced he gathered the files either for his own entertainment or, worse, blackmail. Said Senator Gale W. McGee, "Obviously [the sex files were] to be held in reserve for some kind of blackmail. The Gestapo operated that way, too. They were just collecting records."

Hoover was especially preoccupied with homosexuality in government. In a 1976 *Washington Post* article, John M. Goshko reported that " . . . homosexuality runs through the files like a connecting thread. Reference after reference is made to allegations that various politicians, government officials and other well-known people were homosexuals." The irony of Hoover's life remains that although he was obsessed with collecting sex data on everyone else, there is much to suggest that J. Edgar Hoover may have been a homosexual.

No one can say if Hoover was a practicing homosexual or if his sexual preference remained latent. If anyone could shield his privacy, it was the director of the FBI. But the fact remains that J. Edgar Hoover had a lifelong intimate relationship with Clyde Tolson, his number-two man at the Bureau. Neither man ever married, and they worked together every day, dined together every evening, and vacationed together, alone, for more than forty years. They had no other close personal friends but each other.

J. Edgar Hoover and his right hand man, Clyde Tolson, vacationed together for forty years.

Reports of their living arrangements conflict. Some say that each night after dinner, Hoover's chauffeur would drive Tolson home, then pick him up again the next morning en route to the office. Others say both men shared Hoover's home. Those who dared repeat the rumors nicknamed the FBI director and his assistant ''J. Edna'' and ''Mother Tolson.''

When Hoover died he willed Tolson the bulk of his half-million dollar estate. None of the estate—which included a $100,000 house; antique furnishings; stocks and bonds; forty oil, gas, and mineral leases; and cash—was left to his next of kin, who included four nieces and two nephews. The day Hoover died, Tolson resigned from the FBI in a terse, one-sentence statement. He was too emotionally shattered to accept a condolence call from the man appointed to act as Hoover's temporary replacement.

Second only to Hoover's interest in the homosexual activities of politicians was his fascination with interracial and/or group sex. His perverse curiosity also led to some of the worst abuses of his power. Between 1963 and 1966, the FBI bugged and wiretapped Martin Luther King in his Atlanta home and offices, and in the hotel rooms he occupied while carrying the banner for the civil rights movement across the country. The tapes were originally authorized by Attorney General Robert Kennedy after Hoover convinced him that King's top adviser was a communist. So scandalous were the results of the surveillance that in 1977 the Federal District Court in Washington ordered all recordings, transcripts, logs, and quotations sealed in the National Archives until the year 2027. But, as usual, much of the information has already leaked.

The most damaging of all the tapes were the first ones, recorded in the Willard Hotel in Washington, D.C., between January 5 and January 7, 1963, just weeks after Martin Luther King had been named *Time* magazine's Man of the Year. The FBI recorded a lively, drunken party involving King, some colleagues, and two black women who worked at the Philadelphia Naval Yard. The tape was garbled, but the sounds unmistakably included those of people having sex. The following morning, domestic intelligence chief William C. Sullivan wrote a lengthy memo to Hoover's number-three man in which he said, "King must, at some propitious point in the future, be revealed to the people of this country and to his Negro followers as being what he actually is—a fraud, demagogue and moral scoundrel.'' When Hoover was played highlights of the surveillance tapes, he is said to have replied gleefully, "They [the tapes] will destroy the burrhead.'' From that point on, surveillance was intensified by Hoover, who was determined to destroy the man he had also referred to as "a 'tom cat' with obsessive degenerate sexual urges.''

Subsequent surveillance included bugs in hotel rooms in Hawaii, Los Angeles, Sacramento, and Las Vegas. In Las Vegas, local officials gave the FBI a detailed memo of a rendezvous between King and a prostitute who was a police informer. The FBI, in turn, passed along the memo to Lyndon Johnson, who was always eager to hear Hoover's latest sex gossip.

While Kennedy had been close to dumping Hoover as FBI director, Johnson welcomed him back into power. Hoover once again reported directly to the president, and in May 1964, LBJ waived the mandatory-retirement-age regulation for the seventy-year-old Hoover. One reason for the honor might have been Johnson's gratitude to Hoover for turning over to him 1,200 files on Johnson's political enemies. There is no evidence, however, that Johnson, who signed the 1964 Civil Rights Act into law, ever condoned the surveillance of King. On the other hand, there is no evidence that he tried to stop it.

Towards the end of 1964, the FBI bugs of Martin Luther King were no longer used for Hoover's entertainment. Copies of transcripts and photos from the Willard Hotel surveillance were given to reporters representing *Newsweek*, the *Los Angeles Times*, the *New York Times*, the *Atlanta Constitution*, the *Augusta Chronicle*, and others. When it was apparent that no one was going to use the material, a "highlight" tape was sent to Martin Luther King's wife, Coretta. The tape was garbled, but the sounds unmistakably included those of people having sex. Upon learning of the blackmail, King said, "They [the FBI] are out to break me.''

Although shaken by the FBI's sexual blackmail Martin Luther King was never discouraged by it. On the road about twenty-five days each month, he considered sex a way to "reduce anxiety.'' Although his advisers cautioned him that disclosures of his affairs could ruin him, he continued to have many extramarital encounters.

While many of his aides at the time concentrated on keeping Dr. King out of trouble, others, such as Jesse Jackson, took the offensive, publicly denouncing Hoover's obsessive pursuit of the black leader. Jackson called Hoover's actions the ''sick and Peeping Tomism interest of the white male in black sexuality, especially as it concerns the intimate, bedroom activities of the black male.'' At one point, Jackson actually demanded that the FBI director undergo a psychiatric evaluation.

Hoover was no doubt a racist, as the employment rolls of the FBI graphically attested. In 1964, out of 6,014 special agents working for the bureau, only twenty-eight were black. And out of the twenty-eight, many were actually Hoover's personal chauffeurs and staff put on the public payroll. What's more, it was impossible to right any of his racial injustices. For his entire reign, J. Edgar Hoover answered to no one.

Hoover's financial abuses went unchecked, as did his staff abuses. He commonly took perks and freeloaded in the finest hotels around the country, and his employees were constantly pressured by Tolson to buy Hoover expensive gifts. When Hoover wanted something, such as a new appliance for his home, a collection was taken up among the agents. The money was carefully counted to make sure everyone contributed. This went on not only for each Christmas and birthday, but for more obscure occasions such as Hoover's anniversary with the bureau.

As no one dared challenge him, perhaps because of his blackmail files, Hoover's clout continued until his death in 1972, during the second administration of Richard M. Nixon. Nixon, it might be noted, had been filed under ''Obscene Matters'' after three agents reported the president's ''friendship'' with a cocktail lounge hostess he met in Hong Kong.

"I Am Not a Crook"

Scandals in the Life and Times of
Richard M. Nixon

RICHARD M. NIXON WAS involved in two of the most widely reported political scandals in American history. One he survived in memorable fashion. The other proved to be his undoing. But in between the "Checkers" speech and Watergate, there was one intriguing scandal that escaped everyone—except the agents of the FBI. Virtually unknown to the public until a 1976 *New York Times* account was the story of Marianna Liu, a beautiful Chinese cocktail-lounge hostess whose relationship with Richard Nixon became part of J. Edgar Hoover's "files."

The tale was one of international intrigue with exotic rendezvous in Hong Kong and Saigon, with flowers and perfume, and a citizenship for Marianna. When she emigrated to the United States from Hong Kong in 1969, she moved to Whittier, California, Richard M. Nixon's hometown. The following year, she visited the president in the White House on two separate occasions. The FBI might not have taken much notice except for one small fact— Marianna Liu had once been investigated to find out whether she was a communist spy. Although Marianna Liu was ultimately cleared of all suspicion, Nixon was socializing with her during the height of the FBI's investigation.

Nixon and Marianna first met in a Buddhist Temple near Shatin (outside of Hong Kong) in 1958 when he was vice president under Eisenhower and she was a part-time tour guide for a Hong

221

Richard Nixon and Marianna Liu in Hong Kong in 1966.

Kong travel agency. As all of the vice president's time was accounted for, the secret service was able to confirm there was no "hanky panky" at that time.

Marianna later told the press that it's possible they met again in 1964 and 1965 when Nixon returned to Hong Kong as a private attorney in connection with his law firm, Nixon, Mudge, Rose, Guthrie, Alexander & Mitchell. And they certainly renewed their acquaintance during another visit in 1966. Unbeknownst to either of them, the Royal Hong Kong Police observed their meetings as a result of their own investigation of Marianna's affiliations.

While admittedly hazy on the details of their earliest meetings, Marianna told the press she remembered one specific night in 1966 when Nixon came into The Den, the cocktail lounge in the Hilton Hotel where she worked as a hostess. Later that evening, by her own account, she and a waitress friend visited Nixon, along with his friend, Bebe Rebozo, in a suite in the Mandarin Hotel. The foursome shared drinks and fruit. A few months later, when Nixon returned to Hong Kong, he looked up Marianna and learned she was in the hospital. When she woke up from emergency surgery, she found a bouquet of flowers, a bottle of her favorite perfume, and a card with Nixon's New York address. She maintains, however, that there was never any intimacy.

While the Hong Kong Special Branch continued to keep a close eye on Marianna, the FBI ignored the first dispatches from their agent stationed in Hong Kong. According to an FBI source, it was a detailed account of Nixon's sexual activities. Although the bureau classified them as "hi-levs," or high level reports, the FBI didn't get officially involved until 1968, when Nixon declared his candidacy for the presidency.

"The reason the FBI investigation began was because secret meetings with Nixon [were] the exact type of blackmail Marianna would need if she was a spy," said the source, adding "The main reason the FBI felt Marianna Liu could possibly be a spy was not because of any direct action. It was more guilt by association." The most suspicious connection investigated by the FBI was Marianna's daughter, Lily, who had grown up in an orphanage. When Lily was 14, she was taken in by a communist family. Years later, Marianna and Lily were reunited. Actually there was no proof that Lily was really her daughter.

Since Marianna had fled the mainland during the Chinese revolution, she had neither a birth certificate nor official documentation. She was married (her husband had emigrated a few years after her to the United States), but no one knew whether or not they were separated. The FBI was also suspicious because the father of one of Marianna's closest friends was a general in the Red Army in China. It was also noted that Marianna owned quite a bit of real estate in Hong Kong, more than her Den salary might have afforded her.

The FBI concluded the investigation into Marianna's possible communist ties in 1969 when, according to one FBI source, President Nixon learned about the investigation and killed it. According to the FBI source, by that time there was little reason to keep it open. "We were satisfied that the allegations of her communist leanings were unfounded," the source said.

In 1969, Marianna was admitted to the United States as a permanent resident. One of her sponsors was listed as William Allman, a man at whose luxurious Hong Kong home Nixon had been a guest. Another sponsor was listed as Raymond Warren, a senior immigration official in the Nixon administration who resided in Whittier, California, Nixon's hometown. Marianna became a naturalized citizen in 1975.

In 1970, Marianna visited Nixon twice in the White House. At the time, the secret service ran a routine check with the FBI and suggested they pay close attention to the situation. Nixon, however, soon ended the relationship. In the opinion of one source, it was not because of the FBI, but because Pat "was on to it." "The FBI [was] not sure Pat knew who he was seeing, but like most wives, she knew it was someone."

The Marianna Liu file may also have influenced Nixon in 1971 to keep J. Edgar Hoover as FBI director. At that time, the president was at odds with the FBI director over his new China policy. In what still remains as one of his greatest achievements, Nixon ended the longstanding hostility with China and established diplomatic relations. In February 1972, he became the first U.S. president to travel to China, where he met with Chairman Mao Tse-tung and Premier Chou En-Lai. After Nixon returned, he called for the admission of The People's Republic of China into the United Nations.

When Hoover learned of this plan, he was outraged and told a House Appropriations Committee, "The potential threat to our national security posed by Red China still exists . . . the United States is Communist China's No. 1 enemy." Nixon wanted to fire Hoover so badly that he even rehearsed how to do it. But for some reason, perhaps Hoover's file on Marianna Liu, Nixon allowed the FBI director to remain in office until he died on May 2, 1972, at age 77. When the story first broke, Marianna denied there ever was any intimacy with Nixon. Nixon had no comment.

★ ★ ★

If the press had missed the scandal of Marianna Liu, they

certainly made up for it with their exhaustive coverage of Nixon's next scandal, Watergate. Considered the worst scandal in American history, it became the first to drive a president from office in disgrace. It also changed dramatically the role of the press in our political system.

It began on June 17, 1972, when a security guard named Frank Wills discovered a piece of tape on a latch of a door in the Watergate complex in Washington, D.C. He called the police, who caught five agents of the Committee to Reelect the President (CREEP) burglarizing the Democratic National Headquarters. For 784 days, the American public endured some of the most devastating political exposés ever, unraveled by *Washington Post* reporters Bob Woodward and Carl Bernstein, along with a Senate committee headed by Sam Ervin (D.-N.C.). Although many questions remain unanswered today, and an overabundance of conspiracy theories exist, the basic facts are still shocking:

• Nixon campaign officials ordered the break-in and installed eavesdropping devices to monitor Democratic Party activities.

• White House officials, including the president, authorized a cover-up of criminal acts and authorized payment of hush money to Watergate defendants.

• A team of Republican dirty tricksters, including Donald Segretti, wreaked havoc with various Democratic campaigns. Some of their actions were silly, such as sending unordered pizzas to Muskie headquarters. Others, such as the malicious letters Segretti distributed claiming Henry "Scoop" Jackson was a homosexual and Hubert Humphrey had consorted with a call girl, were less amusing and particularly offensive.

• A White House "Plumbers Unit" was established to plug the leaks of classified information to the press. On September 3, 1971, a date which many regard as the unofficial beginning of "Watergate," the "plumbers" broke into the Los Angeles office of Dr. Lewis J. Fielding, a psychiatrist who was treating Daniel Ellsberg. The object of the break-in was to find information to discredit Ellsberg, the government official turned anti-war activist who had leaked the Pentagon Papers, a top-secret study of the origins of the Vietnam War.

• Nixon kept an "Enemies List." According to one White House memo, its purpose was to "use the available federal machinery to screw our political enemies." The list included Carol Channing, Bill Cosby, Jane Fonda, Paul Newman, and Tony Randall, along with CBS newsman Daniel Schorr, and John Conyers of Michigan, a black congressman who was on the list with the notation, "Has known weakness for white females."

Because of modern technology, the public learned much about Nixonian politics firsthand—through audio tapes that the president made and, oddly enough, never destroyed. Presidents Kennedy and Johnson had secretly taped their visitors at the White House, as had FDR, but the practice was unknown until Alexander Butterfield revealed it to the Senate investigating committee during the Watergate hearings. Nixon at first refused to turn the tapes over, citing executive privilege. When the Supreme Court voted unanimously that he relinquish the tapes, he grudgingly relented.

It was soon discovered that one tape contained a mysterious 18½-minute gap, which sound experts agreed had been deliberately erased. The rest of the tapes only further discredited Nixon and tended to support the chain of events described by John Dean, Nixon's legal counsel, who became the star witness in the Senate hearings after he decided to give evidence of the Nixon cover-up. In one tape, the president was heard to say, "I don't give a shit what happens, I want you all to stonewall it, let them plead the Fifth Amendment, cover-up, or anything else, if it'll save it, save the plan."

★ ★ ★

The question of ethics aside, it is ironic that the Watergate break-in was completely unnecessary. Even with the events of Watergate unfolding in the daily papers, Nixon had been guaranteed a landslide victory over Democratic opponent George McGovern. McGovern's campaign began to destruct on its very own because of "The Eagleton Affair," the first scandal in United States history to topple a vice presidential nominee.

On Tuesday, July 25, 1972, Senator Thomas Eagleton of Missouri, McGovern's running mate, held a news conference in a resort lodge in the Black Hills of South Dakota and revealed that he had been hospitalized three times for mental disorders. Two Knight newspaper reporters were about to break the story and Eagleton chose to scoop them himself. While Americans had elected Warren G. Harding president despite his nervous breakdown at the age of twenty-four, Eagleton's revelation proved to be devastating. Although fully recovered, his admission of having undergone shock treatment on two separate occasions was too much for the public. And no matter how he tried to dismiss his problem as "nervous exhaustion," it was doubtful Americans were willing to place a man with a history of mental illness "a heartbeat away."

The behavior of the press created almost as much scandal as the press conference. One observer described the media as "a mob scene out of Shakespeare . . . [displaying] all the tyrannous powers that our country has traditionally feared to be vested in the hands of government." Another said, "In the Eagleton Affair, the nation had a taste, more of a taste than it liked, of the media's capacity for inhumanity to man."

The individual most eager to top the original Eagleton story proved to be syndicated columnist Jack Anderson. While Anderson has been a leading watchdog of government for decades, this incident proved to be a great public embarrassment. The afternoon following the press conference, Anderson heard that Eagleton had been arrested eleven times for drunk driving in Missouri. His source was True Davis, former ambassador to Switzerland and undersecretary of the treasury during the Johnson Administration. Although Anderson's reporter, Brit Hume, could not corroborate the information, Anderson reported it on national radio anyway.

Eagleton, who was by then in Honolulu, immediately called another news conference and denounced Anderson's story as a "damnable lie." As it turned out, True Davis said he was given the information at a political rally by a state trooper who wasn't in uniform. He wasn't even certain he was really a state trooper. To make matters worse, the *Washington Post* had ignored a similar tip from an alleged highway patrolman when "repeated checks with authorities in Missouri did not substantiate the report."

On Sunday, Anderson and Eagleton squared off on "Face the Nation." The following day, Anderson appeared on the "Today Show" to deliver a thirty-minute retraction and apology. Anderson's goof initially helped bolster Eagleton's support, but its long-term effect was minimal. On August 1, 1972, Thomas Eagleton resigned, leaving Jack Anderson's credibility and George McGovern's presidential campaign damaged in the wake. Presumably, Eagleton wasn't planning to forget about the ordeal. After he stepped down, he bought 5,000 McGovern-Eagleton buttons, 2,000 bumper stickers, and 2,000 lapel pins.

★ ★ ★

So, exactly what did Nixon know about Watergate and when did he know it? In the final analysis, no one—including the Ervin Committee, the House Judiciary Committee (chaired by Representative Peter Rodino, (D-N.J.)), the special prosecutor's office, or the hordes of reporters led by Woodward and Bernstein—could prove that Richard Nixon knew about the Watergate break-in in advance. But in the final analysis, it really didn't matter. His order of a cover-up was deemed a far worse crime than the original sin of Watergate. In televised proceedings in July 1974, Rodino's committee approved three articles of impeachment for obstruction of justice, abuse of power, and failure to comply with congressional subpoenas. "In all of this," the committee concluded, "Richard M. Nixon has acted in a manner contrary to his trust as president and subversive of constitutional government, to the great prejudice of the cause of law and justice and to the manifest injury of the people of the United States. Wherefore, Richard M. Nixon by such conduct, warrants impeachment and trial, and removal from office."

Facing an almost certain impeachment, President Nixon took off to Camp David with his speech writers. But there were no rabbits, or "Checkers," to pull out of the hat. On August 9, 1974, Richard M. Nixon resigned as president, only owning up to some "errors in judgment." A few years later, in a televised interview with David Frost, he revealed where he might have gone wrong, explaining, "When the president does it, that means it is not illegal."

Nixon was succeeded by Gerald R. Ford, who had served as vice president since 1973, when Spiro T. Agnew resigned amidst his own political scandal. Agnew had been warned of an investigation by the U.S. Attorney in Baltimore, Maryland for as many as fifty possible violations of federal bribery, extortion, conspiracy, and tax laws. The illegal activity was alleged to have taken place during his term as Baltimore County executive, from 1962 to 1967, and as Maryland governor from 1967 to 1969. Agnew was suspected of taking kickbacks totaling $250,000 from contractors during that time in exchange for construction projects. Some payments were alleged to have continued while Agnew was vice president. Agnew was also suspected of accepting a $2,500 payment in 1969 in exchange for a high-level appointment to the General Service Administration. Other payments, such as $15,000 from a retired tool manufacturer, were said to be gifts to help Agnew make ends meet over-and-above his $62,500 salary and $10,000 expense account.

The list of freebies Agnew accepted was equally scandalous. The vice president had paid a cut-rate rent on his apartment while attempting to do official favors for the corporation that owned the building. And a local supermarket chain supplied him regularly with groceries and liquor.

Faced with possible indictment, or impeachment, or both, Agnew drew upon the experience of vice president John C. Calhoun who, 146 years earlier, had been accused—and cleared—of profiting from an Army contract while serving as secretary of war. Like Calhoun, Agnew claimed he was the victim of an "ever-broadening stream of rumors." But there was one major difference between the cases; Calhoun was exonerated and Agnew was not. After a plea-bargain on tax-evasion charges, Agnew paid a $10,000 fine and received three years probation. He was also later asked to repay the State of Maryland nearly $250,000 he had received in kickbacks from state contractors.

★ ★ ★

In September 1974, President Ford granted Nixon his highly controversial pardon "for all offenses against the United States which he . . . has committed or may have committed or taken part in" during his term.

Of the rest of the Watergate alumni, twenty-five went to jail and all are free men today. None served more than fifty-two months. Several have become rich writing Watergate books and touring on the lecture circuit. Some characters have had amusing television appearances—Senator Sam Ervin in an American Express ad, John Ehrlichman on Divorce Court, and G. Gordon Liddy on Miami Vice. In real life, Liddy, the former FBI agent who planned the Watergate break-in, volunteered to be shot. His refusal to cooperate with prosecutors earned him the longest prison term of all the alumni. His book, *Will*, was made into a television movie. E. Howard Hunt, who planned the break-in with Liddy, pleaded guilty and served thirty-three months. To date, he has written fifty-six novels and nonfiction books. In 1981, he won a $650,000 libel judgment against the Liberty Lobby, which had falsely linked him to John Kennedy's assassination.

At least two key Watergate figures found God. Former deputy CREEP director Jeb Stuart Magruder became an associate pastor of the First Presbyterian Church in Burlingame, California, after serving seven months in prison for pleading guilty to conspiracy to obstruct justice. White House aide Charles W. Colson, known as Nixon's "hatchet man," most recently turned down the leadership of the PTL ministries. Colson found God in 1973, after which he pleaded guilty to the charge of obstruction of justice for his role in providing misinformation on Daniel Ellsberg. After serving seven months in prison, he wrote two books, *Born Again* and *Life Sentence*, and today works without pay as president and founder of Prison Fellowship, a nonprofit organization formed to help rehabilitate prisoners and ex-convicts.

The five Watergate burglars who were arrested at the Democratic National Committee headquarters served prison terms from thirteen to fifteen months. Bernard Barker took an early retirement from his job as a Miami building inspector in 1982 after it was discovered he was punching in more hours than he really worked. Virgilio Gonzalez, the master locksmith, became a discount shop-keeper. Eugenio Martinez became a manager at a Chevrolet dealership in Miami, and Frank Sturgis became a partner in a video-electronics store while continuing to work with rebel Cuban and Nicaraguan exiles. In 1981, he plotted a bizarre attempt to invade the U.S. naval base at Guantanamo Bay. James McCord, the electronics expert, runs a small solar-energy firm in Fort Collins, Colorado.

Former Attorney General John Mitchell, who resigned from his cabinet post in 1969 to become director of CREEP, was convicted of conspiracy, obstruction of justice, and lying under oath to cover up the Nixon administration links to Watergate. He served nineteen months before his parole on January 19, 1979, which made him the last conspirator to get out of jail. Upon his release, he told reporters, "Don't call me, I'll call you." Disbarred from the practice of law, he became a business consultant. He is one of the few Watergaters never to publish a book. Oddly enough, he tried, but when he didn't deliver a suitable manuscript, Simon & Schuster asked for their $50,000 advance back. An undisclosed settlement was negotiated. Mitchell's colorful wife, Martha, who claimed she was drugged and kept as a political prisoner throughout the Watergate period, died in 1976.

H. R. Haldeman, Nixon's chief of staff, served eighteen months in prison for conspiracy, perjury, and obstruction of justice in the Watergate cover-up. Bitter over Nixon's refusal to pardon him, Haldeman wrote *The Ends of Power*, in which he accused the president of being behind the cover-up "from Day One." His estimated earnings from the book are $500,000.

John D. Ehrlichman, Nixon's number two White House aide, was also convicted of conspiracy, obstruction of justice, and perjury, and was suspended from the practice of law. In addition, he was convicted of conspiracy in the 1971 raid on the office of Daniel Ellsberg's psychiatrist. He, too, served eighteen months in prison and has written three books: *Witness to Power*, which was about his White House days, and two novels.

John W. Dean III, Nixon's legal counsel, pleaded guilty to

conspiracy to obstruct justice and served only four months in prison due to his heroic cooperation with prosecutors. Also disbarred,
Dean made a small fortune writing and lecturing about Watergate.
Blind Ambition, his bestselling memoir, was made into a television
miniseries.

Dirty trickster Donald H. Segretti served nearly five months
for distributing illegal campaign literature and resumed his law
practice in Newport Beach, California. George A. Hearing also
pleaded guilty to distributing illegal campaign literature and
served nine months.

Dwight L. Chapin, an appointments secretary to Nixon,
served nearly eight months for lying to a grand jury about his
knowledge of campaign tricks. After his prison term, he became
publisher of a Chicago-based magazine, *Success Unlimited*.

Herbert L. Porter served twenty-seven days in jail for lying to
the FBI about the disposition of campaign funds. Frederick C.
LaRue, an aide to John Mitchell, served four and a half months for
conspiracy to obstruct justice. Herbert W. Kalmbach, Nixon's
personal lawyer, pleaded guilty to soliciting money for an illegally
formed campaign committee and to offering an ambassadorship in
return for political support. He served six months. Former Assistant Attorney General Robert C. Mardian, who went to work for
CREEP, was convicted of conspiracy in the Watergate cover-up. It
was overturned on appeal.

Egil (Bud) Krogh Jr., the Ehrlichman aide who directed the
plumbers unit from the White House, was disbarred and served
four months in prison in connection with the Ellsberg break-in. He
was readmitted to the bar in 1982.

Maurice Stans, CREEP finance chairman, was fined $5,000
on five charges of election-campaign violations.

At the age of seventy-five, former president Richard M. Nixon lives in Saddle River, N.J., with his wife, Pat. Although he was
permanently disbarred from practicing law, it is estimated that he
has made more than $3,000,000 from his books and television
appearances. In addition, he draws an $85,000 annual federal pen-
sion and receives free offices, secretarial help, and secret service

protection. Whatever his net worth is today, it is far greater than it was at the time of his humble "Checkers speech." For one, the federal government paid for security improvements on his homes in Florida and California worth $17 million, as estimated by a House committee. When he sold the properties at their new inflated value, he kept the difference. The IRS wasn't as generous with the ex-president. On April 3, 1974, they claimed Nixon owed almost $500,000 in back taxes and interest penalties for a phony deduction he had taken. Nixon had made a gift of his vice-presidential papers, many of which were mere refusals of speaking engagements. While Nixon once again stayed out of the mess, Frank De Marco, Jr., his tax preparer, and Ralph G. Newman, his appraiser, were indicted by a Watergate grand jury on charges of helping Nixon falsify his tax return by backdating the gift of the papers. Charges against De Marco were dismissed on the grounds that he had not received a fair trial. Newman was found guilty of preparing a false affidavit and of giving false information to the Internal Revenue Service.

★ ★ ★

No scandal redefined the course of American history more than Watergate, a time when the presidency saw its darkest hour. But in the bleakness of the moment, the system survived. A post-Watergate morality emerged and new laws were created. The Campaign Reform Law of 1974 provided for strict limits on campaign spending and individual campaign contributions; it also established public funding of campaigns through an optional one dollar contribution taxpayers can provide for on their income tax returns. As a direct result of the battle over Nixon's tapes, Congress declared presidential records to be federal property, a legal move that formed the basis of the Presidential Records Act of 1978. Also as a result of Watergate, Congress established the Freedom of Information Act, allowing everyone access to government files—including their own. Both the Senate and the House of Representatives strengthened their ethics committees, and in 1978, Congress passed the tough Ethics in Government Act. For a while, at least, the FBI and CIA were brought under tighter control. The new morality also filtered down to the state level, where at least four-fifths of the legislature passed financial-disclosure and conflict-of-interest laws.

Watergate ultimately redefined the virtues voters wanted to see in their president. Just as Lincoln had been elected in response to the corruption of James Buchanan, Jimmy Carter was the choice for reform-happy Americans. After promising, ''I will never lie to you,'' the humble peanut farmer won the first election of a post-Watergate president.

Post-Watergate Morality

Scandals in the Life and Times of Gerald R. Ford

MARK TWAIN ONCE said, "There is no distinctly native American criminal class except for Congress." In light of the growing number of congressmen investigated for criminal and unethical activities in the period following Watergate, he wasn't too far from the truth.

In the House of Representatives, Andrew Hinshaw (R-Calif.) was convicted of bribery, misappropriations of public funds, and petty theft. James Hastings (R-N.Y.) was convicted on twenty-eight felony counts involving kickbacks from his staff members. Wendell Wyatt (R-Ore.) pleaded guilty to violating federal campaign spending laws. Allan T. Howe (D-Utah) was arrested in Salt Lake City after soliciting two undercover policewomen who were posing as prostitutes. And the list went on, supporting the general perception: if it's a sex scandal, you're more likely to find a Democrat involved; if it's a financial scandal, you're more likely to find a Republican. But, then again, even that rule of thumb had some glaring exceptions.

With the presidency of Gerald R. Ford, Americans hoped to put the Nixon era of scandal and corruption behind them. But even more stories of political wrongdoing came to light as the climate for political purging lingered on. Reporters were more zealous than ever, and journalism schools were flooded with the next generation of Woodwards and Bernsteins. Even the politicians began

235

to police their own. While some investigations were quite noble
and reform-conscious, others proved to be costly and self-serving.
But they all had one thing in common. They were all fueled by
post-Watergate morality.

The times had clearly changed. *Everything* was reported, dis-
sected, and dealt with more firmly than ever before. In 1968, Spiro
Agnew had caused only a minor stir when he asked, ''What's the
matter with the fat Jap?'' in reference to a Japanese-American
journalist who was sleeping on a press plane. But in 1976, when
Agriculture Secretary Earl Butz uttered his racist remark: ''I'll tell
you what coloreds want. It's three things: first a tight pussy; second, loose shoes; and third, a warm place to shit, that's all,'' the
secretary was forced to resign amid the resulting uproar.

As president, Gerald Ford set a higher moral and ethical
standard for himself than previous chief executives, as did his
wife. Early on, First Lady Betty Ford established a refreshing at-
mosphere of candor in the White House when she told an inter-
viewer that she suspected her four children had probably tried pot
and that she wouldn't be surprised if her eighteen-year-old daughter, Susan, told her she was having an affair. While her comments
caused a minor scandal in their own right, Betty Ford's openness
actually helped return credibility to the White House. But while
the executive branch was finally shaping up, the legislative branch
suffered some blows—starting with a scandal which became
known as Koreagate.

Koreagate actually began with a Justice Department investigation of bribery and influence-buying by South Korean rice
broker Tongsun Park. Since as many as one hundred Democrats
appeared to be implicated, the Watergate-weary Republicans encouraged a full probe.

Park had been courting Democrats since 1967. By his own
estimate, he had given about $850,000 in gifts and cash to thirty-
one congressmen over the following decade. On August 26, 1978,
a grand jury indicted him on thirty-six counts of conspiracy, bribery, mail fraud, racketeering activities, failure to register as a for-

eign agent and making political contributions as a foreign agent. In exchange for his testimony, however, all of Park's charges were dropped. But even with his evidence, Koreagate was hardly the great Democratic financial scandal the Republicans hoped it would be. As it turned out, many of the Democrats under suspicion had received nothing more than a night on the town when they visited Korea.

In the post-Watergate spirit, the House considered disciplinary actions against eleven members. However, only three Democrats, all from California, were officially reprimanded: John McFall, for not reporting his $4,000 contribution and for making personal use of the money; Charles Wilson, for lying to the Ethics Committee in claiming he received only $100 from Park in 1970 when he had received $1,000 from him in 1975; and Edward Roybal for not reporting a $1,000 cash gift, converting it to his personal use, and lying about it. The House cleared the eight other congressmen of misconduct charges, including House Speaker Tip O'Neill, for whom Park had thrown two birthday parties costing a total of $7,500. In the end, only one congressman went to jail because of Koreagate: Richard T. Hanna (D-Calif.) had pleaded guilty to one count of conspiracy to defraud the government and served one year of his thirty-month sentence.

Although the Democrats escaped relatively unscathed from the financial scandal of Koreagate, sex scandals led to the downfall of two of the party's most powerful members. The first was Representative Wilbur Mills (D-Ark.), who, as chairman of the Ways and Means Committee for sixteen years, was one of the most formidable and important legislators in Congress.

Since the late 1960s, Mills's power had been unquestioned. His ability to steer legislation and influence fellow representatives earned him the respect of his colleagues and even the media. He was often mentioned as a presidential hopeful—until an incident which occurred at two a.m. on October 7, 1974. Mills had been stopped in his black-and-silver Lincoln for speeding and driving with no headlights. His passenger, much to the surprise of the Park

Representative Wilbur Mills visited stripper Fanne Foxe in her dressing room on December 2, 1976.

Police, was a thirty-eight-year-old stripper named Fanne Foxe. Even more surprising was that she leaped off Kutz Bridge into the Tidal Basin in what appeared to be a suicide attempt. One officer jumped in after her while the other threw a spare tire into the water to assist them to shore. No arrests were made, but the police reported that both the congressman and the stripper, who was also known as the "Argentina Firecracker," were intoxicated and displayed some mysterious injuries. Mills had a bloody nose and some scratches on his face, and Fanne had two black eyes.

The police chose not to pursue the matter any further. But as the incident was not only post-Watergate, but also the first sex scandal after Chappaquiddick, it was aggressively covered by the press. In no time, reporters unearthed most of the facts, including that Fanne, whose real name was Anabell Battistella, lived with her husband in the same luxurious apartment building where Mills lived with his wife. The night Fanne jumped into the Tidal Basin, she and the sixty-five-year-old congressman had spent a few hours in a nightclub with other friends, but not their spouses.

For a few days after the incident, Mills was absent from Congress, presumably to let the scratches on his face heal. Still, no one really took the incident too seriously. That November, after cautioning his Arkansas constituents against "drinking champagne with foreigners," he was reelected to his seat.

On December 2, however, the truth emerged when Mills appeared with Fanne on stage and backstage at the Boston Burlesque Theater. Mills said he hoped his visit to the theater would stop "innuendos" about his relationship with her. But those who witnessed his display understood more—Wilbur Mills was an alcoholic.

Fortunately, Mills finally acknowledged his problem. And the following day, as House Democrats voted away much of his power as chairman of the Ways and Means Committee, he checked into Bethesda Naval Medical Center, telling friends, "I'm terribly tired." He really must have been. Mills had spent half of his time in Congress in an alcoholic stupor. He had no recollection of many meetings at the White House and many meetings of his committee. He often read about his contributions in the next morning's paper. And while his reputation as a problem drinker preceded him in Washington circles, neither his colleagues nor the press had publicly called any attention to the matter.

Ironically, once he sought treatment, he got more attention than he needed. Mills faced a rollercoaster ride to recovery. After the congressman was released from Bethesda at the end of January, he didn't drink for two weeks. But on February 13, he bought two quarts of one-hundred-proof vodka, drank them both, and was back in the hospital within twenty-four hours. After his second stay at Bethesda, he went to the Palm Beach Institute in Florida, a private alcoholism treatment center where he had greater success. When he returned to Congress the following May, however, he had been stripped of his Ways and Means chairmanship. After four decades in the capital, he served out the remainder of his term and retired from public life.

After his political career was over, Mills became a six-figure tax consultant for Shea Gould Climenko & Casey. Fanne Foxe went on to star in "Posse From Heaven," a $17,000 feature film that was pulled from a theater in Washington the day after it premiered. And when no customers showed up for its premier in Jacksonville, Florida, it was pulled from that theater, too.

While the front-page exposure of the Fanne Foxe affair wasn't enough to inspire sweeping reform on the Hill, it was certain to make at least some congressmen just a bit more nervous. At the height of the scandal, one Democrat pointed out the window to the Potomac River and warned his mistress that if any of his women "ever did that to me, they'd be down there—down there, six feet under." It turned out to be an idle threat. Two years later, when Elizabeth Ray blew the whistle on her affair with Ohio's Wayne Hays, the only thing that sank to the bottom of the Potomac River was his thirty-year career. And few people were sorry to see it happen.

Stories of Wayne Hays's arrogance and abuse of power had been legion. The House barbers hated him because, as chairman of the House Administration Committee, he had eliminated their tips.

The elevator operators hated him because he had removed their stools. One day, when he was dissatisfied with a hamburger in the House dining room, he walked in the kitchen and fired the chef on the spot. His treatment of fellow congressmen wasn't any better. He once called Don Riegle (D-Mich.) "a potato-head." Another colleague explained, "[Carl] Albert may be the Speaker, but Wayne Hays is the czar." Needless to say, when the story broke in the *Washington Post* on May 25, 1976, that Wayne Hays, at the age of sixty-five, not only had a thirty-three-year-old blonde mistress named Elizabeth Ray, but that he kept her on the federal payroll as a secretary for nearly two years—despite her claims that she couldn't type, couldn't file, and couldn't even answer the phone—many agreed it couldn't happen to a nicer guy.

At first, one of the most surprising aspects of the scandal was that it broke just five weeks after Hays had married Pat Peak, his legislative aide in his hometown office in Ohio. But it was this second marriage, in fact, that triggered the chain of events which led to the disclosure. When Elizabeth asked Hays what was to become of her after the nuptials, he replied, "Well I guess that'll make you mistress #1." Not surprisingly, Ray caused such a scene in his office that Hays ordered the police to escort her off the Capitol grounds. Immediately afterwards, she phoned Marion Clark at the *Washington Post* who, with Rudy Maxa, broke the story.

Once the scandal hit the front pages, Hays immediately denounced the report as the fantasy of "a very sick young woman." It seemed easy to attack her credibility. Elizabeth Ray claimed she had been romantically involved with many other congressmen— and even former vice president Hubert Humphrey—before Hays. Unfortunately, none had treated her much better. The vice president arranged for her to sleep with a doctor friend first. One congressman suggested that they have an intimate dinner in her Arlington, Virginia, apartment. Although he promised to supply the food, he arrived with an open bottle of wine and a slab of melted brie wrapped in a napkin, all of which he had lifted from a banquet he had attended on the way over. For this, she had set the table with candlesticks.

Elizabeth Ray in 1973, when she was Miss Virginia at the International USA pageant.

Within hours of the publication of the *Post* exposé, the FBI began an investigation into the charges that Hays had placed Elizabeth in her staff job with the Oversight Subcommittee in exchange for sexual favors. More than two dozen members of the House, both Democrats and Republicans, filed a letter with the Ethics Committee calling for an investigation of possible violations of the new House code of official conduct that was created after Watergate. Two clauses seemed to be in violation: one, that a member shall conduct himself at all times in a manner which shall reflect "credibility" on the House, and the other forbidding members to hire employees who do not "perform duties commensurate with the compensation" received.

Finally, after two days of insisting Elizabeth's story was a fabrication, Wayne Hays admitted that he did, indeed, have a "personal relationship" with her. He denied, however, that she was on the payroll as his mistress for her $14,000-a-year salary. In an address before the House of Representatives, he said:

> I stand by my previous denial of Miss Ray's allegation that she was hired to be my mistress.
>
> I further stand by my statement that Miss Ray is a seriously disturbed young lady, and I deeply regret that our relationship, and its termination, has apparently greatly aggravated both her emotional and psychological problems. I am now sixty-five years old, and I have been privileged to serve in this House for twenty-eight years. I know my days on earth are numbered, and my service in this body may well be also . . . but I stand here before you today . . . with my conscience now clear.
>
> To my other staff members, to my colleagues in the House, and to the people of Ohio, who have all stood by me in this hour of need, you have my undying gratitude. Only time will tell whether Miss Ray will be successful in destroying my marriage.
>
> I hope that when the time comes to leave this House, which I love, Wayne Hays may be remembered as mean, arrogant, cantankerous and touchy, but I hope Wayne Hays will never be thought of as dishonest.

A few weeks later, Hays took an overdose of sleeping pills. Although he recovered from his suicide attempt, he decided he could not rescue his political career and resigned from the House of Representatives. Elizabeth Ray wrote a novelization of her experiences in Washington called *The Washington Fringe Benefit*. She is still pursuing an acting career in New York.

★ ★ ★

While the House was busy policing its own during the post-Watergate period, the Senate had its hands full probing the CIA which, in 1975, was the target of an investigation by the Select Committee to Study Government Operations chaired by Frank Church (D-Idaho). After taking more than 10,000 pages of sworn testimony from over one hundred witnesses, Church issued a report laden with tales of illegal and unethical activities. These activities ranged from assassination attempts on foreign leaders to drug experiments on unwitting citizens. In at least one of these experiments a man killed himself while under the influence of LSD.

The CIA had regularly abused civil rights, compiling files on 10,000 American "dissidents." Protest groups were infiltrated, mail was monitored, and average citizens were targeted by surveillance units with such names as Cable Splicer, Garden Plot, Leprechaun, and Chaos. At its peak, Operation Chaos had fifty employees, who accumulated an estimated 7,200 "personality" files; over 11,000 memoranda, reports, and letters from the FBI; over 3,000 disseminations to the FBI; and almost 3,500 memos for internal use only. In addition, 12,000 cables were generated to high-level government officials. The Chaos computer system indexed 300,000 names of members of organizations which had nothing to do with espionage. At least eight studies were conducted to discern whether or not the anti-war movement was being controlled by a foreign country. Although there was never any evidence to support this contention, private mail was opened, phones were tapped, and people surreptitiously photographed.

On the international front, CIA activities were equally disturbing. As early as 1953, the CIA had mounted its first covert operation to overthrow a foreign government, targeting the prime minister of Iran, Mohammed Mossadegh. A popular and legitimate leader, Mossadegh had strained American relations when he nationalized his country's oil fields. But in spite of the full support of his people, the CIA (with President Eisenhower's approval) paid money to street gangs, police, and soldiers to overthrow him for the Shah, who allowed American oil companies to take over almost half of Iran's oil production.

That covert operation was just the beginning. As Church's report outlined, there were at least five more CIA attempts to overthrow and/or assassinate foreign leaders, including Cuban Premier Fidel Castro, Dominican Dictator Rafael Trujillo, Congolese Nationalist Leader Patrice Lumumba, Chile's Salvador Allende, and South Vietnam President Ngo Dinh Diem.

TRUJILLO: After thirty-one years of his corrupt, dictatorial rule over the Dominican Republic, General Trujillo was assassinated on May 30, 1961. The CIA is alleged to have supplied the rifles to the assassins who had not been able to steal any from their heavily guarded military bases.

LUMUMBA: In February, 1961, Lumumba was kidnaped by Katanga tribesmen and murdered. The CIA is alleged to have supported President Moise Tshombe of Katanga over Lumumba, whom they feared had Soviet sympathies.

DIEM: On November 1, 1963, Diem was killed after a military coup, which allegedly had been planned with the knowledge of Dean Rusk and Averell Harriman at the State Department, Robert S. McNamara and Roswell Gilpatric at the Defense Department, and Edward R. Murrow at the U.S. Information Agency.

ALLENDE: On September 11, 1973, Allende reportedly killed himself following a military coup, which had been financed by the CIA.

CASTRO: At least eight plots were hatched against Castro in the late spring or early summer of 1960, ranging from poison cigars and skin-diving suits dusted with lethal powder, to seashells charged with explosives, and a substance created to make Castro's trademark beard fall out. One assassination attempt by an old girlfriend of Castro's failed when the poison pills she carried in her cold-cream jar melted. Through Chicago crime boss Sam Giancana, the Mafia was offered $150,000 for a successful hit on the Cuban leader. Well over a quarter of a century later, Castro is alive and well, having outlived almost everyone who tried to kill him.

★ ★ ★

Long after the Ford Administration had departed from the White House, there were two last scandals brought before the public, both of a highly personal, rather than political, nature. The first involved Nelson Rockefeller who had filled the vacancy of vice president in 1974 after Nixon resigned and Ford became president. Rockefeller had escaped the slightest hint of scandal throughout all his years of public service, first as governor of New York, then as a member of the House of Representatives, and finally throughout his tenure as vice president. At the time of his nomination, his record and personal finances were closely scrutinized at House Judiciary Committee hearings. Although a financial adviser testified that the Rockefeller family had total assets of $1.034 billion, no scandals were to be found. He maintained his reputation until January 26, 1979—the night he died of a fatal heart attack in the company of a twenty-five-year-old blonde aide named Megan.

Megan Marshak had worked for Rockefeller since joining the vice president's staff in 1976 as assistant press secretary. After Rockfeller completed his term as vice president in January 1977, Megan remained on his staff as a $60,000-a-year special assistant, working on his extensive art collection. When he had his heart attack at 10:15 p.m., Marshak and Rockefeller, a married father of six (four children were from his first marriage), were allegedly working alone on an art book.

The story might have ended there had not a Rockefeller family press spokesman said that the seventy-year-old former vice president was "having a ball" when he died. No doubt, it was an unfortunate choice of words. But if the press found the comment amusing, they took their investigation of it very seriously. For the following two weeks, reporters untangled the many mysterious and contradictory reports surrounding Rockefeller's death with investigative intensity. Their efforts were not in vain. By the time they were finished, the Who, What, Why, Where, and When had all changed from the original report.

Daily News columnist Jimmy Breslin was the first to question what work the two were actually doing. While there was food and wine on a table in the room, he reported, there were no books or papers about. On February 4, the *Sunday New York Times* was credited with brightening brunches across New York City when they added a clothing report. Megan was wearing "a long, black evening gown," they said, and Rockefeller was "lying on the floor, clad in dark trousers and socks but no shoes," when a paramedic team arrived on the scene.

It was also discovered that the call to the police was not made by Megan, as originally reported, but by a girlfriend she asked to help in the emergency. What's more, that call occurred an hour later than first stated. Of that little disclosure the *Sunday Washington Post* quipped, "Copious in all things, Nelson in the end produced a sixty-minute gap where Nixon could only manage 18½."

Despite the press's post mortem, Megan Marshak remained silent on her relationship with Rockefeller and the mysterious circumstances surrounding his death. In the end, perhaps, Rockefeller revealed more. His will forgave a $45,000 interest-fee loan he once made to Megan so that she could buy an apartment. The family, however, seemed to take it all in stride. When Rockefeller's eighteen-year-old grandson, Steven, was asked on a morning talk show what he would say to Megan Marshak if he met her, he simply replied, "I hope you made my grandfather happy."

★ ★ ★

The final tale of the Ford years was one that tested the personal courage of the entire first family. Six years after leaving Washington, former First Lady Betty Ford revealed the inside story of her battle against alcohol and drug addiction. It was one of the most inspiring stories to come out of the White House. Had it not been for Betty Ford's integrity and candor, it might have also been one of the most scandalous; but what Mrs. Ford did for women who shared her experience of mastectomy, she was determined to do for those trapped by drug abuse. What would have been an embarrassment for other first ladies became a noble crusade for her.

Betty Ford's addiction began thirty years earlier, when she was first prescribed daily medication for a pinched nerve in her neck. It became a problem when she began to mix vodka with her daily dosage, a combination that allowed her to move ''into a wonderful fuzzy place where everything was fine'' and she could cope.

Hers was a quiet addiction that passed largely unnoticed. She wasn't loud or embarrassing nor did she act out any other characteristics common of a drunk. It wasn't until the Fords left the White House in 1977 that her health deteriorated and her family noticed she was shuffling around, falling down, drinking her dinners and slurring her speech. In her 1987 book *Betty, A Glad Awakening*, she recalled the depths to which she had fallen: ''April 1, 1978. I was dying and everyone knew it but me. I sat on the couch in the living room of our Palm Springs house, my husband's arm around me and I cried.''

Betty Ford cried as the former president and their children— Mike, Jack, Steve, and Susan—along with two doctors and a nurse and a couple of friends, gathered around her for an ''intervention,'' the event in which she was confronted, with love and care, about her addiction. Each family member gave testimony, helping to define the problem through vivid examples such as the night she fell and cracked her ribs and chipped a tooth.

The technique worked. Immediately after the intervention, Betty Ford began a week-long, supervised detoxification. On April 7, she entered a treatment program in Long Beach, California. Years later, after a full recovery, she would raise money for another treatment center there, named the Betty Ford Clinic in her honor. Today Mrs. Ford continues to serve as a role model for other former drug and alcohol abusers, many of whom were celebrities. One alumni of Long Beach was even a first family member like herself. After creating a series of scandals for the next administration, Jimmy Carter's brother, Billy, sought treatment there, too.

"I've Committed Adultery in My Heart Many Times"

Scandals in the Life and Times of Jimmy Carter

ELECTED IN 1976, JIMMY Carter proved to be one of the most moral men ever to occupy the highest office. While the God-fearing Baptist president was destined to be criticized for other shortcomings, no one could ever show the slightest impropriety in his personal or public morality. That doesn't mean no one tried, however. During his 1976 campaign for president, Carter found himself, like many candidates before him, in the midst of a sex scandal. Unlike his predecessors, however, he was hounded not for an affair in which he participated, but rather, for one he had only thought about.

In the November 1976 issue of *Playboy Magazine*, which hit the stands just weeks before the election, Carter revealed that throughout his life he had lusted after women other than his wife—in his mind! The comments only meant to reflect his interpretation of Christian teachings, but the article, which became known as the "lust-in-my-heart interview," was seen as a disgrace in the climate of post-Watergate morality.

Early on in the campaign, his religious upbringing had, in fact, helped Carter jump to the head of the pack of eighteen Democractic candidates. But once he secured the nomination, his strong Baptist beliefs became controversial. Questions emerged concerning Carter's religion and how it influenced his stand on such key issues as birth control, abortion, and homosexual rights. To address the growing concerns, Carter decided to grant an in-depth interview to *Playboy* magazine. He apparently chose *Playboy* after he saw the successful results of an interview that the magazine had conducted with California Governor Jerry Brown. Brown had announced his candidacy the week his own interview was published and actually beat Carter in the first few primaries.

Carter's *Playboy* interview was designed to cover a variety of issues. On the personal side, he was asked questions regarding his marriage—if he ever had trouble adjusting, and if he ever spoke to his wife about the possibility of assassination. On the political side, he addressed issues such as apartheid and the Middle East crisis. Many of Carter's responses were expressive, thoughtful, even lively, but none compared to his comments regarding religion.

When the issue of personal morality was first broached, Carter set out to explain how his religious beliefs, as president, would translate to political action. He said he believed, for example, that civil laws that govern personal behavior such as marijuana use, sodomy, and homosexuality should be left to individual states, not the federal government. The discussion of religion continued as Carter explained more personal aspects of his religious practices, such as how he used daily prayer to help control his blood pressure. As the interview was winding down, no one was prepared for the dramatic turn that was about to come. As the two *Playboy* interviewers stood in the doorway of Carter's living room, ready to leave, the 1976 Democratic nominee tried to explain, for one last time, the influence of religion in his life. His effort went like this:

> I try not to commit a deliberate sin. I recognize that I'm going to do it anyhow, because I'm human and I'm tempted. And Christ set some almost impossible standards for us. Christ said, ''I'll tell you that anyone who looks on a woman with lust in his heart has already committed adultery.''
>
> I've looked on a lot of women with lust. I've committed adultery in my heart many times. This is something that God recognizes

I will do—and I have done it—and God forgives me for it. But that doesn't mean that I condemn someone who not only looks on a woman with lust but who leaves his wife and shacks up with somebody out of wedlock.

Christ says, Don't consider yourself better than someone else because one guy screws a whole bunch of women while the other guy is loyal to his wife. The guy who's loyal to his wife ought to not be condescending or proud because of the relative degree of sinfulness. One thing that Paul Tillich said was that religion is a search for the truth about man's existence and his relationship with God and with his fellow man; and that once you stop searching and think you've got it made—at that point, you lose your religion. Constant reassessment, searching in one's heart—it gives me a feeling of confidence.

I don't inject these beliefs in my answers to your secular questions.

(*Carter clenched his fist and gestured sharply.*)

But I don't think I would ever take on the same frame of mind that Nixon or Johnson did—lying, cheating, and distorting the truth. Not taking into consideration my hope for my strength of character, I think that my religious beliefs alone would prevent that from happening to me. I have that confidence. I hope it's justified.

Weeks before the interview was due out on the newsstands, *Playboy* released "preprints" to Associated Press and the Today Show, under the condition they agree to summarize the entire interview and not lead with the "lust" quotes. They agreed, but by midafternoon on September 20, headlines coast-to-coast blared, "SEX, SIN, TEMPTATION!" and "I'VE COMMITTED ADULTERY IN MY HEART!"

Perhaps because he had used the word "screw," or perhaps because it had been a dull campaign, the *Playboy* interview created such an uproar that it brought Carter's presidential campaign to a halt. The effects, however, were only temporary. In the end, voters believed in his personal integrity and elected Jimmy Carter the thirty-ninth president of the United States.

★ ★ ★

As president, Carter fulfilled his campaign promise to bring a voice of conscience to the White House and never lie to the American people. But while Jimmy Carter never suffered any direct charges of misconduct, key members of his White House staff were investigated for criminal and ethical wrongdoings. Even his own brother came under scrutiny.

Earlier "first brothers" had raised an eyebrow or two. Lyndon Johnson's brother Sam drank too much, wrote a bad check or two, and, at one point, was assigned a secret service agent to keep him out of trouble. Richard Nixon had his brother Donald's phone tapped for more than a year in order to keep him in line after learning of Donald's involvement in a number of suspicious business deals, one of which included a $205,000 loan from billionaire Howard Hughes. But none of the other first brothers ever matched the level of embarrassment caused by Jimmy Carter's brother Billy.

At first it looked like the president's brother had brought the Beverly Hillbillies to the White House. The public seemed fairly amused by his redneck charm, which was highlighted by such efforts as the Vancouver World Belly Flop and Cannonball Diving Contest and "Billy Beer." He was perhaps just a slight presidential annoyance. But all that changed with the revelation that he had accepted $220,000 from the Libyan government.

Relations with the Arab nation had been strained since 1973 when Nixon blocked the $60 million sale of eight C-130 Hercules military jet-transport planes to Libya. President Carter had stalled the transfer of three Boeing 747s, two 727s, and 400 trucks already bought for $300 million. Supporting the Libyan terrorist regime of Muammar Qaddafi was much too risky, especially for Carter, whose efforts were more sharply focused on the Camp David peace accord between Israel and Egypt.

If the Libyans were looking for a messenger to plead their case to the president, they could not have made a more unlikely choice than Billy Carter. But as one State Department expert said, "It simply shows a standard Mideast mind-set—the back door to a leader is through his family."

Billy Carter posed with a Libyan official in front of a photograph of Qaddafi in 1978.

The first overture was easy enough. Billy was offered a free trip to Libya, which he accepted. When he returned, he founded the Libyan-Arab-Georgia Friendship Society, although it was never incorporated. If his public relations efforts on behalf of the Libyans didn't get enough attention, Billy certainly did. In January 1979, while awaiting the arrival of a delegation of Libyans, Billy

Carter urinated on the airport runway and made headlines around the world.

One unexpected result of the attention, however, was the Justice Department's demand that Billy register as a foreign agent, as required by a 1938 law. That request was ignored, as was the second. Billy stirred up even more bad feelings later, when he explained why he was involved with such a faction in the first place. "There's a helluva lot more Arabians than there is Jews." When the American Jewish community responded with outrage, Billy huffed, "They can kiss my ass."

For the president, "Billygate" had become a serious liability. On February 27, 1979, President Carter tried to distance himself by explaining that his brother was seriously ill and that he had no control over him. But the damage had been done. As one leading Democratic fundraiser explained, "The Billy Carter connection is the killing blow [for reelection]. It finishes off President Carter with the Jewish vote all over the country. I'm sorry about that because he deserves better."

Driven by the momentum of an election year, Billygate culminated in a full-fledged Senate inquiry. It didn't even matter that on March 6, Billy checked into the Long Beach Naval Hospital's Alcohol and Drug Rehabilitation Service, the treatment center where former First Lady Betty Ford had been hospitalized. The country wanted to know why Billy accepted $220,000 from the Libyan government and what, if anything, he did in return. Just as delicate an issue was the president's role in protecting his brother from prosecution following Attorney General Benjamin Civiletti's revelation that he had personally discussed Billy's situation with the president on June 17. While it turned out that Billy did very little for the Libyans and never had any influence on foreign policy whatsoever, cries of "cover-up" echoed through the Republican ranks and the public approval rating of Jimmy Carter sank to 22 percent, the lowest rating of any president since the poll began in 1939. Even Richard Nixon had a 25 percent rating before he resigned over Watergate.

Of course, the Iranian hostage crisis certainly had a great deal to do with his poor rating, but, then again, so did the other serious scandals which tainted his personal staff. There was, in fact, a fair share of misconduct going on all around this same president who had promised reform. But as in the administration of Ulysses S. Grant, many scandals were exposed in the first place because of the president's desire to clean up the government. Under Carter, new laws and rules of ethics made it easier to do. What he didn't expect, however, was that many investigations would start right under his own nose—or at least the noses of two of his closest aides.

Perhaps as a sign of the times, two key Carter aides wound up in the middle of the first official cocaine investigation in American politics. First, White House Chief of Staff Hamilton Jordan was accused of using the drug, once at a party in Beverly Hills in 1977, and once at New York's Studio 54 in 1979. Jordan's case marked the first time a special prosecutor was appointed to investigate a government official, an option only made possible by the 1978 Ethics in Government Act.

Jordan had been the subject of some criticism ever since it was reported that he spit a drink on a woman in a bar, certainly a tasteless act. But through it all, President Carter stuck by his man, as did the first lady. In what was described as a "spirited defense" of Jordan amidst the cocaine allegations, Rosalynn Carter described him as "a very clean-cut, very decent young man." She added, "Hamilton Jordan is as different from his image as anybody I know." By 1980, the charges were dismissed for lack of evidence. But the investigation had already contributed to a decline in public confidence in the president during a critical election year.

It didn't help election matters any more when President Carter's campaign manager resigned on September 14, 1980, after it was revealed that he, too, was under investigation by a special prosecutor for the use of cocaine. The allegations against Tim Kraft, who had been senior White House aide to Carter before taking his campaign post, had grown out of the Hamilton Jordan investigation. Kraft was alleged to have used cocaine on August

10, 1978, in New Orleans, and on November 18, 1979, in San Francisco. Like the Jordan probe, the Kraft investigation fizzled out quickly. On March 21, 1981, the special prosecutor closed the inquiry and filed court papers, which said the evidence against Kraft did not warrant an indictment.

A separate investigation into the financial activities of Budget Director Bert Lance, on the other hand, led to an indictment on thirty-three counts ranging from conspiracy, to falsifying financial statements, to the misapplication of bank funds. Lance was forced to resign in the wake of the three-year government investigation, which cost $7 million. His 1980 trial involved 20,000 documents and 173 witnesses. When it was over, Lance was exonerated— sort of. The judge dismissed fourteen counts because of insufficient evidence and the jury acquitted Lance and three business associates on all but six of the rest. One of the remaining charges was that Lance, while employed as a Georgia bank president, had improperly secured one million dollars in loans to his wife, son, and friends by falsifying financial statements. The prosecution claimed that Lance had hidden $810,000 in debts to appear more wealthy than he actually was.

In lieu of a retrial on the remaining charges, Lance agreed to sign a consent agreement promising not to violate banking laws in the future. In February 1986, he agreed to pay a $50,000 fine and was barred from holding any post in a federally insured bank. One positive result of the scandal was that Congress enacted a law to put stricter limits on banks' transactions with their executives.

Although the investigation had ended, Bert Lance's troubles were far from over. In a classic political gaffe, 1984 presidential candidate Walter Mondale hired the controversial Lance as the general chairman of his political campaign. Mondale had "personally underestimated" the problems the appointment would cause. When the negative response poured in, Lance resigned.

★ ★ ★

Outside of the president's personal staff and family, seeds for more post-Watergate scandals were planted. During the Carter years, drug abuse had become a more pronounced problem on

Capitol Hill. Few details surfaced, however, until 1982, when a
House Ethics Committee investigation into drug use reported sub-
stantial evidence that three members of Congress—John L. Burton and Barry Goldwater, Jr., both of California and Frederick W.
Richmond, of New York—used cocaine and other drugs while
they were in office. In addition, the report said there was evidence
that twenty Senate employees and twenty-two House employees
were involved in illicit use or distribution of drugs, and that several
pages had used marijuana, cocaine, or pills since 1978.

Burton and Richmond admitted their drug use after being
granted immunity from prosecution. Goldwater denied he ever
bought or used drugs of any kind. Although the report said, "Evidence obtained by the special counsel indicates that he purchased
drugs on one or two occasions in 1979 or 1980," Goldwater said,
"I deny it uncategorically." At the time the report was released,
Goldwater had already lost a bid for a senate seat and was pursuing
a career in finance. Burton and Richmond had also retired from
public service. Burton began a law practice in San Francisco after
attending a drug and alcohol treatment program in Arizona. Richmond, a millionaire from Brooklyn, served nine months in a federal prison for income-tax evasion and possession of marijuana.
When he pleaded guilty to those charges, the government agreed
not to prosecute him on potential charges of purchasing marijuana
and cocaine. In 1983, Goldwater was cleared of suspicion by the
Justice Department.

If the emergence of marijuana and cocaine in politics signalled changing times for the Congress, "Abscam" heralded a
new era of investigative fervor for the FBI. The dramatic twenty-
three-month undercover operation showed that the bureau had certainly come a long way since the death of J. Edgar Hoover. No
longer was the FBI interested in personal, or sexual, misconduct.
They were looking for corruption and conflict of interest on the
public payroll.

When Abscam first broke in February 1980, everyone snickered at the thought of a phony Arab sheik enticing congressmen
into accepting bribes—on videotape. But there was little else fun-

ny about it. Abscam, shorthand for Arab-scam, cost the FBI close to one million dollars, as one hundred agents set out on their "sting" in an elaborate series of hoaxes and disguises. A "sheik" named Kambir Abdul Rahman (actually an ex-convict in disguise) set out to buy influence in Congress. And one by one, congressmen showed up at the FBI's rented house on W Street in Washington, D.C., ready to sell their influence.

Some of the Abscam images were appalling. Raymond Lederer (D-Pa.) and John Murphy (D-N.Y.) were videotaped taking $50,000 each. Frank Thompson, Jr. (D-N.J.) was also on tape accepting a bribe. In addition, Michael "Ozzie" Myers (D-Pa.) was heard boasting, "Bullshit walks, money talks." John Jenrette (D-S.C.) was videotaped telling an undercover FBI agent, "I've got larceny in my blood." Richard Kelly (R-Fla.) was taped at the sheik's house stuffing $25,000 into his suit, coat, and pants pockets, asking: "Does it show?" Only Senator Larry Pressler (R-S.D.) performed honorably on tape, telling the Abscam sheik, "Wait a minute, what you are suggesting may be illegal."

Pressler had been tested by the FBI because, basically, they thought he might be vulnerable to payoffs during the time when he was trying to run for president but was in serious need of cash to continue his campaign. On the other hand, the others became Abscam targets because they had more questionable reputations to begin with. On January 16, 1979, a year before Abscam, Myers had been charged with assault and battery when a cashier in an Arlington, Virginia, hotel bar accused him of hitting and kicking her. Myers pleaded no contest to the charges and received a six-month suspended sentence.

Murphy had been the subject of numerous federal investigations and two House Standards Committee probes in the five years prior to Abscam. In 1973, he was investigated for his role in arranging a meeting between an alleged Mafia official and the secretary of the Interstate Commerce Commission. He also was investigated for taking kickbacks from the foundation established to manage the financial interests of the deposed Shah of Iran—while he served as the director. In 1977 and 1978, he was scrutinized for his role in Koreagate, although the Standards Committee found no evidence of wrongdoing. And in 1978 he was suspected of pressuring the Navy to settle a cost overrun claim against the government made by a private firm in his hometown district.

Jenrette had also been the subject of numerous FBI and grand jury probes before Abscam. In 1975, he was accused of taking a contribution from a contractor who was later hired to do work on a South Carolina federal building. (The FBI never found evidence of criminal activity.) In 1976, Jenrette's business partner charged that he had converted company profits to personal use. (They settled out of court.) That same year, Jenrette's real estate company was alleged to have sold underwater land to unsuspecting buyers, although the grand jury never issued any indictments. And in 1979, the FBI investigated Jenrette's possible connection to a drug smuggling operation in Darlington County, South Carolina, after a close friend of Jenrette's was arrested for smuggling 1,400 pounds of marijuana into the state. It was suspected that Jenrette might have used his influence to help the smuggler gain access to key airstrips.

As a Florida state circuit judge, Kelly had once been impeached for harassing lawyers and fellow judges (the impeachment was dismissed). He was later ordered to undergo psychiatric tests for which he was given a clean bill of health. Years later, his mental health report enabled him to boast: "I'm the only member [of the House of Representatives] certified to be sane." But those who watched his Abscam defense strategy in motion must have thought he was crazy. Kelly claimed that he had only been playing along with the sheik, trying to make him believe that he was on the take as part of his own investigation of the influence-peddlers whom he presumed were backed by organized crime. Unfortunately for Kelly, the only Republican snared by Abscam, his jurors didn't play along with him and he was convicted.

Ray Lederer's response was almost as innovative. After the scandal broke, he declared the $50,000 given to him by the "FBI Arab" to the House of Representatives' Finance Office. He claimed he was convinced that it was all right to take the money under the rules of the Ethics Committee, which permitted a congressman to earn up to $10,000 beyond his salary. His constituents believed his story and reelected him for another term. Soon after, however, he resigned his seat, as did Harrison Williams (D.-N.J.), the only senator stung in the operation. Williams, indicted on nine counts including bribery, conspiracy, and accepting outside compensation to perform official duties, became the fourth U.S. senator ever convicted of a crime while in office.

With Williams convicted on all nine counts, the final body count for Abscam was nineteen sentenced to jail, including six congressmen and some local politicians and businessmen.

Lederer, Myers, Williams, Thompson, and Murphy were each sentenced to three years. Jenrette got two years, and Kelly was sentenced to eighteen months. Most were paroled early for good behavior and none ran for reelection, closing the chapter on what finally emerged as the most serious financial scandal for 20th-century Democrats.

★ ★ ★

Although Abscam recalled some of the bleak moments of Watergate, it did have a somewhat lighter side. Livening up the front pages throughout the ordeal was Rita Jenrette, the beautiful, blonde, congressman's wife from South Carolina. While her husband, John, was sent off to a Federal prison in Atlanta, Rita parlayed his downfall into a new career, which included a *Playboy* layout, a paperback book called *My Capitol Secrets*, a few B-movie roles, and a country-western song, "It Gives Me the Low Down Blues Ever Since You Found Money Stashed in My Shoe." The song had been inspired by her real-life drama of finding $250,000 of FBI bribe money in her husband's brown suede shoe.

For a while after her husband's arrest, Rita remained the dutiful Washington wife, blaming John's actions on alcoholism, which she said caused him to do a variety of terrible things. On one occasion, she recalled, she found her husband "drunk, undressed, and lying on the floor in the arms of a woman . . . old enough to be his mother." But John went through rehabilitation and all was forgiven. At the time Rita said, "John's sober. We're happier now than we've ever been."

While John Jenrette talked with reporters following his 1980 guilty verdict in the ABSCAM trial, a tear streamed down wife Rita's cheeks.

In part to raise the $250,000 Jenrette needed for her husband's legal fees, and in part as a way of getting back at the Washington wives who had snubbed her for being a little too blonde and a little too attractive, Rita posed for *Playboy* magazine and confessed that she and her husband had once made love on the steps of the Capitol. That wild abandon would become little more than a memory as Rita soon found John reverting to his old womanizing ways. Only this time, she divorced him. When she appeared on the Phil Donahue Show, John phoned in and their breakup was broadcast nationally.

For Rita, life after Abscam also included a few television guest spots and a low-budget horror film called *Zombie Island Massacre*, followed by an involvement with churches and charities and a stint in a Wall Street brokerage firm. But for better or for worse, she did manage to brighten a dark moment in politics.

Lobbyist Paula Parkinson sparked an FBI ''sex for votes'' investigation of Congress.

★ ★ ★

At the same time Rita Jenrette's *Playboy* issue was sizzling on the newsstands, another blonde bombshell was sending shock-waves across Capitol Hill. Newspapers across the country revealed that Paula Parkinson, a lobbyist from 1978 to 1981, had been scoring a lot more than votes around Washington. The scandal had such far reaching implications that the FBI quickly stepped in to investigate.

The investigation of whether or not Paula had traded sex for votes began in March 1981, after the *Wilmington* (Del.) *News Journal* printed a sensational account of a Florida golfing vacation Paula took with three congressmen and six other men, fourteen months earlier. At the time there was also speculation that the thirty-year-old lobbyist had secretly videotaped several congressmen in compromising positions. If that wasn't enough, Paula's husband, Hank, granted an interview in which he apologized for creating "a sexual Frankenstein." As the story unfolded, the latest Capitol Hill sex scandal was nicknamed "Parkinson's disease," because, as local humorists noted, it really makes your hands shake.

The three congressmen with the shakiest hands turned out to be Illinois's Tom Railsback, Indiana's Dan Quayle, and Delaware's Thomas B. Evans, Jr., all Republicans. They were identified as the men who shared the Florida cottage with Paula. Railsback readily admitted that he and two colleagues "made a big mistake." He confessed, "When we got to the house and saw that Paula was there, we should have either asked her to move out, or we should have moved out. . . . Not moving out was my first mistake. Not telling my wife about it when I got home was the second." Quayle was pleased to reveal to the press that he had shared his room with tobacco lobbyist William Hecht. "I guess you might want to make something homosexual out of it," he joked.

Evans, on the other hand, went into seclusion after the story broke and denied he had been improperly lobbied. He said, "I deny any of the vicious implications. . . . I have never let any influence other than the best interests of the citizens of the state of

Delaware and my country affect my vote." According to Paula, she and Evans shared the only room in the house with a king-sized bed and private bath. She also revealed that she and Evans had begun their "romantic lark" two months before the Florida vacation.

For her part, Paula could not understand what all the fuss was over. By her own estimate, she had had affairs with "less than a dozen" congressmen. More specifically, it was one senator and seven congressmen. All but one were Republicans, and several were supporters of the Moral Majority. According to Paula, she had sex with three in their offices. "The whole thing was knowing that someone could burst in at any moment," she said, explaining the reasoning behind their unusual choice of locale. Paula engaged in sex with another congressman several times in the garage of his office building. "The only way I could reach him was on the floor [of the House]," she recalled. "The secretaries would never put me through to his office, so I'd send him messages. We'd have sex until the bell rang for the vote."

Still, Paula maintained that she never influenced votes—at least not directly. The night before the vote on the bill to bail out Chrysler, she threw a party for a few of her friends. Some congressmen were so hungover the next day, they didn't make the vote. Although Paula was a lobbyist for farm crop insurance, not Chrysler, she was offended by the negligence just the same. "Here was a bill that would affect millions and millions of lives," she said, "and these congressmen were using their power to get laid, not get votes."

Eventually, Paula quit her lobbying job after becoming disillusioned. "I truly cared about making changes in government," she said, adding, "In the three years I spent in Washington I watched 535 members of the House. Only fifteen percent of them are legitimate." She claimed one congressman who had voted against abortion issues actually gave her $500 so that she could have one. "At least I'm honest. I've never changed my story and I don't carry on and then have my picture taken with the wife and kids. My morals might be low, but at least I have principles."

★ ★ ★

If the Republican party felt the heat of a sex scandal for the first time with the Paula Parkinson affair, it really got burned during the next two rounds. The party's two subsequent sex scandals were not the usual variety; they involved homosexuals.

Despite the more liberal climate of the Carter years, homosexuality was still considered a political taboo. But in 1980, one incumbent congressman decided to seek voter acceptance of his gay lifestyle. The self-appointed guinea pig was Jon Hinson (R-Miss.).

Hinson had long been haunted by the fear that someone would discover and publish his secret. There was good reason to believe his homosexuality would some day be leaked to the press. Some clues were already on public record. In 1976, while serving as an administrative assistant for Republican Thad Cochran (R-Miss.), Hinson had been arrested in an Arlington, Virginia, park on a charge of committing an obscene act. Although the charge was dropped, Hinson paid a one-hundred-dollar fine for "creating a public nuisance." A year later, Hinson was one of three survivors of a fire that swept through a movie house in Washington's gay district. When he won the Mississippi House seat in 1978, he was astonished those reports had not yet surfaced.

By the time he ran for reelection in 1980, however, Hinson had grown tired of worrying when and if his political opponents would dig up his past. On August 8, 1980, in a bold and unprecedented move, the congressman called a press conference in his Jackson, Mississippi, district office to reveal his homosexuality. Although his advisers thought it would mean political suicide, Hinson argued it was "better to just get it out there and hope people understood."

Given the gay-bashing climate of the times, Jon Hinson's press conference was certainly a novel, if not a courageous, idea. As one reporter described it: "Had UFOs landed with aliens singing the Osmonds' greatest hits, the astonishment of those gathered would not have been greater." But the press conference worked. When the damage was assessed shortly after, the polls showed

Hinson still maintained a twenty-point lead over his opponent. Even after local newspapers printed more sordid details than Hinson would have liked, he won reelection handily. He had rallied support by telling his constituents: "We've always said that we want honesty from our public officials. I've been more honest with you than any politician I can remember. Here's the chance to prove that candor is what we truly want from the politicians who will lead us into the 1980s." Unfortunately, Hinson did not justify the voters' faith in him. In April 1981, Jon Hinson resigned from the House after pleading no contest to a charge of attempted oral sodomy after police observed him with a twenty-nine-year-old male in a public restroom of a House office building.

While Hinson had won his 1980 election in spite of his homosexuality, for Robert Bauman (R-Md.), it meant defeat and the end of a promising political career. Bauman, one of the most conservative Republicans on the Hill, had been charged with soliciting sex from a sixteen-year-old, nude, male dancer in a gay bar just four weeks before the 1980 election. Some analysts believed that had he faced the voters as directly as Hinson, he might have recovered in the polls. But Bauman wasn't really ready to face the truth himself.

Instead, Bauman blamed the incident on alcoholism and agreed to enter a treatment program. The charges were dropped but no one was fooled. As one observer said, "I've been drunk lots of times and never ended up in a gay bar on Ninth Street." It would be a long time before Bauman, married twenty years and the father of four, came to terms with his own homosexuality. By the time he finally did, he had lost his career, his wife and family, his home, and his conservative friends. He even contemplated committing suicide. In 1986, he wrote a book about his experiences, *The Gentleman from Maryland: The Conscience of a Gay Conservative*, because, he said, he needed the money. In it he chronicled his twenty-year rise from page to lawmaker to alcoholic who was beaten and rolled by homosexual hitchhikers and more. To many of his friends in the "Moral Right," Bauman's secret life was unbelievable.

At the time the charges were made public, Robert Bauman was considered a leading ultraconservative. In 1968, he had served as executive director of the Citizens for Nixon-Agnew. Later, as president of the 200,000-member American Conservative Union, he had been an active watchdog for conservative causes. During his three terms in Congress, he firmly backed the legislative efforts of the New Right and the Moral Majority. He even co-sponsored the Family Protection Act, a bill which allowed overt discrimination against gay men and women and permitted their exclusion from jobs and housing. In letters to his constituents, he wrote that he did not want his children to be taught or influenced by gay people if it could be avoided. As it is said about many gay-bashers, the homosexuality he was fighting was in himself.

Unbeknownst to him, Bauman had been under investigation for his homosexual activities for some time. When he had started visiting Washington's gay bars in the late '70s, local police had just formed a Juvenile Sex Exploitation Unit to look into rumors of organized male prostitution among the growing population of runaways in Washington.

When questioned by the vice unit, frightened young homosexuals often dropped names of powerful men they thought would help them get out of trouble. Among those mentioned were Bauman and nine other members of the House and Senate, as well as other high government officials and aides to Carter's White House staff. Considered too hot for the local police to handle, a special task force was organized with twelve FBI agents, the Secret Service, members of the U.S. Attorney's staff, and local police representatives from the vice, sex, juvenile, and prostitution squads. Bauman was an accident waiting to happen. Apparently, he wasn't alone. Bauman wrote in his book, "The closets of Washington are full of gay Republicans and gay conservatives. Many of them serve in high Reagan administration posts, some in the White House."

As even more homosexuality within the political community was brought into the spotlight, many turned to the "cross-section theory" for an explanation. If Congress reflects a cross-section of society, then it follows that 10 percent of the House and Senate are gay. Although many scoffed at the theory at the time, admissions of homosexuality by a number of legislators in subsquent years have given credence to it. Many have survived their admissions quite well. Notably, Barney Frank (D-Mass.) and Gerry Studds (D-Mass.) both came out of the closet and kept their jobs. Not all, however, have elected to be as open. In 1987, when the first congressman died of AIDS, it was suggested that Rep. Stewart B. McKinney (R-Conn.) had contracted the deadly virus from a blood transfusion he received during bypass surgery in 1979. But the *Washington Post* thought the source of the AIDS virus might have been different and reported that McKinney, who was married and father of two children, was a homosexual. Controversial as it may have been, it was the first obituary of its kind involving a congressman.

"Country Club Morality"

Scandals in the Life and Times of
Ronald Reagan

IT HAS BEEN SAID THAT IF earlier presidential scandals like Watergate and Teapot Dome seemed to spread from a single cancer, then the Ronald Reagan Administration has suffered a breakdown of the entire immune system. At the last count of the House Subcommittee on Civil Service, over 225 Reagan appointees have faced allegations of ethical or criminal wrongdoing. While not all of the charges are of a serious nature, the sheer number of scandals in the Reagan Administration is unprecedented in American history.

When Ronald Reagan was first elected, Johnny Carson joked that the new president had filled all his cabinet posts with a minority—old millionaires. Unlike other presidents, who turned to the academic sector to fill key political positions, President Reagan turned to the business sector. And that's where at least some of the trouble began. The higher percentage of businessmen in government alone increased the odds for conflict of interest charges.

The official party line regarding Reagan administration scandals is that they are all isolated incidents. Vice President George Bush explains, ''Our administration has been the victim of individuals who haven't had the judgment or integrity to put the public's business above their own selfish interest.'' The scandals, however, have become too widespread to be viewed as individual aberrations.

If Harry S Truman was right that the buck stops with the president, then the vast number of scandals—conflict of interest, financial wrongdoing, abuse of expense accounts, office decorating overrides, the use of government staff for personal use—can only reflect a low ethical standard set by Reagan himself. But an even more serious problem is Reagan's blatant disregard for the rules, a recurring theme throughout his administration. From the questionable lobby efforts of the president's most trusted aides to the covert White House operations known as the Iran Contra Affair, many members of the Reagan team seem to have marched to their own constitutional drummer. When and how did it all start? One only has to look to the 1980 presidential campaign to find the event which foreshadowed it—''Debategate.''

During the final throes of the 1980 campaign, Ronald Reagan had mysteriously come into possession of a looseleaf notebook containing Jimmy Carter's debating strategy notes. The Carter team later maintained the notebook was stolen. The Reagan camp explained it was sent to them, unsolicited, by a disgruntled worker. But while Reagan workers insisted there was no organized effort to gather information from the opposition, others confirmed, off the record, an operation to gather inside data. William Casey, who became Reagan's CIA director after the election, was alleged to have been directly involved, although he denied it. Whether or not the notebooks were stolen was only part of the issue. Ronald Reagan had benefitted by the incumbent president's private notes, and that wasn't part of the rules.

When Debategate was eventually disclosed during the first year of the Reagan Administration, the president had his own way of dealing with the situation—he chose to ignore it. His advisers argued on his behalf; look what happened to Richard Nixon when he looked into Watergate. In the final analysis, the public wasn't interested anyway. After six years of the public purging that had followed Richard Nixon's resignation, enough was enough. They preferred that Ronald Reagan bring swashbuckling—not Senate hearings—back to the presidency. This public attitude helped President Reagan sail through not only Debategate, but the endless stream of scandals that have continued to surface throughout his administration. Thus ended the post-Watergate morality.

Interestingly, few Reagan Administration scandals have been those reflecting personal or "character" issues. Interior Secretary James Watt was forced to resign after a crass and arrogant comment on the makeup of a new commission: "Three Democrats, two Republicans, every kind of mix you can have. I have a black, a woman, two Jews, and a cripple. And we have talent." No one in the Reagan administration was caught cheating on his wife, but John Fedders, chief of enforcement for the Securities Exchange Commission, admitted beating his—seven times during their eighteen-year marriage. According to Charlotte Fedders, the attacks left her with a broken eardrum, a wrenched neck, several black eyes, and many bruises. When the reports became front-page news in the *Wall Street Journal*, Fedders was forced to resign. When Mrs. Fedders wrote a book about her ordeal, titled *Shattered Dreams*, he sued her and won 25 percent of the profits.

President Reagan's personal decency, however, has never been questioned. The most serious scandal to emerge within the first family was when Nancy Reagan revealed that the president and his son Michael had been "estranged" for three years. But quicker than you could say "all-the-kids-had-better-be-at-the-inauguration," the family feud was neatly patched up. Nancy Reagan came under fire in 1983 when it was disclosed that she accepted expensive clothing as gifts from American designers. But the public opinion polls stayed high and everyone seemed to take the attitude that these things always happen, even in the best of first families.

So how does a basically moral president wind up with over 225 scandals in his administration, many of a serious nature? Perhaps Reagan's personification of the Republican dream, combined with his hands-off style of management, festered elitism, greed, and the "country club morality," seen time and again.

Early in the administration, National Security Adviser Richard Allen resigned, after it was revealed that he accepted one thousand dollars for helping Japanese journalists arrange an interview with Nancy Reagan, although later exonerated of wrongdoing. In 1981, Max Hugel, the number-two man at the CIA, resigned over allegations of questionable stock transactions, although no charges were ever brought. In 1983, Thomas C. Reed resigned as White House counselor on national security and repaid $427,000 he made on an illegal inside stock trade. More recently, Deputy Defense Secretary Paul Thayer resigned when the SEC filed a civil suit regarding insider trading that allegedly took place before he entered government. The suit, which is still pending, claims Thayer illegally traded stock of LTV Corp., a defense company he headed.

Two other top Reagan officials were investigated, but cleared, of questionable financial practices. In 1982, Attorney General William French Smith was investigated for an impermissible oil and gas tax shelter and for taking a $50,000 severance check, after his nomination was announced, from a company he had served as director. Smith renounced the write-off and returned the severance check, which turned out to be a higher fee than he earned in the six years he served on the board.

In 1983, CIA Director William Casey was investigated for insider trading of stocks of companies that had contracts with the CIA. Also investigated was his sale of more than $600,000 in oil stocks during 1981, a year oil prices plummeted. Casey at the time was the only high-ranking official with access to intelligence estimates on worldwide oil production who hadn't either sold his holdings or set up a blind trust before taking office. The furor died down when he agreed to place all his holdings in a blind trust. It was also discovered that Casey once failed to file as a foreign agent for Indonesia, and that he was once ordered to pay punitive damages as the results of a plagiarism suit.

Secretary of Labor Raymond Donovan became the first U.S. cabinet member in history to be indicted while in office. He resigned after being charged with defrauding the New York City Transit Authority of $7.4 million. He was acquitted, however, following a nine-month trial. Earlier, Donovan was investigated by special counsel for ties to union corruption and organized crime, but no charges were brought.

Although some of the other Reagan Administration scandals may seem more frivolous in nature, they are just as serious in principle. A year before his unfortunate comments, James Watt was accused of misusing government funds to pay for two private parties. He was ordered by the General Accounting Office to reimburse the government, but had the Republican National Committee pay them back instead. Attorney General Smith repaid the government $11,000 for government limousines his wife took to luncheons, art galleries, and other assorted social events. The wife of Treasury Secretary Donald Regan was alleged to have misused a government car on seventy-five occasions over a twenty-month period, as Regan's chauffeur shuttled her back and forth across Washington regularly on personal trips to such places as the Kennedy Center, the Smithsonian Institution, the Corcoran Gallery, and exclusive clubs and restaurants.

Robert Nimmo, the head of the Veterans Administration, resigned after disclosures that he spent $54,183 for decorating his office and that he misused charter aircraft and government cars for personal business. Edgar Callahan, chairman of the National Credit Union Administration, was forced to repay $21,250 in improper moving and living expenses. Emanuel Savas resigned his post as assistant secretary of housing and urban development after it was discovered that he used his agency staff to work on his book titled, funnily enough, *Privatizing the Public Sector.*

A variety of scandals in the Environmental Protection Agency led to the resignations of Administrator Anne Burford and more than a dozen of her senior aides. Burford was charged with agency mismanagement, political manipulation and possible conflict of interest. The EPA was said to have ignored violations by certain chemical companies with whom they were friendly. In addition, clean-ups of hazardous waste dumps were allegedly sped up or delayed to help Republicans in the 1982 elections. Under Burford's auspices, the EPA also kept lists of political leanings of agency employees.

The EPA scandals led to the first felony conviction in the

Reagan administration. Rita Lavelle, the head of the toxic-waste clean-up program, first came under fire for taking expensive lunches from firms that had regulatory matters pending with the EPA. She was accused of showing favoritism toward certain companies with whose executives she discussed pending EPA enforcement cases. When agency actions involved her former employer, Aerojet General Corporation, she refused to remove herself from direct involvement. In 1983, she was ultimately found guilty of perjury before Congress. She eventually served three months of a six-month jail sentence.

★ ★ ★

By Reagan's second term, special counsels were hired to investigate the mounting scandals among key Reagan officials including Theodore Olson, Lyn Nofziger, Michael Deaver, Edwin Meese III, and those involved in the Iran Contra Affair. As of February 1988, the cost to tax-payers for all of these investigations had risen to more than $8 million.

Former Assistant Attorney General Theodore Olson came under investigation by a special prosecutor for allegedly misleading the House Judiciary Committee investigating the EPA scandals in 1983. Olson had advised Anne Burford to withhold certain documents, under executive privilege, which had been subpoenaed by the House Energy and Commerce Committee. Olson, along with two other deputy attorneys general, allegedly gave false testimony to Congress by refusing to identify certain documents in their possession.

On January 22, 1988, however, Olson's investigation by independent counsel Alexia Morrison was voided when the U.S. Circuit Court of Appeals for the District of Columbia ruled that the independent counsel provision of the 1978 Ethics in Government Act was unconstitutional. It will be argued before the Supreme Court shortly. Both Nofziger and Deaver were indicted on charges that stemmed from other provisions of the 1978 Ethics in Government Act, which states that senior government officials who join the public sector are forbidden to lobby anyone at their former agencies for one year. Regarding matters in which they participated "personally and substantially," they are forbidden to lobby for life.

Deaver, a lifelong associate of the president who was often called the Reagans' "honorary son," was investigated for his lobby efforts on behalf of Trans World Airlines and other clients he represented just a few months after leaving office. The former White House aide had been paid $250,000 by TWA during the time when it was working to block a hostile corporate takeover by Carl Icahn. Although investigated for possible violations of the ethics law, Deaver was ultimately indicted on five counts of perjury, a charge legal experts felt was easier to prove. On December 16, 1987, a U.S. District Court jury convicted Deaver on three of five counts. His conviction, however, could be influenced by the Supreme Court decision on the independent counsel law, as could the conviction of Lyn Nofziger.

Lyn Nofziger was indicted on a more direct charge of violation of the ethics law. In 1982, Nofziger opened up a lobby firm after quitting his post as White House political director. Four months later—eight months less than the year required by law—he wrote a letter to James E. Jenkins, deputy to Attorney General Meese, asking for help in securing a $32-million Army contract for his client, Wedtech Corporation. Wedtech, which was later shown to have misrepresented itself as a minority-owned firm to qualify for certain government benefits, had grown from a tiny South Bronx machine shop to a defense contractor with $100-million annual revenues. The company had been barred from competing for the contract because of a poor performance history. But miraculously, they won this one and Jenkins soon after signed on as a Wedtech consultant. Nofziger's firm received Wedtech stock reported to be worth between $720,000 and $1 million.

The Wedtech scandal led to the guilty pleas of four company executives who admitted stealing $2 million from the firm and bribing federal, state, and local officials; the conviction of two Maryland politicians for accepting $50,000 to stop a congressional investigation; and the indictment of a New York congressman for racketeering. On February 11, 1988, Nofziger was indicted on four counts of violating the federal ethics law. He was later fined $30,000 and sentenced to ninety days in jail.

Attorney General Edwin Meese III was also under investigation by a special prosecutor for his alleged involvement with the Wedtech lobby efforts and other questionable activities. In 1982, while counselor to the president, Meese allegedly had intervened to help Wedtech secure the $32 million Army contract at the request of E. Robert Wallach, his longtime friend. Three years later, Meese and his wife invested $50,000 in a partnership run by W. Franklyn Chinn, who became a Wedtech director. In two years, the Meeses earned a profit of $45,857, or 90 percent. Although Meese's role has not yet been defined or judged, Wallach, Chinn, and a third associate were indicted for fraud, racketeering, and conspiracy in connection with the Wedtech scheme.

In 1984, Meese was investigated by another special counsel. At the time, Meese had recently been nominated as attorney general. That investigation focused on his financial dealings and relationships with these men:

Thomas J. Barrack, Jr.: When Meese had trouble selling his home in La Mesa, Calif., this wealthy real estate developer contributed $70,000 to the sale. Three months later, he was named deputy under secretary of the interior.

Gordon C. Luce: As bank chairman, he allowed Meese to fall fifteen months behind in his mortgage payments while the house was stuck on the market. He was later named an alternate representative to the United Nations.

Edwin J. Gray: As vice president of another bank, which held more than $420,000 more in mortgages, he also allowed Meese to fall behind in payments. He became chairman of the Federal Home Loan Bank Board. As chairman, Gray repaid $26,000 in travel costs for himself and his wife.

Edwin W. Thomas: Thomas had once given Meese's wife, Ursula, a $15,000 interest-free loan. He became Meese's deputy at the White House. His wife and son also ended up with government jobs.

John R. McKean: As a San Francisco tax accountant,

McKean arranged for $60,000 in unsecured loans for Meese. He was later nominated as governor of the U.S. Postal Service and became chairman of its board of governors.

In the final analysis, the Senate Judiciary Committee accepted that Ed Meese had not peddled influence for personal gain. Although these men were his longterm friends, Meese had built a strong case that they would have been offered federal jobs anyway. Even after becoming attorney general, Meese's political and legal difficulties have continued.

Most recently, independent counsel James McKay expanded his investigation of Meese to include the attorney general's alleged failure to take action on a memo from his friend E. Robert Wallach, which discussed a possibly illegal payment to former Israel Prime Minister Shimon Peres or members of his Labor Party in return for their support of a one-million-dollar oil pipeline for Israel's longtime enemy, Iraq. The pipeline plans were ultimately scrapped and Peres had denied knowledge of any payments. Still, the question remains whether or not Meese shirked his responsibility, as attorney general, to see if the plan cited in the memo was a violation of U.S. law, which makes it illegal to bribe officials of foreign governments.

In addition to the pipeline probe, McKay is also investigating Meese for a possible violation of conflict of interest laws relating to an investment he and his wife made in ninety-one shares in seven regional telephone company stocks. During the time they owned the telephone stocks (they sold them last year for approximately $14,000), Meese endorsed legislation intended to end federal regulation of the seven "Baby Bell" companies, which were created after the breakup of American Telephone and Telegraph Co. He had been urged to support the legislation in meetings with several company executives. Only after the Justice Department formally endorsed the legislation (which was ultimately defeated in U.S. District Court) did Meese obtain a waiver letter from the counsel to the president, which allowed him to participate in the case. Despite wave after wave of scandals in the attorney general's office, President Reagan stuck by his close friend of twenty years.

Meese's staff wasn't as loyal. By the end of March 1988, two senior aides resigned amidst the turmoil at the Justice Department, as did their four closest advisers. Smart money, meanwhile, awaited McKay's final report before laying odds on Meese's political survival.

★ ★ ★

Out of all scandals in recent memory, there is probably none more bizarre than the Iran-Contra affair. It revealed that a shadow government, operating right out of the White House, had embarked on a scheme to trade arms with Iran for American hostages in Lebanon, and then use the profits to fund the rebel Contras in Nicaragua. This violated, if not the letter, then certainly the spirit of the 1981 Boland Amendment, which banned U.S. military aid to the Contras. It also was in violation of the unwritten, but well publicized, Reagan policy of never negotiating with terrorists.

The disclosures of the Iran-Contra affair were first made by Meese, on the heels of a magazine exposé published in Beirut. Soon after, on November 12, 1986, President Reagan insisted, "We did not—repeat—did not trade weapons or anything else for hostages—nor will we." Six days later, however, he admitted there was a secret project that involved a third country. February 11, 1987, he said he had not approved the arms trade. Nine days later, as press and congressional questioning intensified, the President declared, "I don't remember—period!" By the time two federal investigations were underway, the cry turned from "What did the president know and when did he know it," to "What did Reagan forget and when did he forget it?" Meese apparently had memory lapses, too. During the Iran-Contra hearings he replied, "I don't recall," or made similar statements 187 times. (Meese's memory failed him twenty-nine times in the Nofziger trial.)

As the Iran-Contra scandal unfolded, National Security Council aide Oliver North was fired, National Security Adviser John Poindexter resigned, and National Security Adviser Robert McFarlane tried to commit suicide with an overdose of valium. Retired Air Force General Richard Secord was suspended, but reinstated, after fraud charges were brought. CIA Director William Casey was suspected of lying to Congress about CIA involvement, but died before Senate hearings concluded. According to journalist Bob Woodward, he confirmed the Agency's involvement in a deathbed interview.

For at least a few, however, the Iran-Contra scandal marked not a defeat, but a new beginning. After his crowd-pleasing testimony at the televised hearings, Oliver North received millions of dollars worth of endorsement offers, as well as book and movie offers. North's wife, Betsy, won the "National Full-Time Homemaker of the Year" award from an antifeminist group. North's secretary, Fawn Hall, boosted the Nielsen ratings during her testimony, was signed by the William Morris talent agency, and began dating Rob Lowe. John Poindexter had a street in Odon, Indiana named after him.

On the down side, however, Richard Secord watched one business go under (although he quickly started another). White House chief of staff Donald Regan took the brunt of the blame for the disarray in the White House that had been portrayed in the hearings, and was asked to step down. Regan's resignation also marked the end of his two-year running battle with Nancy Reagan. During their feud it was reported that Regan hung up on the first lady and, in another rancorous exchange, she hung up on him.

Two big losers in the private sector were John Lee and Shanna Hudson, entrepreneurs from San Francisco, who lost their shirts manufacturing Oliver North dolls. They had hoped to sell 450,000 at $19.95, but only managed to get orders for 230. Hudson thought the doll's failure reflected the public's intellectual rather than their emotional reaction to North. He said, "People felt sorry for the soldier North, but when it came down to buying a doll they basically said, 'We are not going to buy an image of someone who has disrespect for the Constitution.'"

Perhaps that was comforting to the Senate chairman for the hearings, Daniel K. Inouye (D-Hawaii), who said in his closing statement: "The story has now been told. Speaking for myself, I see it as a chilling story, a story of deceit and duplicity and the arrogant disregard of the rule of law. It is a story of withholding vital information from the American people, from the Congress, from the secretary of state, from the secretary of defense, and, according to Admiral [John M.] Poindexter, from the president himself.''

On March 16, 1988 a federal grand jury indicted North, Poindexter, Secord, and his business colleague, Albert A. Hakim on twenty-three counts of conspiracy to defraud the United States and theft of government property in connection with the Iran-Contra scandal. While criminal charges could possibly take years to get through the system, it was clear to the public that this time the Reagan team had gone just a little bit too far. When the Iran-Contra affair first broke, the President's public approval rating sank to 40 percent, the lowest it had been since 1983, when the country was caught in the grip of an unemployment and financial recession.

As for the reaction of the press, the Iran-Contra affair seemed to rekindle the fervor of the Watergate years. A controversial, heated exchange between Vice President George Bush and CBS's Dan Rather, broadcast live on January 26, 1988, created as much news as the scandal they were attempting to discuss.

While the full effect upon George Bush's presidential campaign remains to be seen, the Iran-Contra Affair at least temporarily wounded Reagan. Perhaps the first evidence of the real damage was the Senate rejection of Judge Robert H. Bork, the president's nominee for the Supreme Court seat vacated by Justice Lewis Powell. The televised confirmation hearings gave a black eye to the president, who was aggressively working behind the scenes to help push the nomination through. Even with the assistance of Howard Baker, his new chief of staff, noted to be one of the great dealmakers on Capitol Hill, Reagan had run out of steam. Bork was rejected, as was, in a very real sense, Ronald Reagan himself. The Senate Judiciary Committee had not only questioned Bork's qualifications and ideology, they seemed to question Ronald Reagan's judgment and decision-making ability as well.

If Bork's rejection was a blow to the president, the scandal surrounding his second choice for Supreme Court was an outright humiliation. Douglas Ginsburg had to step down from his nomination after admitting he had been a pot smoker—not just as a college student, but as a law professor at Harvard. In light of the first lady's "Just Say No" campaign against drugs, there was nothing left to do but say "no" to Judge Ginsburg. Reagan's third choice, Judge Anthony M. Kennedy, received unanimous Senate approval.

Reagan, however, was a long way from setting the record for the most Supreme Court nominees rejected or withdrawn. The Senate killed five out of six nominations by John Tyler. Millard Fillmore saw three of his nominations fail and Ulysses S. Grant and Lyndon Johnson each had two nominations rejected in their last year in office.

Ginsburg, however, marked the first time a Supreme Court nominee was withdrawn because of drug use, a situation that touched off a few other confessions. To help limit the potential damage that forced disclosures might cause in an election year, two Democratic candidates for president stepped forward. Former Arizona Governor Bruce Babbitt admitted he tried marijuana twenty years ago. Senator Albert Gore, Jr. (D-Tenn.) said he and his wife had smoked it when they were younger.

In addition, Senator Clairborne Pell (D-R.I.) said he tried "several puffs off a marijuana cigarette" but didn't like it. Conservative Rep. Newt Gingrich (R-Ga.) said he tried it nineteen years ago but it didn't have any effect. Senator Lawton Chiles (D-Fla.) and his Republican challenger Representative Connie Mack also admitted having smoked pot.

★ ★ ★

Besides the Reaganites mentioned earlier, here are just a few more who have come under fire for ethical or criminal wrongdoing.

> James Beggs, chief administrator of NASA—indicted on criminal charges for allegedly defrauding the government while serving as an executive with General Dynamics (the indictment was dropped).

> Robert Burford, director of the Interior Department's Bureau of Land Management—obtained a waiver from regula-

tions to own an interest in grazing land administered by the Bureau.

Carlos Campbell, Assistant Secretary of Commerce for Economic Development—resigned over allegations that he awarded grants to firms operated by personal friends.

Joseph Canzeri, White House Assistant to the President—resigned after disclosures that he double-billed the government and the Republican National Committee for expenses.

Michael J. Connolly, General Counsel to the Equal Employment Opportunity Commission—resigned amid allegations that he conspired to end an E.E.O.C. enforcement action of a company represented by his brother.

Guy Fiske, Deputy Secretary of Commerce—resigned after conflict of interest allegations that he negotiated a sale of weather satellites to COMSTAT, a corporation with whom he was seeking a job.

Robert Funkhouser, EPA director of international activities—resigned after allegations that he helped a Dow Chemical company representative influence trade negotiations on toxic chemicals.

Louis Giuffrida, Director, Federal Emergency Management Agency—resigned amid allegations of misuse of government property.

Arthur Hayes, Food and Drug Administration Commissioner—resigned while under investigation for overlapping travel reimbursement from outside groups and his agency.

William S. Heffelfinger, Assistant Secretary of Energy—accused of falsifying his résumé, deceiving federal investigators, and violating civil service merit protection principles.

John W. Hernandez, Acting EPA Administrator—resigned after his staff disclosed he had allowed Dow Chemical to review a report naming the company a dioxin polluter.

Robert Hill, Economic Development Administration—resigned after his staff disclosed he had allowed Dow Chemical to "edit" a report naming the company a dioxin polluter.

John Horton, Assistant EPA Administrator—fired for using government employees and telephones for personal business.

Donald Hovde, Undersecretary of Housing and Urban Development—took trips to Italy and Puerto Rico paid for by realtors and builders. Repaid the government $3,000 for private chauffeur expenses.

John McElderry, Denver regional administrator for the Department of Health and Human Services—resigned after allegations that he used his position to promote and sell Amway products.

Marjory Mecklenburg, Deputy Assistant Secretary of Health and Human Services—resigned after being cleared of allegations of travel voucher irregularities, which cost taxpayers $12,938.69.

Jonathan Miller, Deputy Assistant to the President—resigned after being accused of helping move cash to the Contras in Lt. Col. Oliver North's operation.

Robert Nimmo, Head of Veterans Administration—resigned after disclosures that he spent $54,183 for decorating his office; that he sent his old furniture to his daughter, Mary, who worked for the Commerce Department; that he misused charter aircraft; and that he used government cars for personal business.

Matthew Novick, EPA inspector general—dismissed after allegations that he used government employees to work on personal business.

Robert Perry, EPA general counsel—resigned after participation in a settlement involving a subsidiary of his former employer.

J. William Petro, U.S. Attorney in Cleveland—fired and fined for tipping off a friend to a grand jury indictment.

Armand Reiser, Counselor to the Department of Energy—

resigned after disclosures that he failed to reveal $106,000 in earnings from five energy-related companies.

Bill Sloan, California regional director of the Department of Housing and Urban Development—reprimanded and forced to repay $6,800 he charged the government in travel and meals. $1,026 was for meals he ate in his home in Fresno.

John Todhunter, assistant EPA administrator—resigned after allegations of private meetings with chemical lobbyists.

Peter Voss, Postal Service governor—received a four-year prison sentence and a fine after pleading guilty to charges of a kickback scheme and expense account fraud, which amounted to $43,817.

Faith Ryan Whittlesey, U.S. Ambassador to Switzerland— investigated by the Justice Department and the House Subcommittee on International Operations for bad judgment in hiring practices and in administration of a fund which was supposed to enhance American representation. The subcommittee found that she used the fund "as an augmentation of her personal wealth." Before the State Department took the "Enhanced Representation Fund" out of her control, she had used it for such expenses as flying a guitar player, round trip from the U.S., to play at a July Fourth party. A Justice Department investigation concluded it was unnecessary to appoint a special prosecutor. However, the House Subcommittee on International Operations concluded that she showed poor judgment in her hiring policies.

Charles Z. Wick, Director, U.S. Information Agency—reimbursed the government two-thirds of the cost of a $31,713 security system in his home after a White House ethics adviser suggested the expense might be "misunderstood." He also secretly taped telephone conversation without permission, and was caught lying to reporters who investigated the charge.

As the Reagan Administration wraps up its eighth and final year, the picture has changed for the president. While the public had once been eager to overlook some scandals and forgive even more, they were not able to ignore the Iran-Contra affair—no matter how hard they tried. Yet, while Reagan's popularity as a president has weakened considerably, his personal popularity in many ways remains intact. The list of scandals in his administration did not really match the wholesale corruption seen in the Nixon or Buchanan administrations. But neither did it match the picture of morality for which Ronald Reagan once said he would like to be remembered. How many of the Reagan Administration scandals were the result of partisan politics? Perhaps a fair share. How many investigations by House and Senate committees were instigated and led by Democrats? Probably a lot. But, then again, thank heaven for the two-party system.

"Let the People Decide"

Scandals of
the 1988 Presidential Campaign

E
VEN IN THE BEST OF
times, scandals are difficult for politicians to overcome. But when
they hit in the middle of a presidential campaign they are especially
brutal. While the candidate is hard at work trying to create—and
control—a certain image, the media uncovers a scandal and de-
stroys it. It's been the American way for more than 200 years,
although recently, the effect has been greatly intensified by television. Ever since the 1960 televised presidential debates, analysts
have known that a candidate could be just one sweaty lip, or one
five-o'clock shadow, away from victory, as was Richard Nixon.
In 1972, there was Thomas Eagleton's demise over his mental
health record, and Ed Muskie's fall after he was photographed
shedding a tear (which he said was a melted snowflake). In 1984,
there was Geraldine Ferraro's anguish as charges of her husband's
real estate fraud unraveled. That anguish turned to anger when the
press dug up a gambling scandal alleged to have involved her father over forty years before. While most journalists agreed it was
in poor taste to question the background of Ferraro's father, who
died when she was just eight, the report served as a presage for
campaign coverage in the years to come.

So far in the 1988 presidential campaign, investigations of
personal scandals have shown no boundaries at all. Perhaps be-

cause of the vast numbers of White House scandals still unfolding, or simply because of the arrogance of certain candidates, the focus of the first post-Reagan election has become the "character issue," a catch-all phrase for any incident or utterance that would reveal a candidate's inner self. Much like the 1884 presidential campaign, there is no one overriding issue, such as war or depression. And just as with Cleveland and Blaine, journalists in the 1988 campaign began uncovering everything from mistresses and bastard scandals, to how a candidate grew rich in office.

Needless to say, in 1988, the media has flexed its muscle, showing off a capability to break a candidate just as easily as it makes one. No one learned this lesson more clearly than Gary Hart. In 1984, the media had helped turn this little-known Democratic senator from Colorado into a leading presidential candidate. But just four years later, they ended his second bid in one fell stroke. In fact, on May 3, 1987, when the *Miami Herald* reported that Hart had spent the night with a twenty-nine-year-old Miami woman named Donna Rice, it set the tone for the entire campaign.

Hart's reputation as a womanizer had dogged him for many years. So when a *Herald* reporter received an anonymous tip of the rendezvous, the newspaper embarked on a stake-out of Hart's Washington, D.C., townhouse. Unbeknownst to the *Herald* team, Hart had issued an independent challenge to journalists, inviting them to follow him to prove that he had nothing to hide. Ironically, Hart's "dare" appeared in the *New York Times Magazine* the same day as the Donna Rice story hit the front page of the *Herald*. If the *Herald* needed a justification for their stake-out, Hart's challenge seemed to take care of it. But even so, an ethics controversy was ignited. And as people gathered for Gary Hart's campaign vigil, the question arose: Does a presidential candidate have any right to privacy?

It was difficult to find anyone in the media who thought Gary Hart had any such right. Even when his wife, Lee, arrived on the scene to lend Hart badly needed support, journalists continued to press harder. Hart repeatedly denied any impropriety, but it was already too late. The final blow came when the *Washington Post* reported another story about an unnamed woman with whom Hart had had an affair. By May 8, just five days after the initial report, Hart threw in the towel and told his wife, "Let's go home."

Hart's quick withdrawal from the race didn't stop further investigation of the scandal. The *National Enquirer* quickly followed with exclusive color pictures of Hart, Rice, Lynn Armadt (Rice's girlfriend), and Hart fundraiser William Broadhurst drinking and partying the night away in Bimini weeks before. The happy foursome had taken a cruise there aboard a boat aptly called the "Monkey Business." In a *People* magazine exclusive, Lynn Armadt revealed that Donna and Gary had shared the master stateroom, a different story than Hart's account of the girls staying on one boat and the boys staying on another. A Gail Sheehy article in *Vanity Fair* added further to the scandal by noting that—in addition to her other romantic larks with Prince Albert of Monaco, Tony Curtis, and Don Henley of the Eagles—Rice had also enjoyed the company of Adnan Khashoggi, the Arab arms trader once considered the wealthiest man in the world, and a convicted drug dealer named James Bradley Parks, who had been sentenced to ten years in Eglin Federal Prison in Florida.

Not surprisingly, Gary Hart's December reentry into the race became not just a piece of political history, but a bit of political theater as well. Despite a new womanizing scandal or two and a few more about possible campaign finance law violations, Hart forged ahead with the battle cry, "Let the people decide." At first, he showed a new strength in the polls as a result of his celebrity status, as short-lived as it would be. By mid-March, Hart withdrew from the race again.

★ ★ ★

Senator Joseph Biden (D-Del.) was also sidelined by the "character issue," having dropped out of the race on September 23, 1987, amid charges of plagiarism and résumé enhancement. Biden had been considered an up-and-coming favorite of the baby-boomer vote. His role as chairman of the Senate Judiciary Committee during the televised Bork confirmation hearings was expected to boost his support. But when plagiarism charges were first reported, they undermined his presidential campaign and threatened the Bork hearings as well.

Biden's scandal began with the mildly embarrassing disclosure that the senator, often praised as a topnotch orator, had been using other politicians' campaign speeches as his own. It soon grew to include an incident in law school where Biden once flunked a course for copying five pages of a paper without accrediting them to its rightful author. If that wasn't damaging enough, a C-SPAN cable network videotape showed Biden misrepresenting his academic résumé. In an angry exchange with a reporter in Claremont, New Hampshire, Biden boasted that he graduated from University of Delaware with three degrees. He also claimed he went to Syracuse University Law School on a full academic scholarship and that he graduated in the top half of his law school class. Actually, Biden had only one undergraduate degree, he went to law school on a half scholarship given for financial need, and he graduated seventy-sixth out of a law-school class of eighty-five. His undergraduate ranking was 506th in a class of 688.

Biden was not the first senator to be embarrassed by his university record. In 1962, Ted Kennedy admitted that he had asked a friend to take a Spanish exam for him at Harvard. But as Kennedy proved so clearly, the scandals the public might find acceptable for a senator are far different from what they'll consider for a president.

Although Biden's demise was cause for celebration amongst some fellow Democratic candidates, for Massachussett's Governor Michael Dukakis, it touched off yet another minor scandal. After initially denying any involvement, Dukakis eventually confirmed that his campaign manager had been the one to leak the Biden scandal to the press. Not only did his manager tip off the press that Biden was lifting campaign speeches, he actually prepared a videotape, which dramatically juxtaposed Biden's speeches with those of British labor leader, Neil Kinnock, their rightful author. Once Biden had resigned, however, the scandal suddenly backfired on Dukakis, who was pressured into firing his campaign manager for unethical behavior.

Dukakis ultimately survived the incident, perhaps with some

expert guidance from his wife. Kitty Dukakis had already proved to have the best scandal strategy of the '88 presidential campaign when she voluntarily revealed her twenty-six-year-long battle with amphetamine addiction. She quickly learned that beating the press to the story in the first place takes the sizzle out of the exposé.

Mrs. Dukakis had kept her 1982 treatment at a Minnesota drug rehabilitation clinic a secret because of her husband's close race for governor of Massachussets that year. But in July 1987, in the wake of the Donna Rice scandal, she decided it was best to go public. If the timing of Mrs. Dukakis's disclosure was not calculated, it was instinctively savvy. The earlier a scandal is publicized, the quicker it is usually forgotten. If the Dukakises benefited from this phenomenon, so did candidates Albert Gore, Jr. (D-Tenn.) and Bruce Babbitt, former Arizona governor, who, during the Douglas Ginsburg scandal, quickly revealed they had smoked pot, too.

Once in a while, however, a campaign scandal just refuses to die. Such was the case with Republican hopeful Jack Kemp who has been haunted by a sordid scandal for over twenty years. The story had originally plagued his former boss, Ronald Reagan, who some say postponed his own plans for the presidency because of it. But with Jack Kemp's entry into the 1988 presidential race, Reagan's "gay sex scandal" was suddenly all his.

The scandal dates back to 1967, when Kemp was athletic adviser to Ronald Reagan, then governor of California. At the time, the controversy actually centered around Kemp's immediate supervisor, who was forced to resign amidst rumors that he had secret trysts and gay orgies in a Lake Tahoe cabin. The scandal eventually tainted Kemp's reputation, too, as he co-owned the property in question with his supervisor.

As it turned out, the scandal was really a product of internal staff politics. As Reagan tested the waters for the 1968 Presidential campaign, various sides had embarked on their individual plays for power. One such maneuver, spearheaded by Lyn Nofziger, turned into a witch-hunt for a "homosexual ring." Nofziger, then Reagan's press secretary, set out to document various rumors, seeking support from other aides such as Ed Meese, who became attorney general, and William Clark, who later became Reagan's national security advisor and then secretary of the interior. Nofziger also enlisted the expertise of Arthur Van Court, a former detective who served as Reagan's bodyguard and travel secretary. Although no conclusive proof was ever found, and Court's efforts to tape record the "orgies" failed, six men, including Kemp, were ascertained to be gay. Proclaiming fear of vulnerability to blackmail, Nofziger and ten top aides handed Governor Reagan a report of their findings in a secret meeting in the Hotel del Coronado in San Diego. Reagan reportedly exclaimed, "My God, has government failed?"

The following Monday, Kemp's boss turned in his resignation and Kemp soon returned to his football career. Although the press at first missed the story, the truth eventually filtered out. On October 30, 1967, *Newsweek* reported: "A top GOP presidential prospect has a potentially sordid scandal on his hands. Private investigators he hired found evidence that two of his aides had committed homosexual acts. The men are no longer working for the GOP leader, but the whole story may surface any day."

The following day, columnist Drew Pearson wrote: "The most interesting speculation among political leaders in this key state of California is whether the magic charm of Governor Ronald Reagan can survive the discovery that a homosexual ring has been operating in his office." The column also revealed another scandalous element of the story—that Nofziger had leaked it himself. Denials were issued by everyone. At his regularly scheduled press conference that day, Reagan insisted the report was untrue and Nofziger called Drew Pearson a liar. It was a standoff according to public opinion— until the *New York Times, Washington Post, Time,* and *Newsweek* all confirmed that Nofziger was, indeed, their source.

Although personally wounded by the scandal, Reagan was apparently happy the suspected gays were gone and praised Nofziger for his discoveries. Reagan even joked about it, once suggesting they trawl Truman Capote through the halls "to see if there are any of them left." Some say the scandal ultimately influenced his presidency, and that as a result of Nofziger's report Reagan would never again trust anyone he didn't know personally for a long time. From that day forward, he restricted his inner circle to a few trusted friends, all of them followed him to the White House.

Kemp's boss returned to the private sector, where he quietly raised a family. Kemp, married since 1958 with four children, went on to become a successful congressman in New York. And while the "gay sex scandal" has never ruined his political career, it has lingered like a dark mist over his presidential campaign just the same. As early as December 1985, *Newsweek* reported: "Kemp aides know they must also deal—publicly—with a . . . delicate personal matter: a persistent rumor, for which no evidence has ever surfaced, that Kemp is or was a homosexual."

Today, Kemp still denies any wrongdoing and explains the Lake Tahoe cabin was a financial investment and that he never stayed there. Despite the lack of evidence to dispute his denial, until he withdrew as a presidential candidate on March 10, 1988, Kemp was still expected to answer questions regarding whom he slept with twenty years ago.

★ ★ ★

The only candidate with scandals dating back further than Kemp was Republican Pat Robertson, who managed to acquire a sex scandal and a résumé scandal in one campaign. The *Wall Street Journal* dredged up this old controversy when they revealed that the former television evangelist conceived his son out of wedlock and then fudged the date of his marriage to hide the fact. In circumstances that recalled the James Blaine shotgun wedding scandal of 1884, Robertson maintained that he had married his wife, Adelia, on March 22, 1954, when he was really married five months later, on August 27. Their first son, obviously conceived out of wedlock, was born ten weeks later. Even though Robertson had regularly preached against sex before marriage, the report had little impact on his campaign. The Robertsons, after all, had been married for thirty-three years and had four children together. Robertson's résumé scandal, however, wasn't as easily dismissed. His "graduate studies at the University of London" turned out to be a summer arts course for American tourists. His questionable claim of combat duty in Korea was far more controversial.

The first to dispute Robertson's war record was not the press, but Representative Paul N. (Pete) McCloskey (R-Cal.), a highly decorated, combat veteran who was severely wounded in the Korean War. McCloskey, who knew Robertson during the war, claimed the former television evangelist was never under fire or even near the front lines. Instead, he declared, Robertson's father, the late Senator A. Willis Robertson (D-Va.), pulled political strings to keep his son away from the fighting. As a result of the charge, Robertson filed a $35 million libel suit against McCloskey to prove to the public that he never shirked his military responsibilities. In addition, Robertson also filed a $35 million libel suit against Representative Andrew Jacobs, Jr. (D-Ind.). Jacobs, another Korean combat veteran, had circulated a letter from McCloskey, outlining his claims against Robertson, among various news organizations. Interestingly enough, by placing the résumé scandal in the hands of the lawyers, Robertson had taken it out of the hands of the media. By early March, Robertson had dropped both suits, but by that time eager journalists were already pursuing the campaign scandals of George Bush and Robert Dole, the Republican frontrunners.

★ ★ ★

From the beginning of the campaign, George Bush was fighting a no-win battle over questions concerning his role in the Iran-Contra scandal. If he claimed he had not been apprised of the arms-for-hostages plan, he might appear to be a do-nothing vice president. If he claimed he did know what was going on, he might be criticized unless he voiced objections. Then again, if he voiced objections and the president ignored him, he might appear to be a do-nothing vice president. With no clear-cut winning road to travel, Bush tried a different path—media bashing.

Bush first tested his new combative approach during a televised GOP debate in early January. When asked about his Iran-Contra role by the editor of the *Des Moines Register*, Bush raised his voice and won over the Iowa audience. Editor James P. Gan-

non asked, "How can you expect [the public's] trust if you won't
tell them plainly what you thought, what you did?" Bush angrily
replied, "You ask about diversion. I didn't know about diversion
of funds to the Contras. The Congress had a $10 million hearing
and never suggested I did. The Tower report said I didn't. And
you, your paper today, had that question raised as if I hadn't answered it. And I resent it frankly, and I think you owe me now to
ask the question you say I haven't answered. You owe me in fair-
ness." Although Bush made a lot of noise, he had wiggled out of
the issue.

If the strategy worked well in Des Moines, it worked like
magic on the *CBS Evening News* with Dan Rather. The nine-min-
ute heated exchange that was broadcast live and unedited on January 25 was an interview that defied description. As Rather fired
Iran-Contra questions at the vice president, Bush argued that CBS
misrepresented the purpose of the interview and criticized Rather
for the network's ambush. In the final analysis, the tone of the
discussion made more news than its content and once again,
George Bush had successfully deflected the issue. What's more,
the public's favorable response to Bush helped him gain in the
Iowa polls against Robert Dole (R-Kan.), his strongest GOP
challenger.

Dole, meanwhile, had been trying to deflect a scandal himself
in mid-January after a Kansas newspaper published a report detail-
ing some questionable family finances. And in case anyone was
about to miss it, Bush staff members circulated copies of the article
to the media, conjuring up the ghost of the Biden-Dukakis affair.
The Dole financial scandal had a more distressing historical counterpart in the 1884 campaign. Much like James Blaine, Bob Dole
had grown rich while in office. And reminiscent of the illustrations
comparing Blaine's first humble home to his sprawling mansion in
Washington, newspapers compared the Doles' modest $13,000
frame house in Kansas to their posh apartment in Washington's
exclusive Watergate building.

Over two decades, Dole had transformed himself from a man
of modest means to a senator with a $500,000 annual income.

Unlike Blaine, whose money came from bribes and payoffs, the Dole controversy centered around various financial investments he made with his wife, Elizabeth.

Elizabeth Dole, transportation secretary from 1983 to the fall of 1987, had held the family investments in a blind trust until the scandal broke. During the last three years, the assets of the trust had nearly doubled, increasing from $1.4 million to more than $2.3 million. The growth of the trust was due at least in part to real estate investments, which came under investigation by both the Small Business Administration and the House Small Business Committee.

According to *The Hutchinson* (Kansas) *News* article, which was circulated by Bush, a former Dole aide named John Palmer had bought an interest in a building from the blind trust. Ten months later his company, EDP Enterprises, was awarded a $30-million federal contract to provide food services to an army base in Missouri. Dole admitted he did try to help Palmer get the federal contract awarded by the Small Business Administration's program for minority-owned businesses, explaining, "There wasn't any undue influence," adding that Palmer is "a very bright, outstanding young black entrepreneur and a friend of mine."

Palmer's minority-owned company, however, was suspected by the SBA of being a possible front for a white businessman, David C. Owen, Dole's national financial director for his Presidential campaign. Owen was forced to resign after a series of scandalous disclosures. According to the *Washington Post*, Owen had been receiving $4,500 a month from Palmer since the three-year army contract was awarded in February 1986. In addition, Owen also received $7,000 a month as the result of an army contract to another Kansas businessman.

As the terms of the blind trust established that all business transactions would be conducted without the knowledge of the beneficiaries, neither of the Doles was personally implicated. The scandal, however, still opened a can of worms for the Dole campaign. Bush, for one, issued a challenge to the Doles to release their tax returns for the past ten years, as he had. In response, Dole quickly released not ten, but twenty-one years of his own financial information, telling Bush, "I called you and raised you." Despite a strong start, however, Dole ultimately folded his hand and dropped out of the race.

Thus far in the 1988 presidential campaign, the media has appeared ready to turn over every stone and look under every bed. The press has even reported when George Bush's son was asked about his father's attitude on adultery. *Newsweek* published his immortal line: "The answer to the Big 'A' question is N.O." *New York Magazine* even resorted to a nonscandal of a noncandidate when they debunked the rumors of Mario Cuomo's ties to organized crime. Leading up to the '88 primaries, everything was investigated whether it was fair game or not and no one was immune—except, perhaps, for Jesse Jackson.

Jackson seemed to escape the tough scrutiny the other candidates faced. In stark contrast to the wide press exposure and screaming headlines regarding the Pat Robertson shotgun wedding scandal, the fact that Jacqueline Lavinia Brown was two months pregnant when she married Jesse Jackson in 1962 has been virtually ignored outside of a line or two buried deep in a magazine article. *60 Minutes* correspondent Mike Wallace, who built his reputation on conducting tough interviews, never once asked Jesse Jackson about his reported romantic links with a variety of women. When asked during a recent panel discussion why he ignored the adultery question with Jackson, Wallace explained that the black leader's policy issues were basically far more interesting.

Numerous Jackson scandals had been published as early as 1969 when a gossip columnist linked him with singer Nancy Wilson. After that, Jackson was romantically linked to singer Roberta Flack, who gave Jackson a song credit on her 1971 album, "Quiet Fire." In 1973, Flack recorded a torrid love song called "Jesse," which she sang twice on national television the following year. In her biography, *Jesse Jackson: The Man, the Movement, the Myth*, published in 1975, black journalist Barbara Reynolds reported concern among Jackson's aides about his womanizing. "All of the public crooning was creating quite a stir inside the movement," she noted. "A press aide told me, 'All right, now how am I supposed to cover when the press starts asking the obvious'."

If the press asked the obvious in 1975, they ignored it in 1988 even though the polls showed Jackson the Democratic frontrunner for several months after Hart first dropped out and continued to show strong numbers throughout his neck-and-neck race with Dukakis. This was also despite the fact that many of Jackson's "character issues" had a strong relationship to his quest for the presidency.

For one, Jackson was an illegitimate child. His father, Noah Louis Robinson, lived next-door in Greenville, South Carolina, married to another woman. On October 2, 1943, when Jesse was two years old, his mother, Helen Burns, married Charles Henry Jackson. Although the wedding and subsequent adoption stemmed the tide of small-town gossip among the adults, it did little to stop the childhood insults hurled at Jesse. As a result, he grew up with the strong determination to "be somebody," an idea he nobly used as his motto for the black movement.

As a deputy to civil rights leader Dr. Martin Luther King, Jr., however, Jackson backed himself into a situation that alienated many black associates. Jackson had had a meteoric rise in Dr. King's Southern Christian Leadership Conference, but on April 4, 1968, the day King was assassinated, Jackson had committed a sin that many found unforgivable. Although Jackson was a floor below where King was shot outside of his room at the Lorraine Motel in Memphis, Jesse later told reporters, "I was the last man in the world he spoke to." Technically, he was correct. Moments before the shots were heard, King had called downstairs to invite Jackson to dinner. But that didn't explain why Jackson spoke to reporters wearing a turtleneck covered with blood. The next day, Jackson appeared on two local news shows and NBC's *Today Show* wearing the same bloodstained shirt. For years afterward, the media reported that Jackson had been on the balcony and that he had cradled Dr. King in his arms, which he did not. One eyewitness even speculated that Jackson walked upstairs and smeared the blood on his shirt himself.

Why then has the media been so relatively gentle on Jesse Jackson this time around, while the character and actions of other candidates have been explored in detail? Even his 1984 "hymie-town" slur against Jews was downplayed as was his immortalized embrace of PLO leader Yasir Arafat. Perhaps it was because, as Mike Wallace said, Jackson emerged as one of the only candidates addressing more interesting and relevant issues—or perhaps it was out of fear of being perceived as a racist. But perhaps it is also a reflection of the media's reluctance to acknowledge him as a viable candidate despite his strong showing.

In the final analysis, the highly emotional 1988 presidential campaign won't prove to be any better or worse than the preceding ones. And scandals will most likely continue to heat up right down to the wire. The battle between the press and presidential candidates has been around since the beginning of the republic. It grows with the times and expands with technology, but one thing pleasantly stays the same: On the first Tuesday in November, the United States government really does "let the people decide."

References

★ ★ ★ ★ ★ ★ ★ **CHAPTER 1** ★ ★ ★ ★ ★ ★ ★ ★

Clark, Ronald W. *Benjamin Franklin: A Biography*. New York: Random House, 1983.
De Kay, Jr., Ormond. "His Most Detestable High Mightiness." *American Heritage* 27 (1976).
Fleming, Thomas, ed. "Benjamin Franklin: A Biography in His Own Words." *Newsweek*, 1972.
Ford, Paul Leicester. *Who Was the Mother of Franklin's Son?* New Rochelle, N.Y.: Walpole Printing Office, 1932.
Kammen, Michael. *Colonial New York: A History*. New York: Charles Scribner's Sons, 1975.
Pierce, Arthur D. "A Governor in Skirts." *Proceedings of the New Jersey Historical Society* LXXVIII, January 1965.
Randall, Willard Sterne. *Little Revenge: Benjamin Franklin and His Son*. Boston: Little, Brown, & Co., 1984.
Robbins, Peggy. "History's Lighter Side." *American History Illustrated* 17 (6), 1982.
Schoenbrun, David. *Triumph in Paris: The Exploits of Benjamin Franklin*. New York: Harper & Row, 1976.
Smith, Jr., William. *The History of the Province of New York: From the First Discovery to the Year 1732. Vol. 1*. Cambridge, Mass.: The Belknap Press of Harvard University Press, 1972.
Van Doren, Carl. *Benjamin Franklin*. Garden City, N.Y.: Garden City Publishing, 1941.

★ ★ ★ ★ ★ ★ ★ **CHAPTER 2** ★ ★ ★ ★ ★ ★ ★ ★

Cary, Wilson Miles. *Sally Cary*. New York: The Devinne Press, 1916.
Corbin, John. *The Unknown Washington*. New York: Charles Scribner's Sons, 1930.
Fitzpatrick, John C. "The George Washington Scandals." *Scribner's*, April 1927.
Flexner, James T. *George Washington*, 4 vols. Boston: Little, Brown, 1965–1972.
Ford, Paul Leicester. *The True George Washington*. Philadelphia: J. B. Lippincott Company, 1900.
"George Washington's Presidential Papers." Library of Congress, Reel 96, Series 4, Vol. 21.
Marshall, John. *Life of George Washington. Vol. 4*. Philadelphia, C. P. Wayne, 1805.
McDonald, Forrest. *The Presidency of George Washington*. New York: W. W. Norton, 1974.
Moore, Charles. *The Family Life of George Washington*. New York: Houghton Mifflin Company, 1926.

Prussing, Eugene E. *George Washington in Love and Otherwise*. Chicago: P. Covici, 1925.
Siegeman, John F. "Lady of Belvoir." *Virginia Cavalcade* 34 (1), November 1984.
Woodward, C. Vann, ed. *Responses of the Presidents to Charges of Misconduct*. New York: Delacorte Press, 1974.

★ ★ ★ ★ ★ ★ ★ **CHAPTER 3** ★ ★ ★ ★ ★ ★ ★

Bailey, Thomas A. *Presidential Saints and Sinners*. New York: Free Press, 1981.
Brodie, Fawn. *Thomas Jefferson: An Intimate History*. New York: W. W. Norton, 1974.
Callender, James Thomson. *The History of the United States for the Year 1796*. Philadelphia: The Press of Snowden and McCorkle, 1797.
Emery, Noemi. *Alexander Hamilton: An Intimate Portrait*. New York: G. P. Putnam's Sons, 1982.
Hamilton, Alexander. *Observations of Certain Documents Contained in the History of the United States for the Year 1796*. Philadelphia: printed for John Fenno by John Bioren: 1797.
Hendrickson, Robert. *Hamilton (1789–1804)*. Vol. 2. New York: Mason-Charter, 1976.
Hecht, Marie. *Odd Destiny: The Life of Alexander Hamilton*. New York: Macmillan, Inc., 1967.
McDonald, Forrest. *Alexander Hamilton: A Biography*. New York: W. W. Norton, 1979.
Miller, John C. *Alexander Hamilton: Portrait in Paradox*. New York: Harper & Row, 1959.
Parmet, Herbert S. and Hecht, Marie B. *Aaron Burr: Portrait of an Ambitious Man*. New York: Macmillan, Inc., 1967.
Schachner, Nathan. *Aaron Burr: A Biography*. New York: Frederick Stokes and Co., 1937.
Woodward, C. Vann, ed. *Responses of the Presidents to Charges of Misconduct*. New York: Delacorte Press, 1974.

★ ★ ★ ★ ★ ★ ★ **CHAPTER 4** ★ ★ ★ ★ ★ ★ ★

Brodie, Fawn. *Thomas Jefferson: An Intimate History*. New York: W. W. Norton, 1974.
Brodie, Fawn. "Thomas Jefferson's Unknown Grandchildren." *American Heritage* 27 (6), 1976.
Bullock, Helen Duprey. *My Head And My Heart*. New York: G. P. Putnam's Sons, 1945.
Danbew, Virgnius and Kukla, John. "The Monticello Scandals, History and Fiction." *Virginia Cavalcade* 29 (2), 1979.
Jellison, Charles A. "James Thomson Callender: Human Nature in Hideous Form." *Virginia Cavalcade*, Autumn 1979.
Levin, Phyllis Lee. *Abigail Adams: A Biography*. New York: St. Martin's Press, 1987.
Malone, Dumas. *Jefferson and His Time*. Vols. 1–6. Boston: Little, Brown, 1948.
Malone, Dumas. "Mr. Jefferson's Private Life." *Proceedings of the American Antiquarian Society* 84 (1), 1974.
New York Evening Post, 5 April 1805, p. 1.
Van Pelt, Charles. "Jefferson and Maria Cosway." *American Heritage* 22 (5), 1971.
Woodson, Minnie Shumat. "Researching to Document the Oral History of the Thomas

Woodson Family: Dismantling the Sable Curtain." *Journal of the Afro-American History and Genealogical Society*, 1985.

★ ★ ★ ★ ★ ★ ★ **CHAPTER 5** ★ ★ ★ ★ ★ ★ ★

Adams, George Washington. "A Review of the Year 1825." Adams Papers (Microfilm, Reel no. 427).

Burleigh, Anne Husted. *John Adams*. New Rochelle, N.Y.: Arlington House, 1969.

Clark, Bennett Champ. *John Quincy Adams: Old Man Eloquent*. Boston: Little, Brown & Co., 1932.

Hecht, Marie B. *John Quincy Adams*. Macmillan: New York, 1972.

Levin, Phyllis Lee. *Abigail Adams: A Biography*. New York: St. Martin's Press, 1987.

Musto, David F. "The Adams Family." Massachusetts Historical Society Proceedings 93 (1981).

Shaw, Peter. *The Character of John Adams*. Chapel Hill, N. C.: University of North Carolina Press, 1976.

Shepherd, Jack. *Adams Chronicles*. Boston: Little, Brown & Co., 1975.

Shepherd, Jack. *Cannibals of the Heart: A Personal Biography of Louisa Catherine and John Quincy Adams*. New York: McGraw-Hill, 1980.

Smith, Page. *John Adams*. Vol. 2. Garden City, N.Y.: Doubleday & Co., 1962.

★ ★ ★ ★ ★ ★ ★ **CHAPTER 6** ★ ★ ★ ★ ★ ★ ★

Caldwell, Mary French. *General Jackson's Lady*. Kingsport, Tenn.: Kingsport Press, 1936.

Cullen, Joseph P. "The Madame Pompadour of America." *American History Illustrated* 1 (6), 1966.

Curtis, James C. *Andrew Jackson and the Search for Vindication*. Boston: Little, Brown, & Co., 1976.

Dahl, Curtis. "The Clergyman, the Hussy and Old Hickory: Erza Stiles and the Peggy Eaton Affair." *Journal of Presbyterian History* 52 (2), 1974.

Farrell, Brian. "Bellona and the General: Andrew Jackson and the Affair of Mrs. Eaton." *History Today* 7 (8), 1958.

James, Marquis. *The Life of Andrew Jackson*. Indianapolis: Bobbs-Merrill Co., 1938.

Latner, Richard B. "The Eaton Affair Reconsidered." *Tennessee Historical Quarterly* 31 (3), 1977.

Morgan, William G. "John Quincy Adams versus Andrew Jackson: Their Biographers and the 'Corrupt Bargain' Charge." *Tennessee Historical Quarterly* 226 (Spring 1967).

Parton, James. *The Life of Andrew Jackson*. 3 vols. New York: Mason Brothers, 1861.

Remini, Robert V. *Andrew Jackson and the Course of American Empire, 1767–1821*. 3 vols. New York: Harper & Row, 1977.

Rohrs, Richard C. "Partisan Politics and the Attempted Assassination of Andrew Jackson." *Journal of the Early Republic* 1 (2), 1981.

White, Leonard. *The Jacksonians: A Study in Administrative History (1829–1886)*. New York: Free Press, 1954.

Wiltse, Charles M. *John C. Calhoun, Nationalist: 1782–1828*. Indianapolis: Bobbs-Merrill, 1944.

★ ★ ★ ★ ★ ★ ★ **CHAPTER 7** ★ ★ ★ ★ ★ ★ ★

Alotta, Robert I. *A Look at the Vice Presidency*. Vol. 2. New York: J. Messner, 1981.

Barzman, Sol. *Madmen and Geniuses: The Vice Presidents of the United States*. Chicago: Follet, 1974.

Berger, Raoul. *Executive Privilege: A Constitutional Myth*. Cambridge, Mass.: Harvard University Press, 1974.

Bolt, Robert. "Vice President Richard M. Johnson of Kentucky: Hero of the Thames or the Great Amalgamator?" *Register of the Kentucky Historical Society* 75 (3), 1977.

Chidsey, Donald Barr. *And Tyler Too*. Nashville, Tenn.: T. Nelson, 1978.

Curtis, James C. *The Fox at Bay: Martin Van Buren and the Presidency, 1837–41*. Lexington, Ky.: University Press of Kentucky, 1970.

Lynch, Denis Tilden. *An Epoch and a Man: Martin Van Buren and His Times*. New York: H. Liveright, 1929.

Morgan, Robert J. *A Whig Embattled: The Presidency Under John Tyler*. Lincoln, Nebr.: University of Nebraska Press, 1954.

Rayback, Joseph G. "Martin Van Buren: His Place in the History of New York and the United States." *New York History* 64 (2), 1983.

Seager, II, Robert. *And Tyler, Too: A Biography of John and Julia Gardiner Tyler*. New York: McGraw-Hill and Co., 1963.

White, Leonard D. *The Jeffersonians: A Study in Administrative History, 1801–1829*. New York: Macmillan and Co., 1951.

★ ★ ★ ★ ★ ★ ★ **CHAPTER 8** ★ ★ ★ ★ ★ ★ ★

"Aaron Brown to Sara Polk," letter. Polk papers (Microfilm, Reel #R25 114). 17 January 1844.

Balderston, Thomas. "The Shattered Life of Teresa Sickles." *American History Illustrated* 17 (5), 1982.

Blum, et al. *The National Experience: A History of The United States*. 5th ed. New York: Harcourt Brace Jovanovich, 1985.

Bruns, Roger L. "The Assault of Charles Sumner, 1856." From *Congress Investigates a Documented History, 1797–1974*. Edited by Arthur M. Schlesinger, Jr. New York: Chelsea House, 1975.

Curtis, George Ticknor. *Life of James Buchanan: Fifteenth President of the United States*. Vol. II. New York: Harper, 1883.

Eckoff, Christian F. *Memoirs of a Senate Page, 1855–1859*. New York: Broadway Publishing, 1909.

"First Gay President?" *Penthouse* magazine, November 1987.

Meerse, David E. "Buchanan, Corruption and the Election of 1860." *Civil War History* 12 (2), 1966.

Nicolay, John G. and Hay, John. *Abraham Lincoln: A History*. Vol. II. New York: The Century Co., 1890.

Pinchon, Edgcum. *Dan Sickles: Hero of Gettysburg and Yankee King of Spain*. New York: Doubleday, 1945.
Sellers, Charles. *James K. Polk: Continentalist, 1843–1846*. Vol. 2. Princeton, N.J.: Princeton University Press, 1966.

★ ★ ★ ★ ★ ★ ★ **CHAPTER 9** ★ ★ ★ ★ ★ ★ ★

Barton, William E. *The Women Lincoln Loved*. Indianapolis, Indiana: The Bobbs-Merrill Co., 1927.
Bell, Patricia. "Mary Todd Lincoln: A Personality Portrait." *Civil War Times Illustrated* 7 (7), 1968.
Carruthers, Olive. *Lincoln's Other Mary*. Chicago: Ziff-Davis Publishing Co., 1946.
Croy, Homer. *The Trial of Mrs. Abraham Lincoln*. New York: Dwell, Soan and Pearce, 1962.
Curtis, William Elroy. *The True Abraham Lincoln*. Philadelphia: J. B. Lippincott Co., 1913.
Hackensmith, C. W. "The Much Maligned Mary Todd Lincoln." *Filson Club Historical Quarterly* 44, 1970.
Hertz, Emmanuel. *The Hidden Lincoln*. New York: The Viking Press, 1938.
Neely, Mark E. Jr. and McMurtry, R. Gerald. *Insanity File: The Case of Mary Todd Lincoln*. Carbondale, Ill.: Southern Illinois University Press, 1986.
Nevins, Allan. *The Emergence of Lincoln*. 2 vols. New York: Charles Scribner's Sons, 1950.
Reck, W. Emerson. "The Tragedy of Major Rathbone." *Lincoln Herald* 86 (4), 1984.
Turner, Justin G. and Turner, Linda Levitt. *Mary Todd Lincoln: Her Life and Her Letters*. New York: Alfred A. Knopf, 1972.

★ ★ ★ ★ ★ ★ ★ **CHAPTER 10** ★ ★ ★ ★ ★ ★ ★

Brown, D. Alexander. "The Belknap Scandal." *American History Illustrated* 4 (2), 1967.
Carpenter, John A. *Ulysses S. Grant*. New York: T. Wayne Publishers, 1970.
DeGregorio, William A. *The Complete Book of Presidents*. New York: Dembner Books, 1984.
Joachim, Walter. "Hiester Clymer and the Belknap Case." *Historical Record of Berks County* 36 (1), 1970.
Leish, Kenneth W., ed. *American Heritage Pictorial History of the Presidents*. Vol. 1. New York: American Heritage Publishing Co., 1968.
McDonald, John. *Secrets of the Great Whiskey Ring and Eighteen Months in the Penitentiary*. St. Louis, Missouri: W. S. Bryan, 1880.
Ross, Isabel. *The General's Wife: The Life of Mrs. Ulysses S. Grant*. New York: Dodd, Mead & Co., 1959.
Thayer, William M. *From Tannery to the White House: Story of the Life of Ulysses S. Grant: His Boyhood, Youth, Manhood, Public and Private Life and Services*. Boston: James H. Earle, 1886.
U.S. Congress. House. "Crédit Mobilier Investigation." 42nd Cong., 3rd sess., 1873, S. Rept. 77.

U.S. Congress. House. "Gold Panic Investigation." 42nd Cong., 3rd sess., 1873, H. Rept. 77.
U.S. Congress. House. Judiciary Committee. "Impeachment of W. W. Belknap." 44th Cong., 1st sess., 1867, H. Rept. 345.
U.S. Congress. Senate. "Senate Sitting for the Trial of William W. Belknap." 44th Congress, 1st sess., 1876.
Vann Woodward, C., ed. *The Responses of The Presidents to Charges of Misconduct.* New York: Delacorte Press, 1974.

★ ★ ★ ★ ★ ★ ★ **CHAPTER 11** ★ ★ ★ ★ ★ ★ ★

Cochran, William C. "Dear Mother . . . : An Eyewitness Report on the Republican National Convention of 1876." *Hayes Historical Journal* 1 (2), 1976.
Cook, Theodore P. *The Life and Public Services of Hon. Samuel J. Tilden.* New York: D. Appleton, 1876.
Haworth, Paul. *The Hayes-Tilden Election.* Indianapolis: The Bobbs-Merrill Co., 1927.
Jordan, David M. *Roscoe Conkling of New York: Voice in the Senate.* Ithaca, N. Y.: Cornell University Press, 1971.
Leech, Margaret and Brown, Harry J. *The Garfield Orbit: The Life of President A. Garfield.* New York: Harper & Row, 1978.
Martin, Ralph G. *The Bosses.* New York: G. P. Putnam & Sons, 1964.
Orth, Samuel P. *The Boss and the Machine.* New Haven, Conn.: Yale University Press, 1921.
Peskin, Allan. *Garfield: A Biography.* New York: Harper & Row, 1978.
Smith, Theodore C. *The Life and Letters of James Abram Garfield.* New Haven, Conn.: Yale University Press, 1925.
Stone, Irving. *They Also Ran.* Garden City, New York: Doubleday & Co., 1966.
Williams, Charles R. *The Life of Rutherford B. Hayes.* 2 Vols. New York: Houghton Mifflin, 1914.

★ ★ ★ ★ ★ ★ ★ **CHAPTER 12** ★ ★ ★ ★ ★ ★ ★

Ambrose, Stephan E. "Blaine vs. Cleveland." *American History Illustrated* 1 (6), 1966.
Eaton, Herbert. *Presidential Timber: The Story of How Presidential Candidates Are Nominated.* New York: Free Press of Glencoe, 1964.
Martin, John Stuart. "When the President Disappeared." *American Heritage* 8 (6), 1957.
Nevins, Allan. *Grover Cleveland: A Study in Courage.* New York: Dodd, Mead and Co., 1948.
Rosenberg, Dorothy and Rosenberg, Marvin. "The Dirtiest Election." *American Heritage* 13 (5), 1962.
Schlup, Leonard. "Presidential Disability: The Case of Cleveland and Stevenson." *Presidential Studies Quarterly* 9 (3), 1979.
Tugwell, Rexford G. *Grover Cleveland.* New York: Macmillan, 1968.

★ ★ ★ ★ ★ ★ ★ **CHAPTER 13** ★ ★ ★ ★ ★ ★ ★

Buchanan, A. Russell. *David S. Terry: Duelling Judge*. San Marino, California: Huntington Library, 1956.

Etemadi, Judy Nicholas. " 'Love-Mad Man': Senator Charles W. Jones of Florida." *Florida Historical Quarterly* 56 (2), 1977.

Klotter, James C. "Sex, Scandal, and Suffrage in the Gilded Age." *Historian* 42 (2), 1980.

McCracken, Brooks W. "Althea and the Judges." *American Heritage* 18 (4), 1967.

New York Times, 1 March 1890, p. 1

———. 2 March 1890, p. 1

Roberts, Gary L. "In Pursuit of Duty." *American West* 7 (5), 1970.

Thatcher, Linda. "The 'Gentile Polygamist' Arthur Brown, Ex-Senator from Utah." *Utah Historical Quarterly* 52 (3), 1984.

★ ★ ★ ★ ★ ★ ★ **CHAPTER 14** ★ ★ ★ ★ ★ ★ ★

Cutler, Charles. "My Dear Mrs. Peck." *American History Illustrated* 6 (3), 1971.

Hulbert, Mary Allen. *The Story of Mrs. Peck*. New York: Minton, Bach, and Co., 1933.

———. "The Woodrow Wilson I Knew." *Liberty Magazine*, December 1924 and January 1925 (2 parts).

Link, Arthur S., ed. *Wilson: A Profile*. New York: Hill and Wang, 1968.

———. *Wilson Confusions and Crises, 1915–1916*. Princeton, N. J.: Princeton University Press, 1964.

Seymore, Charles, ed. *The Intimate Papers of Colonel House*. Boston: Houghton Mifflin Co., 1926–1928.

Tribble, Edwin, ed. *A President in Love: The Courtship Letters of Woodrow Wilson and Edith Bolling Galt*. Boston: Houghton Mifflin Co., 1981.

Walworth, Arthur. *Woodrow Wilson*. Boston: Houghton Mifflin Co., 1965.

Washington Post, 9 October 1915, p. 1.

Wilson, Edith Bolling. *My Memoir*. Indianapolis: Bobbs-Merrill Co., 1939.

★ ★ ★ ★ ★ ★ ★ **CHAPTER 15** ★ ★ ★ ★ ★ ★ ★

Adams, Samuel Hopkins. *Incredible Era: The Life and Times of Warren Gamaliel Harding*. Boston: Houghton Mifflin Co., 1939.

Bates, J. Leonard. *The Origins of the Teapot Dome: Progressives, Parties and Petroleum, 1909–1921*. Urbana, Ill.: University of Illinois Press, 1963.

Britton, Nan. *Honesty in Politics*. New York: The Elizabeth Ann Guild, 1932.

———. *The President's Daughter*. New York: The Elizabeth Ann Guild, 1927.

Daugherty, Harry M., with Dixon, Thomas. *The Inside Story of the Harding Tragedy*. Freeport, N.Y.: Books for Libraries Press, 1971.

Day, Donald. *Will Rogers: A Biography*. New York: D. McKay Co., 1962.

DeGregorio, William A. *The Complete Book of the Presidents*. New York: Dembner Books, 1984.

Downes, Randolph C. "The Harding Muckfest." *NW Ohio Quarterly* 39 (3), 1967.
Duckett, Kenneth W. and Russell, Francis. "The Harding Papers: How Some Were Burned . . . and Some Were Saved." *American Heritage* 16 (2), 1965.
Leish, Kenneth W., ed. *American Heritage Pictorial History of the Presidents.* Vol. 2. New York: American Heritage Publishing Co., 1968.
Russell, Francis. "The Harding Papers." *American Heritage* 16 (2), 1965.
———. "The Shadow of Warren Harding." *Antioch Review* 36 (1), 1978.
Stratton, David S. "Two Western Senators and Teapot Dome." *Pacific NW Quarterly* 65 (2), 1974.

★ ★ ★ ★ ★ ★ ★ **CHAPTER 16** ★ ★ ★ ★ ★ ★ ★

Burns, James MacGregor. *Roosevelt: The Lion and the Fox.* New York: Harcourt Brace Jovanovich, 1956.
Faber, Doris. *The Life of Lorena Hickok, E. R.'s Friend.* New York: William Morrow & Co., 1980.
Lash, Joseph F. *Eleanor and Franklin.* New York: W. W. Norton, 1971.
Miller, Nathan. *FDR: An Intimate History.* Garden City, N. Y.: Doubleday & Co., 1983.
Parks, Lillian Rogers with Leighton, Frances Spatz. *The Roosevelts: A Family in Turmoil.* Englewood Cliffs, New Jersey: Prentice-Hall, 1981.
Roosevelt, Elliot and Brough, James. *The Roosevelts of Hyde Park: An Untold Story.* New York: G. P. Putnam & Sons, 1973.
Vann Woodward, C., ed. *Responses of the Presidents to Charges of Misconduct.* New York: Delacorte Press, 1974.

★ ★ ★ ★ ★ ★ ★ **CHAPTER 17** ★ ★ ★ ★ ★ ★ ★

Abels, Jules. *The Truman Scandals.* Chicago: H. Regnery Co., 1956.
Biggart, Nicole Woolsey. "Scandals in the White House: An Organizational Explanation." *Sociological Inquiry* 55 (2), Spring 1985.
Cochran, Bert. *Harry Truman and the Crisis Presidency.* New York: Funk & Wagnalls, 1973.
Donovan, Robert J. *Eisenhower: The Inside Story.* New York: Harper & Row, 1956.
Ewig, Rick. "McCarthy Era Politics: The Ordeal of Senator Lester Hunt." *Annals of Wyoming* 55 (1), 1983.
Fullington, Michael Gregory. "An Organizational Analysis of Scandal in the White House." *Dissertation Abstracts International* 41 (4), 1980.
Greenstein, Fred I. *The Hidden Hand Presidency.* New York: Basic Books, 1982.
"It's Christmas all the Time for the U.S. Presidents." *U.S. New and World Report,* 16 (December 1955).
Michaelson, Judith. "The Blacklist Legacy." Los Angeles Times, 18 October 1987.
Miller, Merle. *Plain Speaking: An Oral Biography of Harry S Truman.* New York: Berkley Publishing Corp., 1973.
Neal, Steve. *The Eisenhowers: Reluctant Dynasty.* Garden City, N.Y.: Doubleday & Co., 1978.

Pearson, Drew. *Diaries, 1949–1959*. New York: Holt, Rinehart and Winston, 1974.
Summersby, Kay. *Eisenhower Was My Boss*. New York: Prentice-Hall, 1948.
————. *Past Forgetting: My Love Affair With Dwight D. Eisenhower*. New York: Simon & Schuster, 1975.
Steele, John L. "How the Press Shot Sherman Adams Down." *Life*, 29 September 1958.
"To the President with Very Best Wishes." *Newsweek*, 16 December 1955.

★ ★ ★ ★ ★ ★ ★ CHAPTER 18 ★ ★ ★ ★ ★ ★ ★

"An Awful Question Revived Again." *Life Magazine*, 14 June 1968.
Blakey, Robert. *The Plot to Kill the President*. New York: Times Books, 1981.
Collier, Peter and Horowitz, David. *The Kennedys*. New York: Summit Books, 1984.
Davis, John H. *The Kennedys: Dynasty and Disaster*. New York: McGraw-Hill and Co., 1984.
Exner, Judith Campbell. *My Story*. (As told to Ovid Demaris.) New York: Grove Press, 1977.
"JFK's 'Close Friend.' " *Newsweek*, 18 September, 1976.
Lasky, Victor. *JFK: The Man and the Myth*. New York: Macmillan and Co,. 1963.
Martin, Ralph G. *A Hero for Our Time*. New York: Macmillan and Co., 1983.
McCarthy, J. *The Remarkable Kennedys*. New York: Dial Press, 1960.
Meyer, Timothy and Shelby, Jr., Maruic. "16 Months After Chappaquiddick: Effects of the Kennedy Broadcast," *Journalism Quarterly* 51 (3), 1975.
Sorenson, Theodore C. *The Kennedy Legacy*. New York: Macmillan and Co., 1969.
Wills, Garry. *The Kennedy Imprisonment*. Boston: Little, Brown & Co., 1982.
Wolin, Howard E. "Grandiosity and Violence in the Kennedy Family." *Psychohistory Review* 8 (3), 1979.
Zeiger, H.A. *Robert Kennedy: A Biography*. New York: Meredith Press, 1968.

★ ★ ★ ★ ★ ★ ★ CHAPTER 19 ★ ★ ★ ★ ★ ★ ★

Caro, Robert A. "The Years of Lyndon Johnson: Longlea." *Atlantic Monthly*, November 1982.
Harwood, Richard and Johnson, Haynes. *Lyndon*. New York: Praeger Publishers, 1973.
Healy, Paul and Volz, Joseph. "Sex and Politics." *New York Daily News*, 15 June 1976.
Janus, Sam; Bess, Barbara; and Saltus, Carol. *A Sexual Profile of Men in Power*. Englewood Cliffs, New Jersey: Prentice-Hall, 1977.
Kearns, Doris, *Lyndon Johnson and the American Dream*. New York: Harper & Row, 1976.
Goldman, Eric F. *The Tragedy of Lyndon Johnson*. New York: Alfred A. Knopf, 1969.
Mollenhoff, Clark R. *Despoilers of Democracy*. Garden City, N.Y.: Doubleday and Co., 1968.
Evans, Rowland and Novack, Robert. *Lyndon B. Johnson: The Exercise of Power*. New York: New American Library, 1966.
Vann Woodward, C., ed. *Responses of the Presidents to Charges of Misconduct*. New York: Delacorte Press, 1974.
"Was LBJ's Final Secret a Son?" *People*, 3 July 1987.

★ ★ ★ ★ ★ ★ ★ **CHAPTER 20** ★ ★ ★ ★ ★ ★ ★

"Close Friend Willed Bulk of Hoover Estate." *Washington Post*, 23 May 1972.
Demaris, Ovid. *The Director: An Oral Biography of J. Edgar Hoover*. New York: Harper's Magazine Press, 1975.
Garrow, David J. *Bearing the Cross*. New York: William Morrow, 1986.
————. *The FBI and Martin Luther King*. New York: W.W. Norton, 1981.
"G-Man Under Fire." *Life Magazine*, 9 April 1971.
Messick, Hank. *John Edgar Hoover*. New York: McKay, 1972.
Nash, Jay Robert. *Citizen Hoover*. Chicago: Nelson-Hall, 1972.
Schlesinger, Jr., Arthur M. *Robert Kennedy and His Times*. Boston: Houghton Mifflin Co., 1978.

★ ★ ★ ★ ★ ★ ★ **CHAPTER 21** ★ ★ ★ ★ ★ ★ ★

"A Decade Later, Watergate's Veterans are Winners, Losers . . . and Everything In Between." *People*, 1 June 1982.
"Aftermath of A Burglary." *Time Magazine*, 14 June 1982.
Einsiedel, Edna F. "Television Network News Coverage of the Eagleton Affair: A Case Study." *Journalism Quarterly* 52 (1), 1975.
"FBI Investigated Hong Kong Woman Friend of Nixon in 60s to Determine if She Was Foreign Agent," *New York Times*, 22 June 1976.
FBI source. Interview with author. 14 July 1976; 15 July 1976.
"How Time Has Treated the Watergate Crew." *U.S. News and World Report*. 14 June 1982.
Hume, Brit. "Jack Anderson and the Eagleton Case." *The Washington Monthly*, July/August 1974.
Lau, Lily (Marianna Liu's daughter). Interview with author. 29 July 1976; 30 July 1976.
"The Legacy of Watergate." *Newsweek*, 1 June 1982.
"Marianna Liu Admits She Knew Nixon." *People Magazine*, 14 October 1976.
Messic, Hank. *John Edgar Hoover*. New York: McKay, 1972.
New York Times, 22 June 1976, p. 19.
Rosenbaum, Ron. "Ah, Watergate!" *The New Republic*, 23 June 1982.
Von Hoffman, Nicholas. "How Nixon Got Strung Up." *The New Republic*, 23 June 1982.
"Where Are They Now?" *Newsweek*, 23 June 1982.
"Watergate's Clearest Lesson." *Time*, 14 June 1982.
White, Theodore. *Breach of Faith: The Fall of Richard Nixon*. New York: Atheneum, 1975.
Wong, Irene. (Marianna Liu's daughter). Interview with author. 30 July 1976.

★ ★ ★ ★ ★ ★ ★ **CHAPTER 22** ★ ★ ★ ★ ★ ★ ★

Koreagate
"All About Koreagate." *Newsweek*, 1 August 1977.

"Final Reckoning." *Time*, 24 July 1978.

"Investigation Into Influence-buying by Korean Figure Comes to an End." *New York Times*, 17 August 1978.

Wilbur Mills

"Back: Wilbur Mills Recalls His Bout With Alcohol." *Washington Post*, 4 January 1978.

"Campaign Strenuous For a Non-Candidate." *Congressional Quarterly*, 30 July 1971.

"From Alcoholism to a New Life." *Parade*, 21 August 1977.

"Mills Hurt, Intoxicated in Incident, Police Say." *Washington Post*, 10 October 1974.

"Returns to Hill." *Washington Post*, 6 May 1973.

"Wilbur Mills' Problems in Ark." *Washington Post*, 23 October 1974.

Nelson Rockefeller

"Megan Marshak's Instant Celebrity." *Washington Post*, 16 February 1979.

New York Times, 7 February 1979, page 1.

"Rocky's Final Hour." *Newsweek*, 19 February 1979.

"Rocky Recalled: A Eulogy and Some Questions." *Time*, 12 February 1979.

Washington Post, 17 February 1979, page [C3].

Washington Post, 4 February 1979, page [C4].

CIA

"The Assassination Plot That Failed." *Time*, 30 June 1975.

Church, F. Forrester. *Father and Son*. New York: Harper & Row, 1985.

"5 Death Plots—Was CIA Involved?" *U.S. News & World Report*, 30 June 1975.

"How the Agency Killed Trujillo." *The New Republic*, 23 June 1975.

"A Kennedy Vendetta." *Harpers*, August 1975.

"Of Darts, Guns and Poisons." *Time*, 30 October 1975.

"A Peak In the CIA's Closet." *Newsweek*, 27 January 1975.

"A Tale of Assassination." *Newsweek*, 12 May 1975.

"The Wounded CIA." *Newsweek*, 17 November 1975.

Wayne Hayes/Elizabeth Ray

"FBI Begins Hayes Inquiry." *Washington Post*, 25 May 1976.

"Grand Jury Gets Hayes Case." *Washington Post*, 27 May 1976.

"Hayes Reverses Himself, Admits Relationship." *Washington Post*, 27 May 1976.

"Hayes Probe Counsel Told to Keep Mum." *Washington Post*, 1 June 1976.

"The Odyssey of Elizabeth Ray." *Washington Post*, 1 June 1976.

"Powerful Hayes Described as a Czar in the House." *Washington Post*, 25 May 1976.

Betty Ford

Ford, Betty and Chase, Chris. *Betty; A Glad Awakening*. Garden City, N.Y.: Doubleday & Co., 1987.

★ ★ ★ ★ ★ ★ ★ **CHAPTER 23** ★ ★ ★ ★ ★ ★ ★

Jimmy Carter

Goldson, G. Barry, ed. *The Playboy Interview*. New York: Playboy Press, 1981.

"The Jimmy Carter Interview." *Playboy*, November 1976.

"This Is the Way It Was." *Washingtonian*, October 1985.

Cocaine

"Hill Drug Probe Implicates 3". *Washington Post*, 18 November 1983.

"Inquiry Set on Alleged Drug Use by Kraft, Carter Campaign Aide." *New York Times*, 14 September 1980.

"Justice Won't Pursue Panel Evidence Linking Goldwater, Jr. to Cocaine." *Washington Post*, 19 November 1983.

"Lawyer Says Woman Reported Jordan Used Cocaine in California." *New York Times*, 16 September 1979.

"Mrs. Carter Firmly Defends Jordan in Cocaine Case." *New York Times*, 22 March 1979.

"Rep. John Burton: Stepping Out of Fast Lane to Walk Tall." *Los Angeles Times*, 13 January 1984.

New York Times, 25 March 1981, p. 1

New York Times, 19 March 1987 [d26]

Bert Lance

"Bert Lance's Banking Woes (Cont)." *Fortune*, 17 March 1986.

"Bert Lance: Crook or Solid Citizen?" *U.S. News & World Report*, 4 February 1980.

"Lance Checks out Politics—Again." *Fortune*, 5 August 1985.

"Latest Chapter in the Bert Lance Saga." *U.S. News & World Report*, 29 January 1979.

"Mondale's Damage Control." *Newsweek*, 13 August 1984.

"We Just Plain Licked 'Em." *Time*, 12 May 1980.

Abscam

"Abscam." *1980 Congressional Quarterly Almanac*, Congressional Quarterly, Inc., Washington, D.C., 1980.

"Abscam Convicts Told to Go to Prison on July 7." *New York Times*, 23 June 1983.

"Abscam Investigation." *Congressional Quarterly's Guide to Congress*. 3rd Edition. Washington, D.C.: Congressional Quarterly, Inc., 1982.

"The Abscam Net Snares a Senator."*Newsweek*, 10 November 1980.

"Abscam's Toll." *Time*, 24 August 1981.

"Abscam: Twist in the Plot." *Newsweek*, 24 November 1980.

"Grand Jury Investigation of Rep. Jenrette Widened." *New York Times*, 9 August 1979.

"Justice Refuse to Hear Appeals in 7 Abscam Cases; 4 Ex-Lawmakers and 3 Others Will Soon Begin to Serve Federal Prison Terms." *New York Times*, 1 June 1983.

"Operation Abscam: The FBI Stings Congress." *Time*, 18 February 1980.

"Profiles of Members Mentioned in Probe." Congressional Quarterly, 9 February 1980.

"Putting Abscam on Trial." *Newsweek*, 26 January 1981.

"Three Ex-Members of House Given Terms in Prison." *New York Times*, 14 August 1981.

Rita Jenrette

" 'Diary of a Mad Congresswife': Why Jenrette Tells All." *The Washington Star*, 4 December 1980.

"Rita Jenrette Granted Divorce." *New York Times*, 23 July 1981.

"The Saga of Rita Jenrette." *Washington Post*, 14 March 1985.

Paula Parkinson

"Congress: An X-rated Tale." *Newsweek*, 16 March 1981.

"Congressmen Shared House with Female Lobbyist." *Washington Post*, 7 March 1981.

"Lobbyist Facing Inquiry Over Her Sexual Affairs." *New York Times*, 27 March 1981.

"Paula Has Some Pearls On Lobbying." *New York Daily News*, 26 March 1981.

"U.S. Plans Inquiry Into Sex-For-Votes Reports Involving Three Congressmen." *New York Times*, 13 March 1981.

Washington Post, 29 March 1981, page F1.

Homosexuality

ABC's "Nightline," Transcript # 1643, 9 September 1987.

"Aids Strikes Down a Congressman." *Newsweek*, 18 May 1987.

"Bob Bauman, After the Fall." *Washington Post*, 6 August 1986.

"Congress Beset by New Sex Scandal." *U.S. News & World Report*, 25 July 1983.

"A Gay Conservative Tells His Story: Bob Bauman is haunted by the past—and future." *Newsweek*, 18 August 1986.

"The Secret life of Bob Bauman." *Washingtonian*, July 1986.

Stevens, Stuart P. "School for Scandal." *Washingtonian*, March 1981.

Billy Carter

"Big Brother Was Listening." *Time*, 17 November 1973.

"Billy Carter is not a Buffoon." *Time*, 1 September 1980.

"Billy Carter Tells His Side of the Story." *U.S. News & World Report*, 1 September 1980.

"Billygate or Mediagate?" *Newsweek*, 18 August 1980.

"The Burden of Billy: The Libyan Caper." *Time*, 4 August 1980.

"Private Lives In Public." *Time*, 4 August 1980.

"What Have You Done, Billy Boy?" (discrepancies in Billy Carter's story). *Time*, 11 August 1980.

"White House Struggles to Clean Up a Mess." *U.S. News & World Report*, 11 August 1980.

★ ★ ★ ★ ★ ★ ★ **CHAPTER 24** ★ ★ ★ ★ ★ ★ ★

Debategate

"Debate Data: Crime or Ethics Lapse." *New York Times*, 11 November 1983.

"Gategrate." *New York Times*, 7 July 1983.

"New 'Debategate' Report Sharpens Focus on Casey Links." *Christian Science Monitor*, 24 May 1984.

"Justice Agency Ends 'Debategate' Inquiry and Says No Evidence of Crime was Found. *Wall Street Journal*, 24 February 1984.

"Reagan Aides Describe Operation to Gather Inside Data on Carter." *New York Times*, 7 July 1982.

"What Price a Political Party's Victory." *New York Times*, 25 July 1983.

Michael Deaver

"Deaver Is Indicted by U.S. Grand Jury on Perjury Counts." *New York Times*, 19 March 1987.

"Deaver Phoned Secretary of Transportation, Jury Told." *Los Angeles Times*, 5 November 1987.

"Deaver Portrayed As Eager to Earn High Pay As Lobbyist." *Los Angeles Times*, 29 October 1987.

"Deaver's Wrong Turn in a Limousine." *U.S. News & World Report*, 28 December 1987.

"The High Price of Friendship: Deaver Faces a Jail Term for Lying About His Lobbying Activities." *Time*, 28 December 1987.

"Jury Convicts Deaver of 3 Perjury Counts." *Los Angeles Times*, 17 December 1987.

Fedders

"Abuse Victims' Reluctant Advocate: Ex-battered Wife Rebuilds a Family's 'Shattered Dreams'." *Los Angeles Times*, 19 November 1987.

"A Private Crisis, a Public Disgrace." *Newsweek*, 11 March 1985.

"Profit From a Shameful Act" *Washington Post*, 21 October 1987.

"SEC Enforcement Chief Beat Wife Repeatedly, Court Told." *Washington Post*, 26 February 1985.

Edwin Meese

"The Ed Meese File Grows Thicker." *U.S. News & World Report*, 8 February 1988.

"$4 Billion Worth of Temptation." *Time*, 15 June 1987.

"Good Connections?" *Newsweek*, 2 April 1984.

"It's Lonely at the Top: Resignations Rock The Justice Department, But Ed Meese Clings to His Job." *Time*, 11 April 1988.

"Meese: Benefit From Fee Paid to Wallach Indicated." *Los Angeles Times*, 10 March 1988.

"Meese's Claim on Wallach Pipeline Memo Questioned." *Los Angeles Times*, 4 February 1988.

"Meese's Friend, 2 Associates Indicted." *Washington Post*, 23 December 1987.

"Meese's Personal Finances Being Probed by McKay." *Los Angeles Times*, 26 March 1988.

"Meese Presence Felt Strongly at Wedtech Trial." *Los Angeles Times*, 28 March 1988.

"Meese Vague in Nofziger Testimony." *Los Angeles Times*, 3 February 1988.

"Pipeline Memo to Meese Gives Plan for Paying Israelis." *Los Angeles Times*, 23 February 1988.

"A Question of Ethics: The Meese Investigation Puts the Reagan Administration Under a Cloud." *Time*, 2 April 1984.

Iran-Contra Affair

"Bush Seen Fully Briefed on Iran Sales, Hostages." *Los Angeles Times*, 7 January 1988.

"The Fall Guy Fights Back: North Fingers His Superiors, But not the President." *Time*, 20 July 1987.

"Iran-Contra Jury Indicts Poindexter, North, Two Others." *Los Angeles Times*, 17 March 1987.

"Memos Suggest Bush Contra Arms Role, Stir Questions on His Candor." *Los Angeles Times*, 28 March 1988.

"Poindexter and North Enter Not Guilty Pleas." *Los Angeles Times*, 25 March 1988.

The Tower Commission Report. New York: Bantam co-published with Times Books, 1987.

"Walsh Hires Legal Expert for High Court Arguments." *Los Angeles Times*, 19 February 1988.

Lyn Nofziger

"Fall of the Californians." *Newsweek*, 27 July 1987.

"Just Say Goodbye, Don; Nancy Reagan Wins Her Campaign Against Chief of Staff Donald Regan." *Time*, 9 March 1987.

"Nofziger's Turn: Another Reagan Aide Is Guilty." *Time*, 22 February 1988.

"Pen Pal: Lyn Nofziger Faces a Probe." *Time*, 17 November 1986.

Miscellaneous

"Country Club Ethics." *Newsweek*, 2 April 1984.

"The First Family Feud" (Cont'd). *Newsweek*, 10 December 1984.

"Ex-Member of Postal Service Board Gets 4 Years: Sentence Follows Voss' Admission of Contract Kickback and Expense Fraud Schemes." *Washington Post*, 25 October 1986.

"Ex-U.S. Attorney Guilty of Disclosing Indictment." (J. William Petro). *New York Times*, 9 March 1985.

"Ginsburg Admits Smoking Marijuana in 60s and 70s." *Los Angeles Times*, 6 November 1987.

"Give Me Back My Reputation." (Donovan) *Time*, 8 June 1987.

"Hard Days for Lame Ducklings." *Los Angeles Times*, 10 January 1988.

"HUD's Sloan Quits Amid New Charges." *Washington Post*, 11 April 1984.

"Indictment of Beggs Dropped." *Science*, 3 July 1987.

"Misuse of Funds Laid to Watt." *New York Times*, 25 February 1982.

"Morality of the Supply-Siders." *Times*, 25 May 1987.

"The Reagan 45." *The New Republic*, 16 April 1984

"Scandal Sheet." *The New Republic*, 20 April 1987.

"A Top Postal Official Admits Guilt in Fraud." (Peter Voss) *New York Times*, 30 May 1986.

"An Unexpected Fall From Grace: NASA's Chief Is Indicted in a General Dynamics Case." (James Beggs) *Time*, 16 December 1985.

"White House Names New EPA Chief: William Ruckelshaus Is Appointed After John Hernandez becomes Embroiled in Charges of Unethical Conduct." *Science*, 1 April 1983.

"Why The President's Men Stumble." *New York Times Magazine*, 18 July 1982.

★ ★ ★ ★ ★ ★ ★ CHAPTER 25 ★ ★ ★ ★ ★ ★ ★

Joseph Biden

"Biden Admits Enhancing School Record." *Los Angeles Times*, 22 September 1987.

"Biden Stirs Row By Using Lines from Briton's Talk." *Los Angeles Times*, 13 September 1987.

"Biden's Stolen Speeches End His Campaign Hopes." *Sunday Times*, 20 September 1987. *New York Times*, 24 September 1987.

"Biden Was Accused of Plagiarism in Law School." *New York Times*, 17 September 1987.

Mario Cuomo

"Cuomo and Those Rumors." *New York Magazine*, 2 November 1987.

Robert Dole

"Dole Aide Leaves Over Real Estate Deal." *Los Angeles Times*, 15 January 1988.

"Dole Hits Bush Tactic on Family Finances." *Los Angeles Times*, 11 January 1988.

"Dole's Now Wealthy—After Modest Start." *Los Angeles Times*, 17 January 1988.

"Ex-Dole Aide Was Paid Large Fees by Firms That Won Army Contracts." *Los Angeles Times*, 25 January 1988.

"Probe of Mrs. Dole's Blind Trust Reported." *Los Angeles Times*, 14 January 1988.

Michael Dukakis

"A Mild Dose of Candor: Kitty Dukakis reveals a Former Drug Dependency." *Time*, 20 July 87.

"Wife Of Dukakis Discloses Abuse of Pills—Now Drug-Free, She Was Addicted 26 Years." *New York Times*, 9 July 1987.

Gore, Babbitt

"Candidates Gore, Babbitt Admit Past Use of Marijuana." *Los Angeles Times*, 8 November 1987.

Gary Hart

ABC's "Nightline." Transcript # 1642, 8 September 1987.

ABC's "Nightline." Transcript # 1643, 9 September 1987.

"Chronicle of a Ruinous Affair; Donna Rice's Monkey Business. Shipmate Lynn Armadt Breaks Her Silence on the Scandal that Toppled Gary Hart." *People*, 15 June 1987.

"Donna Rice: 'The Woman In Question.' " *People*, 18 May 1987.

"Fall From Grace." *Time*, 18 May 1987.

"The Gary Hart Story: How It Happened." *Miami Herald*, 10 May 1987.

"The Grinch Who Stole Christmas." *Time*, 28 December 1987.

"The Road to Bimini." *Vanity Fair*, September 1987.

"The Sudden Fall of Gary Hart." *Newsweek*, 18 May 1987.

Jesse Jackson

"Jackson Aims For the Mainstream." *New York Times Magazine*, 29 November 1987.

"Power or Glory." *Vanity Fair*, January 1988.

Reynolds, Barbara. *Jesse Jackson: The Man, the Myth, the Movement*. Chicago: Nelson-Hall, 1975.

"Taking Jesse Seriously: His Emergence as a Front Runner Changes the Race—and the Nation." *Time*, 11 April 1988.

Jack Kemp

Cannon, Lou. *Ronnie and Jesse: A Political Odyssey*. Garden City, N.Y.: Doubleday, 1969.

"Kemp, New Ideas, Old Questions; Is it Pass or Run in '88?" *Newsweek*, 2 December 1985.

"It Dare Not Speak Its name: Fear and Loathing on the Gay Right." *Harpers*, August 1987. 1987.

"Reagan's Gay Sex Scandal." *The Advocate*, 25 November 1986.

Pat Robertson

"No Big Deal For Robertson." *Washington Post*, 9 October 1987.

"Wild Oats: Robertson Rewrites His Resume." *Time*, 19 October 1987.

INDEX

★ ★ ★ ★ **R** ★ ★ ★ ★

ILLUSTRATION CREDITS

5. Courtesy of The New-York Historical Society, New York; 11. Courtesy of the American Philosophical Society; 13. Virginia State Library and Archives; 18, 27, 30, 36. Library of Congress; 53, 54. Virginia State Library and Archives; 56. Courtesy of The New-York Historical Society, New York; 65, 66. Library of Congress; 76. Culver Pictures; 79, 83. Library of Congress; 88. U.S. Senate; 90, 93, 110. Library of Congress; 113. California Historical Society; 122. Smithsonian Institution, Div. of Political History; 125, 133, 134. Library of Congress; 145. *Salt Lake Tribune*; 149. Mark Twain Memorial, Hartford, Conn.; 161. UPI/ Bettmann Newsphotos; 163. AP/Wide World Photos; 165. Library of Congress; 166. UPI/Bettmann Newsphotos; 171, 173. AP/Wide World Photos; 176, 188, 192, 194, 197. UPI/Bettmann Newsphotos; 199, 204. AP/Wide World Photos; 205, 206. UPI/Bettmann Newsphotos; 217. AP/Wide World Photos; 222. *Hong Kong Standard*; 238. UPI/Bettmann Newsphotos; 242, 253, 261, 262. AP/Wide World Photos

ABOUT THE AUTHOR

Shelley Ross is a seasoned journalist who has written for a variety of newspapers and national magazines since 1973. In 1981, she began working in television and produced an interview with Charles Manson for NBC's "Tomorrow Show Coast to Coast." Taped at the California State Medical Facility at Vacaville, the interview, which was Manson's first in thirteen years of isolation, received the highest rating in the history of the time slot. Since then, Ross has written and produced for many television pilots, specials, and series ranging from magazine shows to sitcoms. In addition to *Fall from Grace*, she has also coauthored an acclaimed self-help medical book with Louis Rosner, M.D., clinical professor of neurology at UCLA.